GOD'S WORD, FINAL, INFALLIBLE AND FOREVER

Compelling Evidence for the Bible's Inspiration and Preservation

by Floyd McElveen

This Book Available Through:
Gospel Truths Ministries
P.O. Box 1015
Grand Rapids, MI 49501

CHRISTIAN OUTREACH
P. O BOX 750
SALT LAKE CITY, UT. 84101

© Copyright 1985 By Floyd C. McElveen.

GOD'S WORD FINAL, INFALLIBLE AND FOREVER

by Floyd McElveen

Floyd C. McElveen is the national evangelist for the Conservative Baptist Home Mission Society. He holds evangelistic meetings nationwide. He served as a missionary for 28 years, 14 of them in Alaska, starting churches in Alaska, Idaho, and Washington. He was listed in Who's Who in Religion in 1977. He and his lovely wife, Virginia, now reside in Port Orchard, Washington.

Contents

Introduction 7
1. Bible Facts Concerning the Inspiration and Preservation of the Word of God 9
2. Evidence That the Bible Really Is the Word of God 21
3. Prophecy Proves the Bible to be the Word of God 30
4. Miracles Attest to the Truth of the Bible and its Christ 45
5. The Miracle of Jesus 56

INTRODUCTION

God's Word, Final, Infallible and Forever, is meant to be a clear, powerful tool to help any honest reader discover the absolute certainty of the Bible being God's Word. It is meant to be an equally powerful tool to show that Jesus Christ was exactly who He claimed to be, Almighty God in human flesh, on a dramatic and bloody rescue mission to redeem rebellious, sinful man. Finally, it is meant to be an extremely powerful and persuasive tool, by God's grace, to lead men to Jesus Christ.

The Title also means that God has given His Word in the Bible. There is no more Word needed and no more to give until He comes for us. His word is without error. His word is preserved as He promised. His integrity is at stake, as this is exactly what He promised to do, not only to give His word, but to preserve it.

Biblical evidence, science, prophecy, Jesus Christ, and His undeniable resurrection, personal experiences, changed lives, mathematical probabilities, incredible answers to prayer, archaeological and historical verification, and convincing illustrations are blended to remove roadblocks to faith and give compelling reasons to believe.

It is our prayer, and our conviction, that there is unanswerable logic supporting the claims of Christianity and that God has allowed us to capture some of this logic for His glory in this book. We do not believe that unbelief logically has anywhere left to stand, in any real encounter with the facts of Christianity. Truth has nothing to fear from error, and Jesus Christ is Truth.

I will be eternally grateful if the Lord Jesus Christ uses this book to open the eyes of many to turn them to Himself and His wonderful salvation.

CHAPTER ONE

Bible Facts Concerning The Inspiration And Preservation Of The Word Of God

We earnestly pray that many will be led to utter and complete confidence in the Bible as the Word of God, without reservation, by the following.

The Bible claims to be the Word of God

Around 3,800 times the Bible claims to be the Word of God. Such terms as 'Thus saith the Lord,' 'The Word of the Lord came unto me,' are common expressions of these claims. 2 Tim:3:16 tells us that, "All scripture is given by inspiration of God, and is profitable for doctrine, for reproof, for correction, for instruction in righteousness." 'Inspired of God' means literally 'God-breathed' from the Greek word originally used, 'theopneustos.' It is a tremendously powerful attestation to the importance and the vital life of the Bible, that God actually created the Scriptures by his Holy Spirit, by a creative act, even as He created the world, and as He created man. Recognition of this very fact insures that just as He did not abandon the world and leave creation an orphan to perish in chaos, and just as He did not leave man in lonely helpless despair, so He did not abandon the Bible, the Word of God, to assault, degradation and dismemberment after having given it! In fact, none of these three entities could perform God's purpose without the other. He gave certain inter-related promises concerning the universe, the earth, man, and the Bible, and these are being and will be fulfilled. 2 Peter 1:21 states: "For the prophecy came not at any time by the will of man, but holy men of God spoke as they were moved by the Holy Ghost." God thus claimed responsibility for the Bible, the Old Testament and the New, and this was corroborated by the teaching of Jesus Christ. The earth was created explicitly for man, and man for the earth, for this time. Can you imagine God losing track of either the one or the other so that earth wound up with no man, or man with no earth until God's will and promises were fully accomplished? Just so, God created the Bible through His Holy men, as a revelation to man, needed to unfold His purposes for man, the earth, and Himself. He would no more permit His word to go unsupervised and perish than He would the earth, or man.

Before we deal with the evidence that the Bible is the Word of God, as it claims to be, let us look at a second claim the Bible makes for itself.

The Bible Claims That It Will Be Preserved by the Lord

Jesus said, in Matthew 5:18, "For verily I say unto you, Till heaven and earth pass, one jot or one tittle shall in no wise pass from the law, till all be fulfilled." Since, in the immediate context, He spoke of the prophets also, the law here seems to apply, as it sometimes does, not just to the 10 commandments, but to the whole revealed Word of God. Jesus here refers to the smallest letter in the Hebrew alphabet, the jot or 'yod', and assures us that not even that tiny portion of God's Word, much less doctrines and books of the Word of God, could pass away! . . . not to mention tittle, which is smaller than a comma! After the Olivet discourse in Matthew 24, in verse 35, Jesus says, "Heaven and earth shall pass away, but my words shall not pass away." While this no doubt speaks of the discourse which He has just given, to limit it to this would be to say this is the most important thing He ever gave and therefore the only thing He is going to guarantee perfect preservation for. This is not true, so by application it applies to the whole Word of God. In fact, He said that, " . . . Man shall not live by bread alone, but by every word that proceedeth out of the mouth of God." Obviously, if man is going to live by every word that comes from God, man must be in permanent possession of every word that comes from God, (Matthew 4:4). Jesus had also said that the Scriptures could not be broken. The Psalmist had already exulted, in Psalm 119:89, "Forever, O Lord, thy word is settled in heaven." Isaiah 40:8 declares, "The grass withereth, the flower fadeth: but the word of our God shall stand forever." I Peter 2:23-25, also speaks of the word of God, living, abiding and enduring forever.

In the light of these plain declarations from God, and from the Lord Jesus Christ, we need to ask ourselves some hard and honest questions. Is it not dangerous to claim that some books are missing from the Bible or that it has been mistranslated? Is this not a direct denial of God Himself, and His Word? Is it not accusing the Lord Jesus Christ of lying? Does it not betray a lack of trust in Almighty God both in His power and in His veracity to preserve that which He has given as He promised?

Some even go so far as to say that every time the Bible mentions a book, such as the Book of Jasher in Joshua 10:13, Books of the Wars of the Lord, Numbers 21:14, and about 18 others, that these are 'lost' books of the Bible. However, Grecian writers and poets are quoted by Paul in Acts 17, Gnostic teaching in Colossians, etc. Certainly just because these pagan writers are alluded too, does not mean that their writings were inspired of God and to be included in the Bible! How could 40 or more writers writing over a period of 1600 years on all subjects to all people NOT mention some of the books of common interest and concern to them and to those to whom they wrote?

When writing about the Bible, I may mention other books, writers or newspapers, but this in no way means that they are 'inspired', or that I believe them to be. Actually the problem anyone has in doubting God's *preservation* of His Word is in essence that this denies the *inspiration,* also. God by inspiration, declares the preservation of His Word!

The truth of the matter is this. Jesus quoted from every part of the Old Testament. He personally superintended or pre-authenticated by His Holy Spirit all of the New Testament. Consider Luke 24:27, given as He spoke to the disciples on the road to Emmaus, after His resurrection. "And beginning at Moses and all the prophets, he expounded unto them in all the scriptures the things concerning himself." The Jews had the Old Testament with the same books we have now. This is what 'in all the scriptures' meant to them. Jesus not only authenticated the whole Old Testament, here and elsewhere as the Word of God, pointing to Him. He never, at anytime, quoted from one of the books some say are missing from the Bible! He quoted from 'all the scripture, the law, all the prophets', God's Word says . . . missing none. Yet He never quoted from these so-called missing books. They were totally unimportant, and they were totally uninspired, never meant to be a part of the Bible, and they never were. Even the apostles ignored them. Jesus was and is Almighty, All-knowing God. It is incredible and unbelievable that He should ignore something of such monumental importance if it were true. Irrefutably, it is not.

Also, the disciples were in close contact with Him day and night for years, and witnessed His life, miracles, death and resurrection. However, he did not depend on that alone, but pre-authenticated the New Testament by telling them that the Holy Spirit would guide them into all truth. He would bring 'all things to their remembrance'. John 16:13-16, John 14:26. He would preserve His word, and guard it as the Word of God, forbidding any adding to it or subtracting from it for any reason. This would include claims of 'living prophets' or new 'revelations'. The Bible is complete. Therefore, 'living prophets' who give 'new revelation' and foretell the future to add to the Bible are no longer needed. This is emphasized by Heb. 1:1, 2a, "God, who at sundry times and in divers manners spake in time past unto the fathers by the prophets, Hath in these last days spoken unto us by his Son . . . "

Remember again, the Old Testament through the prophet, priest and ritual sacrifices foretold and prepared the way for the coming of the Messiah, the Christ. The New Testament contains the New Covenant and fulfills the Old, and shows that Jesus Christ has come. The New Testament recounts in great detail the life of Jesus, His miracles, His death, and His resurrection. All that is pertinent or needed is fully revealed. The New Testament or New Covenant replaces the Old Testament or Old Covenant. Both

Covenants involved a revelation from God. Holy men of God, prophets and apostles, spoke and wrote what God revealed to them. Both the Old Covenant and the New Covenant were fully and adequately explained. The New Testament is the New Covenant spelled out. This Covenant is called the 'everlasting covenant' in Heb. 13:20. There will never be any better or newer covenant. The Old Covenant has been given. The New, everlasting Covenant has also been given. There is nothing missing. There is no gap, no emptiness, no need for anything new or for any new revelation. The book of Revelation provides the capstone, giving information concerning the end of the Church age, the great tribulation, the millennium, and the consummation of all things. The next thing on the calendar for Christians is the return of Jesus Christ for His own. This may occur at any time. If any other 'revelation' is needed He will provide it.

Further proof that the Bible is complete is that since the Bible has been completed, absolutely no 'prophet' has been able to pass the simple test of Deut. 18:20-22, in nearly 2000 years,

> 20. But the prophet, which shall presume to speak a word in my name, which I have not commanded him to speak, or that shall speak in the name of other gods, even that prophet shall die.
>
> 21. And if thou say in thine heart, How shall we know the word which the Lord hath not spoken?
>
> 22. When a prophet speaketh in the name of the Lord, if the thing follow not, nor come to pass, that *is* the thing which the Lord hath not spoken, *but* the prophet hath spoken it presumptuously: thou shalt not be afraid of him.

Consider again Rev. 22:18, 19, "For I testify unto every man that heareth the words of the prophecy of this book, If any man shall add unto these things, God shall add unto him the plagues that are written in this book: And if any man shall take away from the words of the book of this prophecy, God shall take away his part out of the book of life, and out of the holy city, and from the things which are written in this book." Some say this applies only to the Book of Revelation. The warning does apply primarily to the Book of Revelation. However, it is very doubtful that we can limit the application only to the Book of Revelation. Think again of the fact that an Omniscient, all-knowing God, who knows the end from the beginning, knew that under His promised guidance, the Book of Revelation would be placed as the LAST book of the Bible. It is just too much to ask us to believe that it is merely coincidence that the most drastic warning in the Bible concerning adding to its words or prophecies, would be on the LAST page of the LAST chapter of the LAST book of the Bible, in the LAST few verses, by the LAST prophet, unless God wanted this warning to apply to MORE than just the Book of Revelation. He knew the Bible would be compiled, all 66 books, as one whole book, with Revelation appearing as the capstone, the last chapter. He stamped this book, both Revelation and the Bible, as His last prophecies for the Church Age, and took away the power to accurately foretell the future without error that His prophets alone always had, as Deut. 18:20-22 states. This double-barrelled fact emphatically illustrates that the Bible is complete!

Notice also the difference in this warning in Revelation and a similar warning given in Deut. 4:2.a, "Ye shall not add unto the word which I command you . . . " not 'have commanded you or already completely given you'. Obviously, this warning dealt with ongoing revelation. NOT SO the more severe warning given in Rev. 22:18, 19. THIS warning clearly deals with revelation already given, already complete, 'are written in this book' signifying completion. The tense, the wording is different. I say this because some may say that much new revelation was given after the warning in Deut. 4:2, which we acknowledge to be of God and which is recorded in the Bible. Therefore, they may reason, new revelation may be given and added as Scripture after the warning given in Rev. 22:18, 19. But in Deuteronomy God was warning of adding to or taking from Scripture as it was in the process of being given to His people in an ongoing revelation, as well as tampering with that which had been given. In Revelation He is speaking of the revelation which had already been given, a very significant difference. This again underlines the fact that the Bible is now complete, and any 'new' revelation is false revelation as it would violate this terrible warning in Rev. 22:18, 19. Furthermore, 'new' revelation is not needed and does not come from God.[1]

Translations and Manuscripts of the Bible

Some sincere people have expressed doubt that God has preserved His word in view of the transmissions and translations it has been through in its centuries of existence.

Let us look again at the word 'inspired' or 'theopneustia', God used concerning the giving of His word through chosen vessels, in 2 Tim. 3:16. Remember that the word means 'God-breathed'. God breathed the spoken word, and the creation came into being, Gen. Ch. 1. God formed man of the dust of the ground, and God-breathed into a man the breath of life and he became a living soul. Just so, God-breathed His Word through chosen vessels. His Word, the Scriptures, the Bible, is just as much His creation, and just as much to be preserved by Him as He promised, as creation, or man!

The Jews, under God's supervision, preserved the word meticulously, as shown by a comparison of the Masoretic text, and even the Septuagint, a Greek translation of the Hebrew Masoretic text several centuries before Christ, with the Dead Sea Scrolls, discovered in 1947, in a cave about 8 miles south of Jericho. The Dead Sea Scrolls are manuscripts dated by experts about 100 years before Christ. The oldest Isaiah Masoretic text Christians had to depend on for the book of Isaiah in the Bible was dated 916 A.D. How much did the text change in 10 long centuries of transmission, of copying and re-copying the Bible? At last a test could be made!

> Of the 166 words in Isaiah 53, there are only seventeen letters in question. Ten of these letters are simply a matter of spelling, which does not affect the sense. Four more letters are minor stylistic changes, such as conjuctions. The remaining three letters comprise the word "light," which is added to verse 11, and does not affect the meaning greatly.[1]

Also,

> Thus, in one chapter of 166 words, there is only one word (three letters) in question after a thousand years of transmission—and this word does not significantly change the meaning of the passage. This sample is typical of the whole Isaiah A manuscript.[2]

No wonder Dr. W. F. Albright, of John Hopkins University and one of the world's greatest biblical archeologists, called the Dead Sea Scrolls find, the greatest manuscript discovery of all time. God has and is preserving His word as He promised.

Concerning the New Testament, several observations need to be made. According to Geisler and Nix, summarizing Bruce Metzger, in their book, *A General Introduction to the Bible*, there are about 5,000 Greek manuscripts containing all or part of the New Testament. This is far more than for any other ancient text. (Incidentally, Josh McDowell has now documented 24,633 manuscripts of the New Testament alone—as compared to 643 manuscripts for the number two book in manuscript authority, *The Illiad* by Homer.) The New Testament manuscripts are also much older, or nearer to the time of the original autographs, than other ancient books, most of which have only a handful of manuscripts to attest to the authenticity of the originals. Not only is this so, but here is an astounding quote from *Evidence That Demands a Verdict,* by able apologist and scholar, Josh McDowell, concerning an investigation of the writings of the church Fathers, by Sir David Dalrymple. "Look at these books. You remember the question about the New Testament and the Fathers? That question roused my curiosity, and I possessed all the existing works of the Fathers of the second and third centuries, I commenced to search, and up to this time I have found the entire New Testament, except eleven verses."[3] In other words, the New Testament could be reproduced accurately from the quotations of the church Fathers alone, even if we did not have those 5,000 manuscripts! Remember that some of the apostles were around for some time after the writing of the New Testament, and some of their converts were the early church Fathers. Referring to Josh McDowell's book again, Polycarp (A.D. 70-156) was a disciple of John and succumbed to martyrdom at 86 years of age because of his relentless devotion to Christ and the Scriptures. Ignatius (A.D. 70-110), was Bishop of Antioch and was martyred for his faith in Christ. He knew all the apostles and was in the "action group" (in other words a disciple) of Polycarp who was a disciple of the apostle John.[4] Irenaeus, Bishop of Lyons (A.D. 180), was a student of Polycarp, Bishop of Smyrna.

Other church Fathers, to mention a few were Clement

of Alexandria, Tertullian, Hippolytus, Justin Martyr, Origen, Cyprian and Eusebius, carrying us from the 1st and 2nd century to the 3rd and 4th, quoting the New Testament accurately all the way, giving us another check on its accuracy and preservation as compared with the Greek Manuscripts. Interestingly enough, many of these first and second century Fathers, some of them contemporary with or converts of the apostles, and their converts, gave their lives in martyrdom not only for Christ, but for the integrity of the Scriptures, and they knew whether or not they were accurate! Also, the manuscripts had by this time proliferated by the hundreds and thousands. Even if someone deliberately or by accident emended or corrupted a manuscript, it would be corrected by the many other manuscripts available.

To sum up; unless we want to throw a blanket over all of history and say that there is nothing knowable about the past, no history that can be trusted, no Grecian or Roman history, no Aristotle or Plato or Socrates, we had better not make any claims against the historicity and accuracy of the New Testament! The New Testament documents are far more numerous, older, demonstrably more accurate historically, and have been examined by a far greater battery of scholars, both friend and foe, than all the other ancient manuscripts put together. They have met the test impeccably!

Admittedly, this chapter is only a brief summary of the manuscript evidence and other evidence for the inspiration and preservation of the scriptures. Some would also be interested in related subjects such as canonicity. For those who have a deep interest in the subjects touched on in this chapter, meant primarily for the average reader rather than the indefatigible scholar, I recommend *Evidence That Demands a Verdict* and *More Evidence That Demands a Verdict,* by Josh McDowell; *A General Introduction to the Bible,* by

Geisler and Nix; *Basic Christianity,* by John Stott; and *The New Testament Documents: Are They Reliable?* by F. F. Bruce. In addition, many other excellent resources are listed by McDowell and by Geisler and Nix.

Notes

[1] Geisler and Nix, *A General Introduction to the Bible,* 1983, Moody Press Paperback edition, Moody Bible Institute of Chicago. Used by permission. p. 263.

[2] Ibid.

[3] Josh McDowell, *Evidence That Demands a Verdict,* 1972, Campus Crusades for Christ, Inc. p. 54.

[4] Ibid., pp. 66, 67.

CHAPTER TWO

Evidence That The Bible Really Is The Word Of God

Consider the statement by Charles Wesley as given in A

General Introduction to the Bible:

> The Bible must be the invention of either good men or angels, bad men or devils, or of God. 1. It could not be the invention of good men or angels, for they neither would or could make a book, and tell lies all the time they were writing it, saying, "Thus saith the Lord", when it was their own invention. 2. It could not be the invention of bad men or devils, for they would not make a book which commands all duty, forbids all sin, and condemns their souls to hell for all eternity. 3. Therefore I draw this conclusion, that the Bible must be given by divine inspiration.[5]

The Unity and Uniqueness of the Bible

Imagine 40 men, separated by centuries, coming from many different cultures, towns and backgrounds, some having limited access to a part of the work done by the others, some having no such access, working on a statue of Jesus. Each has his particular part of the statue to carve; one a toe; one an ear; another the neck; another the chin; a leg; a shoulder blade; and so on. After thousands of years, all these carvings are brought to one place and put together. Incredibly, they all fit perfectly, and a beautiful statue of Jesus is formed. Impossible, by chance! Possible only by a superintending act of a supervising God. This is exactly what we have in the Bible. Some 40 to 50 authors, working over a period of from 1500 to 1600 years, men educated and uneducated; ignorant to intellectual; from shepherds to statesmen; writing 66 books, come up with a perfectly unified book portraying one perfect person, the Lord Jesus Christ. There is absolutely no dissonance, no contradiction, but perfect harmony. As Dr. Rene Pache says in *Inspiration and Authority of Scripture,*

> To what can one attribute this unity running through the whole Bible: unity of vision, structure, message and doctrine—in spite of the long centuries and the many individuals used as instruments for its completion? To this question there can only be one answer: in reality Scripture has but one author, the Holy Spirit. To Him, it is but one revelation, since it speaks throughout of the only true and proper Object of worship. There is just one salvation: announced, then effected and consummated by one only Saviour. Human nature is the same through all the ages: its needs, weaknesses, and potential will always require this same divine communication. For the everliving, omniscient God, time is as one instant: in other words, eternity means an eternal present, from the first page of Scripture to the last. Finally, truth itself is "one" and could never be contradictory.[6]

Try getting 66 books on psychology together and see what a mess you have! There are now over 10,000 psychological techniques in use, many of them totally contradicting each other, and psychology is a relatively new 'science'. It is impossible for men, even of the same generation, not to challenge or contradict the findings of their fellow psychologists, or scientists, or educators, or religionists or whatever. Most men cannot even agree with their own writings after 10 years! Try getting just 10 science textbooks spread over 20 or 30 years together, and compare them. Just for example: a friend of mine has kept a record, I understand, of the times that science has been wrong in a claim and the Bible right. Not that there is any disharmony between true science and the Bible, but outdated science textbooks often have to be abandoned—some after only a few years. Not so, the Bible. The last I heard, my friend had over 100 examples in which the Bible had proven right and the textbooks wrong. The textbooks had to be changed. The Bible, an ancient book, never. Amazing, isn't it? Here however, I am concerned mainly with showing the inexplicable miracle of the unity, utterly unique, in a Book with over 40 authors, made up of 66 books over nearly 1600 years. Yet not once did Amos 'contradict' Moses, or Isaiah 'correct' Joshua, or Paul 'update' Daniel, because of 'later information' or 'new revelation', or any other reason. This is utterly impossible for human beings, and all of us *know* it! This book, the Bible, has to be from God!

Archaelology and the Bible

As Paul E. Little points out in his book, *Know Why You Believe,* there are over 25,000 sites showing some connection with the Old Testament period located in Bible lands.[7] This does not even include the well known sites and cities mentioned in the New Testament. How thrilling to know, as Terry Winter in his book *Why I am a Christian*, quotes the Jewish archaeologist Nelson Glueck as saying, "It may be stated categorically that no archaeological discovery has ever controverted a biblical reference."

Biblical accuracy is illustrated in the case of the Hittites. There was a time when skeptics ridiculed the Bible, saying that such a city-state never existed. However, on the authority of God's Word, plus the discovery of hundreds of other places by archaeologists that the Bible mentioned, Christians held that the Word of God was true and would be vindicated. It was! In 1906, excavations were made at Bogazkoy, 90 miles east of Ankara, Turkey. This was found to be the capital of the Hittite empire! (The Hittites were mentioned 46 times in the Bible, and, as in hundreds of similar cases, the Bible was right and the critics wrong.) There was a time when men disbelieved in Ur of the Chaldees, Abraham's one-time home, but archaeologists dug it up. As archaeologists have dug into the ruins of Egypt, Palestine, Babylonia, and Assyria, etc. the historicity and accuracy of the Bible has been confirmed a thousand times over. The grandeur of Solomon's reign and wealth was questioned until excavations at Megiddo and discoveries elsewhere confirmed the Biblical accounts.

It was once argued that Luke had erred in the account of the events surrounding the birth of Jesus. There was no census, Quirinius was not governor of Syria at that time, and people did not have to return to their ancestral home, as Luke stated. Again, archaeological discoveries proved every one of these claims to be true. Quirinius was governor according to an inscription found in Antioch. The Romans did have a regular enrollment of taxpayers. A papyrus found in Egypt gives directions for the conduct of a census including the return of people to their ancestral home. Archaeology has proven again the Bible's historicity and accuracy, a fact which also lends supporting credentials to its inspiration and preservation. For further reference, I recommend, *Halley's Bible Handbook,* by Henry H. Halley; *Evidence That Demands a Verdict* by Josh McDowell; *From the Stone Age* by William F. Albright; and *Archaeology and Bible History* by Joseph P. Free.

Science and the Bible

S. Maxwell Coder and George F. Howe, in their book, *The Bible, Science and Creation* contend, "The Bible is the only ancient book that is accurate in all scientific details. Other ancient holy books from the East include legends and errors too childish for consideration. Even comparatively modern books like the Koran abound in historical and chronological blunders."[9] For instance, Plato thought the world to be a living soul, a vast and visible animal, and earthquakes resulted when the creature shook itself! The Greeks believed that a giant, Atlas, stood astride the earth and held the broad heavens with his head and arms, thus we call a book of maps an atlas even today. The Egyptians taught that a sun-god was born on a flower or from an egg on the ocean, and this sun-god had four children,

> . . . two of whom, Shu and Tefnut (together making up the atmosphere), planted their feet on the first, Geb (the earth), and raised their sister Nut (the sky) to the heavens. Geb and Nut (the earth and sky) had four children, Osiris, Isis, Nepthys, and Seth. Osiris married Isis and with her governed the earth; but later he was murdered by his jealous brother Seth, who in his rage cut his victim's body into pieces, burying them in different parts of Egypt. Isis collected the scattered fragments and aided by the jackal-god Anubis, resuscitated the body of Osiris. Osiris, however, was unable

to return to earth and remained in the underworld as a god of the dead and the judge of souls. Isis bore a son, Horus, who took revenge on Seth and won back from the usurper his father's throne.[10]

Remarkably, Moses was "learned in all the wisdom of the Egyptians" (Acts 7:22), but kept from this fanciful account of creation, as the clear, simple and splendid account in Genesis shows. No reasonable explanation but that this book, the Bible, was given directly by God, could explain its scientific accuracy and freedom from the superstitious, mythological, childish accounts of all other ancient religious books, or of any contemporary account of creation from whatever source. Even the Koran says the mountains were created to keep the earth from moving, to hold it fast with anchors and cables! The sacred books of the Hindus have 330 millions of gods. One of the greatest of these gods is Shiva, whose symbol is the organ of reproduction. In Hindu cosmogony, the moon is 50 thousand leagues higher than the sun and shines with its own light. Night worldwide is caused by the sun setting behind the mountain Someyra, situated in the middle of the earth, and several thousand miles high. Our earth is flat and triangular. The earth is in seven stages, each having its own inhabitants and its own sea, one of honey, others of sugar, wine, butter, etc. and the whole mass is carried on the heads of countless elephants, which, shaking themselves, cause earthquakes in the nether world.[11] Have you had enough? Now let us look at the Bible.

In his marvelous little book, *Science Speaks,* Peter W. Stoner M.S. (his co-author was Robert C. Newman S.T.M., Ph.D.) claims that the 13 things listed in Genesis in the creation account are in the same order in which geology finds them, which he claims would be possible by chance only in one chance in 311,351,040![12]

In a day when most people taught that the earth was flat, even up to the voyage of Columbus in 1492, the Bible stated in Isaiah 40:22a, "It is he that sitteth upon the circle of the earth." The word for circle is the Hebrew word meaning 'round' or 'sphere'. In other words, the Bible revealed that the earth was a sphere about 2200 years before man found it out, even though Marco Polo had made some strides in that direction a few centuries before Columbus. But Isaiah wrote about 700 years B.C.! How did he know? He did not, the word came from God!

Job cried out, Job 26:7, "He stretcheth out the north over the empty place, and hangeth the earth upon nothing." What a remarkable statement in the light of all the views held at that time and for centuries afterward! Remarkable too, is the statement of Jesus in Luke 17:34,36, with a strong intimation concerning it being simultaneously night, morning and midday, at His coming. This was clear, but then unknown, reference to the revolution of the earth, since His coming is pictured elsewhere as being instantaneous everywhere. A man named Byron Nelson wrote a book showing how God's statement that everything could only reproduce after its kind was, and is true. The book is called, *After Its Kind,* and supports God's statements in Genesis. At a time when, (and for centuries afterward) men thought they could count the stars. God's word said that they were innumerable. We now know that to be true. Some men, even scientists, will tell you that Heb. 11:3, "Through faith we understand that the worlds were framed by the word of God, so that *things which are seen were not made of things which do appear"* is extremely accurate scientifically. Particularly notice that the *italicized* portion is the best, most succinct description of the atom, the invisible building block of the universe, ever stated.

Isaiah 11:12b, " . . . gather together the dispersed of

Judah from the four corners of the earth." This verse has been used by some to suggest that the Bible teaches a flat earth and is therefore not scientific, not inspired of God. However, we use exactly the same terminology today. We even say the sun is setting, when we very well know better. Newspapers tell us the time of 'sunrise and sunset'. Who uses scientific jargon to speak of these common things? Actually, in *Harmony of Science and Scripture,* Harry Rimmer says, "Isaiah wrote in Hebrew, and when we read his text in the Hebrew, he literally said that 'God would gather together the dispersed of Judah from the four quarters of the earth.'"[13] A perfectly accurate statement for a round earth! Harry Rimmer himself, as Paul Rader had done some years earlier, offered $1,000 to anyone who could prove a scientific error in the Bible. He had some court cases, but won them all! Today, many scientists, such as Henry Morris and Duane Gish, have turned to Jesus Christ and to the Bible as the inspired Word of God. It is in harmony with proven science, not necessarily with unproven scientific postulations.

Suppose just one of the countless foolish errors of other ancient books, or even of scientists within the last century, were in the Bible. It would have been discarded or laughed out of existence long ago by those who demand objective evidence for their faith. Science is another evidence for the inspiration and reliability of the Scriptures.

Notes

5. Geisler and Nix, *A General Introduction to the Bible,* p. 123.

6. Dr. Rene Pache, *Inspiration and Authority of Scripture,* 1969, Moody Press, Moody Bible Institute of Chicago, p. 119.

7. Paul E. Little, *Know Why You Believe,* Victor Books, Scripture Press, p. 103.

8. Terry Winter, *Why I am a Christian,* 1978, Mitchell Press, Ltd., Canada, p. 14.

9. S. Maxwell Coder and George F. Howe, *The Bible, Science and Creation,* 1965 Moody Press, Moody Bible Institute of Chicago, Used by permission, p. 39.

10. Ibid., p. 41

11. Information from Adolph Saphir, *Christ and the Scriptures,* quoted by Rene Pache in *The Inspiration and Authority of Scriptures,* pp. 298 and 299 concerning the Hindu sacred books.

12. Peter W. Stoner, M.S., *Science Speaks,* rev. 1976, Moody Press, Moody Bible Institute of Chicago. Used by permission.

13. Harry Rimmer, *Harmony of Science and Scripture,* 1936, Wm. B. Eerdmans Publishing Company, Grand Rapids, Michigan (20th printing, Oct. 1966), p. 76.

CHAPTER THREE

Prophecy Proves The Bible To Be The Word Of God

Again and again the apostles would declare, 'this is that of which the prophets spoke'. This was calling attention to that which had been given centuries before, and to its literal fulfillment, as evidence that it was of God and that it was incontrovertibly true. Dr. W. A. Criswell, in his book, *Why I Preach That the Bible is Literally True,* says:

> Where is there a god or gods; where is there a founder of religion such as Confucius, Buddha, Muhammad, or Zoroaster; or where is there any statesman who, in these times, can foretell what will be the condition of things in Europe or in America one hundred years from now or even ten years from now? Yea, I can tell any man how he can become a multimillionaire within a relatively short time. If

he can predict even in the course of an hour, he can make himself fabulously rich by playing the market on the New York Stock Exchange. We do not know the future. It is the prerogative of God to know what tomorrow will bring. The fulfilled prophecies of the Bible bespeak the omniscience of its author.[14]

Isaiah 41:21-23 gives a strong challenge for any 'gods' to foretell the future. Since only God can do that with accuracy and consistency, this helps distinguish between the false and the true. The same test is made of those who claim that they are prophets of God:

> 20. But the prophet, which shall presume to speak a word in my name, which I have not commanded him to speak, or that shall speak in the name of other gods, even that prophet shall die.
> 21. And if thou say in thine heart, How shall we know the word which the Lord hath not spoken?
> 22. When a prophet speaketh in the name of the Lord, if the thing follow not, nor come to pass, that *is* the thing which the Lord hat not spoken, *but* the prophet hath spoke it presumptuously; thou shalt not be afraid of him.
> (Deuteronomy 18:20-22)

A prophet was considered false if his prophecies were not 100 percent accurate at all times. It could not possibly be otherwise for a man claiming to speak for God, or God's honor and integrity would be forever compromised. His word could not be trusted.

One false prophecy is all it takes to reveal a false prophet. In Deut. 13:1-5, we are warned that even if some 'dreamer of dreams' did have a prophecy come true, and led away to other gods, than the one true God of the Bible, he was a false prophet! This was another test for a prophet as well as a test for those who claimed to love God with all their hearts. However, on the other hand, fulfilled prophecy is an absolutely sure test, certified by God Himself, to prove Him, His son and His infallible word. Is 46:9-11 declares:

> 9. Remember the former things of old: for I *am* God, and *there is* none else; I *am* God, and *there is* none like me.
>
> 10. Declaring the end from the beginning, and from ancient times *the things* that are not *yet* done, saying, My counsel shall stand, and I will do all my pleasure:
>
> 11. Calling a ravenous bird from the east, the man that executeth my counsel from a far country: yea, I have spoken it, I will also bring it to pass; I have purposed it, I will also do it.

We believe Dr. Stoner's book *Science Speaks* contains absolutely irrefutable evidence that the Bible is the Word of God. In collaboration with students, and their estimates, very, very, conservative estimates, (worked out with more than 600 college students) Professor Stoner has established principles of probability for certain prophecies being fulfilled by chance alone. His basic premise: the principle of probability, a very real principle that has made some insurance companies fabulously rich.

Suppose that one man in every 10 is bald, and one in every 100 has lost a finger. What are the chances of a man being both bald and having one finger missing? By multiplication (10 x 100), we discover that the answer is one in 1000. That is, out of every 1000 men, on the average, there will be a bald man who has also lost a finger. Now let's apply this to the prophecy concerning the city of Tyre, against which very specific prophecies were made in Ezekiel, chapter 26:

> 3. Therefore thus saith the Lord God; Behold, I am against thee, O Tyrus, and will cause many nations to come

up against thee, as the sea causeth his waves to come up.

4. And they shall destroy the walls of Tyrus, and break down her towers: I will also scrape her dust from her, and make her like the top of a rock.

5. It shall be a place for the spreading of nets in the midst of the sea: for I have spoken it, saith the Lord God: and it shall become a spoil to the nations.

7. For thus saith the Lord God; Behold, I will bring upon Tyrus Nebuchadrezzar king of Babylon, a king of kings, from the north, with horses, and with chariots, and with horsemen, and companies, and much people.

12. And they shall make a spoil of thy riches, and make a prey of thy merchandise: and they shall break down thy walls, and destroy thy pleasant houses: and they shall lay thy stones and thy timber and thy dust in the midst of the water.

14. And I will make thee like the top of a rock: thou shalt be a place to spread nets upon; thou shalt be built no more: for I the Lord have spoken it, saith the Lord God.

16. Then all the princes of the sea shall come down from their thrones, and lay away their robes, and put off their broidered garments: they shall clothe themselves with trembling; they shall sit upon the ground, and shall tremble at every moment, and be astonished at thee.

This prophecy was given in 590 B.C. Notice seven specific prophecies concerning Tyre. 1. Nebuchadnezzar to take the city of Tyre. 2. Other nations to participate. 3. The city will be made flat like the top of a rock. 4. It will become a place for the spreading of nets. 5. Its stones and timber and dust to be laid in the sea. 6. Other cities will be afraid because of the fall of Tyre. 7. The old city of Tyre will never be rebuilt.

Tyre was a very strong city-state inhabited by the Phoenicians. Nebuchadnezzar beseiged the city for 13 years, taking it in 573 B.C. The Phoenicians had taken their possessions and themselves to an island, one-half mile off the coast. However, they were not conquered and only one item of the prophecy had been fulfilled, (no. 1). 241 long years rolled by. In 322 B.C., Alexander the Great tried to take Tyre, but had to take other coastal cities and enlist their fleets for help; still he was unsuccessful in taking Tyre. Guess what he did? Alexander mortared out a causeway from the mainland to the island, scraping up the soil in and around Tyre, using the building materials of the old city. He very literally laid the 'stones, the timber and the dust', of Tyre in the sea, exactly as God had prophesied centuries before! In seven bloody months, with the help of his now combined fleet, and a stream of land forces attacking over the causeway, he finally conquered Tyre. In the process, the city of Tyre had been made flat, like the top of a rock. Neighboring cities were so shocked at the conquest of Tyre, they capitulated in fright, opening their gates to Alexander.

Today, as a picture some years ago in *National Geographic* showed, fishermen spread their nets on this very place. Though it is an excellent place for a city with the freshwater springs of Raselain at the site, with a flow of water estimated at 10,000,000 gallons daily, it has never been rebuilt. Dr. Stoner and his students estimated for item No. 1, one chance in three. (If the prophecy were to be fulfilled by chance alone.) Item No. 2, one in five. Item No. 3, one in five hundred. Item No. 4, one in 10. Item No. 5, one in ten. Item No. 6, one in five. Item No. 7, one in twenty. What probability then, is there that the whole 7 item prophecy would come true as prophesied by chance alone? This can be found by our principle of probability; 1 in 3 x 5x 500 x 10 x 10 x 5 x 20. This come to 1 in 75,000,000. This means that there was only one chance in 75 million that this whole prophecy could have come true by chance alone, and this may be a very modest estimate! Every item as you have seen, if you want to review, was perfectly fulfilled, which is always the way God's Word comes true. This is absolute proof, to those not totally blinded by their own unbelief or rebellion, or blinded by the 'god of this world' as the Bible says, that the Bible is inspired. It has been and will be preserved, and its God and its Christ are real.

Dr. Stoner then applies this system to prophecies concerning Samaria, Gaza, Ashkelon, Jericho, The Golden Gate, Zion, Palestine, the Jews, Edom, Babylon, and then finally, to Christ! The results are staggering! There may not be enough numbers to cover the possibility of these detailed prophecies of the Bible, coming true by chance alone. God has to have been the Author of this incredible, infallible book!

The Jews

Deut. 28:25, 26, tells us of the coming suffering and scattering of the Jews, and Deut. 30:1-6, adds to this prophecy, which had indicated that the Jews would be scattered among all nations, but would someday be re-gathered to their own land. These prophecies were given centuries before the full fulfillment. Yet God had given certain very literal prophecies concerning the inheritance of the land of Palestine to Abraham, and to the Jews. Lev. 26:31-33, given 1491 B.C. adds to this prophecy, as does Ezekiel 36:33-35. Luke 21:23, 24 reasserts these prophecies. It was also predicted that Jerusalem would be trodden underfoot of the Gentiles until the time of the Gentiles was fulfilled. From these and other Scriptures let us give a brief summary of what God's Word said the future held for the Jews. 1. Scattering, worldwide among all nations. 2. Intense persecution, suffering. 3. Other, mightier nations around them would be destroyed, but they would never lose their identity as Jews, and a remnant would always survive. 4. They would someday return to their own land and re-establish their own nation. (Though we will not deal with it here, they will also rebuild their temple and Anti-Christ will sign a pact with the nation of Israel for 'peace' just after the coming of the Lord Jesus Christ for His people.)

Now consider these well known facts. Surrounding the Jews were formidable and warlike people, some of them more numerous and more powerful at times than the Jews. Hittites, Canaanites, Philistines, Edomites, etc. Dear friend, when is the last time you met a Hittite? a Philistine? They have long since passed off the scene. Yet the Jews, persecuted horribly, six million dying in Hitler's horrendous Holocaust, remain. For nearly 2,500 years they had no nation, no country of their own. They were scattered world-wide, but instead of being assimilated like the Anglo's, Saxons, and Jutes, for instance, or the Goths or Visigoths, or exterminated like countless others, miraculously, they retain their identity! In Hungary, there are Hungarian Jews, and there are American Jews, Soviet Jews, English Jews, Polish Jews, etc. No totally wiped out, dispossessed nation ever returned to life even after a few hundred years, but God said the Jews would! They did, proving God's Word to be true, and proving the Bible to be God's Word!

Men like Increase Mather saw this truth in the Bible and preached that the Jews would return to Palestine and re-establish their own nation again . . . and he preached it in 1669, as reported by Hal Lindsey in *The Late Great Planet Earth*. This is no 'after the fact' application of some vague generalities to a historical event, but a precise fulfillment of prophecy men of God had been expecting for centuries. Suddenly, it happened! After, and during World War Two, (at one time the Jewish population of Palestine had shrunk to about 10,000!) the Jews returned, fleeing persecution in Germany, Europe and Russia. True . . . but many wealthy Jews around the world, some from America, also . . . returned to Palestine! This inexplicable urge of many to return to a 'homeland' after 2500 years, not because they believed in the Bible, (many did not) fulfilled exactly what God said would happen. The British, in charge of Palestine at the time, put their gleaming warships in the way, but did not know what to do with unarmed men, women and children in merchant ships. Finally, the Jews were allowed in. Miracle of miracles, they declared themselves a nation on May 4, 1948! Against all odds, attacked almost immediately, by forces some say outnumbered them 100 to 1, they survived and conquered. They survived again when they were attacked in 1967 and in the 1970's. The Arabs had controlled Jerusalem, but now that city too is under Jewish control. (See Lk. 21:24). God's Word continues to be fulfilled and will be!

Now Let Us Consider Prophecies Concerning the Lord Jesus Christ

The Bible gives 333 prophecies about Jesus. Most of them, many centuries before He came. For instance, Isaiah's 53rd chapter concerning Him was given about 700 years before He came. John H. Gerstner in his book *Reason For Faith,* says in regard to these prophecies of Jesus: "Someone has taken the trouble to calculate that the possibility of there being fulfilled in one person by sheer coincidence is one over 84,000,000,000,000,000,000,000,000,000,000,000,000,000, 000,000,000,000,000,000,000,000,000,000,000,000,000,000, 000,000,000,000,000,000,000,000,000,000,000,000,000,000, 000,000th of 1 percent."[15] Dr. Stoner takes just 8 of the detailed prophecies concerning Jesus, and shows that the chance of them being fulfilled in one man by chance is the equivalent of covering the state of Texas two feet deep in silver dollars with one of the dollars marked. Then blindfold a man and tell him he has *one* chance to pick out that dollar! When, instead of just 8 prophecies, we consider the whole 333 prophecies concerning Jesus, 33 fulfilled just on the day He died on Calvary, the 'fulfilled by chance' numbers are incomprehensible; the proof irresistible. This reaches about as near the point of absoluteness in evidence as anything in this world can ever be. No wonder Dr. Stoner said "Any man who rejects Christ as the Son of God is rejecting a fact proved perhaps more absolutely than any other fact in the world."[16]

We have mentioned the fact that the place of birth, time of birth, and identifying Virgin Birth was prophesied of Jesus centuries before He was born. A nation waited for this fulfillment. God had also foretold that this nation would reject Him when He came. This was an amazing juxtaposition that came to pass!

Let us look at some of the simplest and best known of the prophecies concerning Jesus. The very fact of the slaying of the lamb, in bloody sacrifice, as God commanded in the Old Testament, pointed for centuries to Jesus Christ, the Lamb of God. The prophecies stated His suffering.

> But he was wounded for our transgressions, he was bruised for our iniquities: the chastisement of our peace was upon him; and with his stripes we are healed.
>
> All we like sheep have gone astray; we have turned every one to his own way; and the Lord hath laid on him the iniquity of us all.
>
> —Isaiah 53:5,6

The prophecies also stated that His hands and feet would be pierced.

> And I will pour upon the house of David, and upon the inhabitants of Jerusalem, the spirit of grace and of supplications: and they shall look upon me whom they have pierced, and they shall mourn for him, as one mourneth for his only son, and shall be in bitterness for him as one that is in bitterness for his firstborn.
>
> —Zechariah 12:10

Then the fulfillment.

> Where they crucified him, and two other with him, on either side one, and Jesus in the midst.
> And again another scripture saith, They shall look on him whom they pierced.
>
> —John 19:18, 37

> The other disciples therefore said unto him, We have seen the Lord. But he said unto them, Except I shall see in his hands the print of the nails, and put my finger into the print of the nails and thrust my hand into his side, I will not believe.
>
> —John 20:25

This is tremendously impressive and exciting. Both the prophecies and the innocent lambs slain by the millions, pointed to and were fulfilled by the bloody death of Jesus Christ on the cross. This is why John the Baptist cried out, "Behold, the Lamb of God that taketh away the sin of the world." When this prophecy about piercing, etc. was given, seven centuries at least before its fulfillment, stoning was the method of execution. Only God could know what method would be used 700 years later to slay His Son on the cross! Amazingly, God said through Isaiah 53:12 that this spotless, sinless one, God incarnate in human flesh, would be numbered with the transgressors; that is, that He would die with criminals as a common criminal. Jesus was crucified between two thieves! Psalm 22:18 declares that His garments would be divided and lots would be cast for His clothing. The hardened, burly soldiers of Rome at the cross centuries later, did not get their Bibles out and say "Hey, fellows, this is our cue. Here is where we are supposed to fulfill prophecy and gamble for the clothes of Jesus Christ!" Nevertheless, they did! They gambled for His garments (Mat. 27:35). It is doubtful they knew or cared about the prophecy at all, but how significant that men even in unbelief perfectly fulfill the Word of God. It impresses me too, that Psalm 69:21 dares to say centuries in advance that He would be offered gall and vinegar to drink. He was! (Matt. 27:34) Only God could know that, centuries in advance. There are thousands of things He could have been offered. He could have been offered nothing! Yet, take a look at Matt. 27:34 and John 19:28, 29! The prediction that He would be buried in a rich man's tomb, is spectacular. That simply did not happen to one who died as a criminal (Is. 53:9). It was the potter's field for them or to the burning refuse in the valley of Hinnon. Yet look at Matt. 27:57-60 and see this 'impossible' fulfillment as Joseph of Arimathaea risked his riches, his reputation, and his life, to claim the body of Jesus to bury in his own unused tomb!

No wonder Dr. Vernon C. Grounds in his book, *The Reason For Our Hope,* has a chapter entitled, "The Difficulties of Disbelief." Some time ago I was dealing with an intelligent but adamant man in his 80's. After He heard the gospel, he said, "Son, it's awfully hard to believe all that stuff!" I replied, "Sir, it takes a lot more faith to believe that all of this happened by chance than it does to believe it's true. Actually it takes a lot more faith not to believe (really, blind faith), than it does to believe." This caught his interest and as I presented some of the evidence to him and then introduced Jesus Christ to him, he opened his tough old heart and Jesus came in!

Let Us Seal This Evidence Now By Illustration

I was talking with a college professor in Vancouver, B.C. He was demeaning Christ and the Bible and telling me how the anthropological concept of God was shallow and outmoded.

I said, "Suppose I gave you 100 pieces of paper, and then you hid these carefully about your home. Meantime, I was being closely attended and watched by several of your trusted friends to see that no trickery is involved. Then, when all the pieces of paper were carefully hidden, suppose I were to return and systematically tell you, in order from 1 through 99, where every piece of paper was hidden, without one failure or mistake. Would you believe I could tell you exactly where you had hidden the 100th scrap of paper? Would you dare risk your *life* on it, as an intelligent human being, that I could *not? Would you risk your soul? Eternity?*"

Then I pointed out to him the fulfillment of Bible prophecies; events hidden in the future that God had unveiled beforehand. For round, conservative figures, let's just take 100. On the scale of God's schedule, 99 have already been fulfilled; relating to cities, nations, the Jews, Jesus Christ. *Now* will *you* my friend, knowing these other prophecies *have* come true—every one of them literally, in detail—risk your whole being, your eternity forever, that what God has said about your future will not come true?

God says that, without Christ, you are a sinner, on your way to hell. Christ died to save you and rose again to conquer death and hell for you. But if you do not receive Him as your Lord and Saviour, you will be lost forever. Will you *risk everything forever* that this is *not* true, that this prediction of God's *will fail* though *His other statements have come true?* Would this be a *reasonable, intelligent* decision?

The professor could only evade that question. He could not give a solid, substantial, logical answer. No, it is not intelligent, but tragically foolish to turn one's back blithely on the tremendous impact of Bible prophecy which is inexplicable, except for this fact. This Book was written by God, through men, as He claimed (2 Timothy 3:16). God will perform all His Words!

Some would argue that Christian faith is wishful thinking, but in reality, unbelief is often *not thinking at all.* That is, unbelief often has never considered the evidences for Christianity. It has simply dismissed faith as intellectually unacceptable.

As a sailor, I had one or two "blind dates" arranged for me. Can't say I heartily recommend them, but that's beside the point. Suppose I agree to meet my blind date at the Greyhound Bus Station, 464 Liberty Street, at 8:00 P.M. She will wear a green hat and a lavender dress and will carry a purple purse. She has yellow hair and blue eyes, but has a black patch over her right eye because of a recent injury. She is one-legged, having lost her left leg, and is missing the little finger of her right hand. She wears a peg-leg. She has painted it a florescent yellow, with a blinking red light built in to keep folks from stumbling over her leg. She will wear a pink stocking on her one good leg and a maroon and white saddle-oxford on her one good foot. Do you honestly think I would have any trouble identifying the right girl at the Greyhound Bus Station at 8:00 P.M.?

Remember, the *time* of Jesus Christ's birth was prophesied. (Dan. 9:24-26). This does away with the otherwise possible objection sometimes made that one could make *any* prophesy and something would eventually occur which you could label as the fulfillment of your prophesy. The time element destroys this objection.

I only gave about 11 marks of identification concerning this girl. Yet the chances are over a million to one against there being another girl with these identification characteristics being in that particular bus station at 8:00 P.M. God gave at least 333 marks of identification about Jesus, concerning the time and place of His birth, and details about His life, death and resurrection. These "MARKS OF IDENTIFICATION" were given centuries before He came so that there could be no doubt about identifying Him WHEN He came! All these 333 "MARKS OF IDENTIFICATION" were perfectly fulfilled in Jesus! Yet some people say Christian faith is wishful thinking!

Remember, everything Christ said came true. He said hell was real and forever. A million years from now, you'll be alive somewhere. Will it be in heaven or will it be in hell?

Notes

14. Dr. W. A. Criswell, *Why I Preach That the Bible is Literally True.* (Nashville: Broadman Press 1969) p. 30. All rights reserved. Used by permission.

15. John H. Gerstner, *Reason For Faith,* p. 115. Reprinted 1967 by Baker Book House and used by permission.

16. Stoner, *Science Speaks,* p. 112.

CHAPTER FOUR

Miracles Attest To The Truth Of The Bible And Its Christ

Miracles . . . what about them? As C. S. Lewis has said, "Christianity is precisely the story of a great Miracle." David Hume has defined a miracle as a "violation of natural law." Christian thinkers however, usually prefer to think of miracles as unusual events caused by God. Some think of miracles as God interposing a higher natural law, unknown to us. Others view miracles as a sovereign act of creation by God in supernatural power. Since Jesus Christ used miracles in part to authenticate Himself as the Son of God, God Himself in human flesh,

> (And without controversy great is the mystery of godliness: God was manifest in the flesh, justified in the Spirit, seen of angels, preached unto the Gentiles, believed on in the world, received up into glory.
> —I Timothy 3:16)

and to cause men to believe on Him (John 20:31), and since if He truly is God and vouched for the Scriptures as the Word of God, miracles have a two-fold significance. To vindicate Jesus, is to vindicate the Scriptures. To vindicate the Scriptures, is to vindicate Jesus. Circular reasoning, to be sure, but in this case justified.

Part of the evidence God gives us through Jesus Christ are the miracles Jesus performed as a divine attestation of His Godhood. These were not cloak and dagger escapades, performed in dim-lit rendezvous, as a cloak for some charlatan of chicanery, but acts of infinite power, mercy and majesty, done in the full glare of day and the brighter glare of publicity.

Take the raising of Lazarus, for instance, recorded in John 11. This man had been dead and deteriorating for four days when Jesus raised him from the dead. The name of the town, Bethany, a small, easily accessible hamlet just outside Jerusalem, is given. The names of Mary, Martha, and Lazarus are given. Jews were present. How easily the enemies of Jesus could have discredited the whole story if it were not true, for it was a simple matter to authenticate or demolish. Yet even His enemies could not deny that Lazarus had been raised from the dead. Neither can we unless we are prepared to assume to call Jesus, Mary, Martha, and Lazarus liars; or the Gospel writer, John, a liar. Many people still alive when his account came out, could have easily disproved the account and laughed or lashed the Gospel into oblivion, if it were not true. It is also thrilling to note that Lazarus spent four days in eternity. He could have come back and denounced Jesus Christ as a liar and an impostor, *if He were not what He claimed to be*—but Lazarus and his family loved Jesus even more! Lazarus knew by actual experience that Jesus Christ was the Son of God and that heaven and hell were real. He had personally visited the eternal home of Jesus Christ.

The supernatural darkness surrounding the Cross for three hours, cloaking the agony of the son of God, baffles men until this day. Science declares that there was an eclipse at that time; and for that length of time; and at that place; but that it could not occur *naturally*. Yet even heathen historians admit such darkness *did* occur. Even Celsus, a bitter opponent of Christianity in the first days of its growth, conceded that the eclipse occurred. Besides, if the Gospel account of the Cross be a myth, why would the Gospel writers include in the account an obviously self-destroying story of three hours of darkness? Thousands were in Jerusalem at that time and could easily have proved it a lie, smearing and ruining the whole account of the Cross. Many of the thousands thronging Jerusalem were still alive when this account was written and circulated. Why did they not challenge this obvious lie, if indeed it was not true, and so crush Christianity? Why? Because it *was* true.

Consider this miracle recorded in all four Gospels. Jesus fed 5,000 people from a little lad's five loaves and two fishes. This miracle aptly portrayed Jesus Christ as the Bread of Life. It proved that He was God the Creator, as was said of Him (John 1:3). It also showed His compassion for the hungry multitude.

This miracle was totally impossible for anyone but God to do and absolutely impossible to fake. Several years ago in Anchorage, Alaska, I led Ian Drummond, a chef at the plush Captain Cook Hotel, to Christ. Though a young man, Ian had been a chef in six different countries and had once cooked for Queen Elizabeth. He had considerable experience in feeding crowds. We calculated about how much food it would take to feed a crowd of 5,000 men, not to mention women and children. We determined five loaves and two fishes were apparently about enough for one small boy. The people had not eaten for quite some time, and had hiked and climbed a mountain. They were probably ravenous. It would have taken 25,000 loaves and 10,000 fishes for just the men to have as much as the lad! It may have required double this amount considering the women and children.

But even if our calculations were off, even if only one-tenth the amount of food were needed (2,500 loaves and 1,000 fishes), a stupendous miracle was required.

Jesus sat on the open mountain, in broad daylight, and fed all these people by breaking up five loaves and two fishes, and having them multiply right before the eyes of the people and His disciples until all had plenty! They then took up 12 baskets full of leftovers!

Ian and I agreed that it would take a *boxcar,* maybe several, full of food to feed that many people, literally thousands of pounds of food! If it were a fake, where did Jesus hide the food? In His robe? To even hint He hid the food is foolish because there is no way to hide that amount of food on a bare hillside before the eyes of thousands.

Apart from the impossibility of faking the miracle, to hint that it was faked, is to accuse the Son of God of lying hypocrisy or to accuse the four Gospel writers, who recorded the event independently, of collusion and duplicity. These disciples and others of that multitude who later became disciples, gave up everything for Jesus. In some cases, even their very lives. Would they show such devotion for a known faker?

Remember, we are not talking about taking a rabbit out of a hat in some dim-lit rendezvous, with loose cloaks and helpful props. We are dealing with thousands of pounds of food, produced in broad daylight, before thousands of witnesses, from five loaves and two fishes. There is *no way* this can be explained except as a direct miracle of God, proving the claims of the Lord Jesus Christ!

This account was published during the lifetime of many who were there. If the event never occurred, the fraud could and would have been exposed by friends, disillusioned disciples, or the bitter enemies of Jesus. To have included such an event in the Gospel record if it had not occurred as presented, would have immediately discredited the New Testament upon its first circulation.

Please consider the evidence. Men who know nothing about electricity do not hesitate to turn on the switch and use the light. They would think you eccentric if you stood in the dark and argued that the whole idea of electricity sounded weird; that you didn't understand it fully; and that you were not about to turn the switch until you did.

Yet many men still approach God's miracles on this basis. God will not cram you with so many facts that you are forced to believe against your will. That would violate your free agency and leave no room for faith. God has ordained that we come to Him by faith (Heb. 11:6). He *does* provide us with abundant evidence so that faith is resting on the credible promises of God.

Since He will not force you, physically or mentally, *you* must make the final choice. But to ignore the evidence and say there is none while believing countless other things with little evidence, may haunt you for a billion years in hell!

Do Miracles Happen Today?

George Mueller proved, incontrovertibly, to any skeptic who would dare to investigate, that the God of the Bible hears and answers prayer. By daily, believing prayer, Mueller supported an orphanage; partly to help orphans; partly to prove to all men forever the reality of the prayer-hearing and answering God of the Bible.

Mueller supported hundreds of orphans over many years. He never asked anyone for a cent or even made his needs known until after God met them. Never *once* did God fail, though some experiences were dramatic.

Many Christians have thrilled to the breakfast episode, when Mueller and his many orphans prayed over empty plates, thanking God by faith that He would provide their food. Just at that moment a milk truck broke down. The driver came in to donate the milk he could not use. Simultaneously a baker came by; God had awakened him early and urged him to bake bread and bring it to the orphanage.

Once, shortly after I trusted in Christ, I was isolated at a lookout tower on Lenhart's Butte in Oregon, almost without food, and with my wife and children. To put God to the test, I asked for three desperately needed items, *that day!* We asked God for meat and bread, which we needed, and for milk, which our baby urgently needed.

Later that day a friend, who never brought us a gift before or since, felt impressed to drive up the 30 or so miles of poor but passable road to see us. On the way he stopped by the home of another Christian family, and they tossed a chicken in the car for us. The thought occurred to him that we might need bread, so he bought some and brought it along. That took care of our meat and bread, but he didn't bring milk. Had God failed us? No! Believe it or not, a neighbor several miles away down the mountainside walked through the woods with some milk. Before sundown we were rejoicing over bread, meat and milk, the exact three items we had requested, and over such a wonderful, loving Saviour.

Miracle After Miracle

I could multiply this story many times. During the years I was attending seminary, we were often in need financially, but I was determined to finish and avoid the temptation to drop out and go to work. I had enticing offers in other fields, but God had laid on my heart the burden of taking the Gospel of Christ to lost men and women. Even to be President of the U.S. would have seemed nothing compared to the joy and responsibility of winning a person to Christ.

As a result we often had little or no food at home as I worked at whatever nighttime jobs were available. We soon learned that, though God does not bless shirkers or loafers, when you honestly are helpless and call on Him, He always hears and answers His own. Time and time again we asked for specific things, *letting no one else know our need*. And time and time again a box was left surreptitiously on our back porch, or an envelope shoved under our door containing exactly what we needed, because we had asked God for the item and trusted Him to respond to our request. Even to attempt to explain this by *chance* or *coincidence* boggles the imagination. The multiplicity of the occasions precludes the possibility.

Among the many indisputable answers to prayer was an experience some years ago when we were in a financial quandary, through medical and other emergencies. I prayed to God for $1,000. A check came in the mail for that *exact* amount. Why did it happen at just that particular time? Because God is real.

Shortly after accepting Christ, I heard my wife Virginia crying one night with pain that had plagued her legs many a sleepless night for twelve years. I prayed hesitantly, brokenly, like a child, in my new faith, wobbling toward God. He heard, and instantly healed her legs. She's had years of trouble-free rest from that problem.

Several years ago my wife came home from a doctor's examination and told me she had to have surgery immediately. She had developed five tumors since her examination ten months before. One was as big as a grapefruit. I tried to keep cheerful before her until she went to bed. There is cancer in her family and I was heartsick. I had promised God I'd thank Him in *all* things, good or bad, as He commanded, but oh, how I loved my wife. I was somehow sure that this was *it,* that I'd lose her.

When she went to bed, I fell on my knees and through my tears thanked God, by faith *not* by feeling, for I was crushed. I told God I gave her to Him willingly, to take or leave, and would thank Him no matter what happened, but please to spare her and give me a verse in my need. I then opened my Bible at random to 2 Kings 20:5b: "I have heard thy prayer, I have seen thy tears, behold I will heal thee." I knew God had answered. I just praised Him that she would be all right. The tumors were benign. My wife recovered completely. Again, marvellously, God met the need!

Of the thousands of verses in the Bible, how can you explain my opening to that verse for the one and only time in a long life of reading the Bible 365 days a year? Just when I desperately needed it! Chance? Sure takes a lot of faith to believe that!

A Rumor of Caribou

I was holding meetings in Ninilchik, Alaska, when Dale Doner and his wife received Christ as Saviour. Dale is a hardheaded businessman, as pragmatic as a ball-bearing. We made plans to go caribou hunting together in an old truck he had purchased, but work and delays forced us to wait until very late in the season, when the Denali Highway, a wild wilderness road to Mt. McKinley, was closed to traffic except at one's own risk.

Because we needed meat and because we were already en route when the closing was announced over the radio, we followed a rumor of caribou nine miles off the road. We turned our truck off the road into the wilderness at about Milepost 84. I was very concerned; we had our wives along, and it was cold and miserable. It had begun to snow. We could easily get stuck in the snow, or get lost and freeze to death. We soon passed an abandoned "swamp-buggy" stuck in the snow. We were going miles farther in. The snow was getting thicker by the minute and darkness would soon overtake us.

I was afraid we were doing something exceedingly foolish, risking the lives of our wives. But we needed meat. Since Dale was a new Christian, I felt he'd take any faltering on my part as a lack of faith. Yet faith and foolhardiness are in two different categories.

We had just about reached the point of no return, several hours before dark, and several, slow, arduous miles off the road in thickening snow, when Dale stopped and motioned me off the open-bedded truck where I was shivering with my wife. "Do you think we should go on?" Dale asked.

"I don't know," I answered honestly enough, "but I know Someone who does."

"Who?" Dale asked quickly.

"God," I answered.

"Yes, but how's that going to help us? I know *He* knows, but *we* don't," Dale declared.

"He'll let us know if we ask Him and trust Him," I said. remembering James 1:5, "If any of you lack wisdom, let him ask of God . . . and it shall be given him."

"How?" he shot back looking both inquisitive and startled. His sharp analytical brain no doubt working overtime.

Sign in the Snowstorm

Then suddenly, I remembered that I had heard someone say that Dale knew God answered prayer spiritually. As a brand-new Christian, he had never seen God answer prayer materially in such a way that there could be no doubt. Immediately it seemed to me that God spoke to my heart. Ordinarily the only "sign" I would have expected from God after praying and claiming His wisdom would be His unmistakable guidance and peace about the decision. But now I turned to Dale, pointed at the sullen, glowering clouds spitting snow on us, motioned to a gray, monolithic rock against the side of a small mountain, which we could only dimly see, and suggested that we ask God to open a hole in the thick cloud layer and let the sun shine through directly on the big rock mass. This was fantastic and he knew it. In quick consultation, we agreed that since our winter's meat supply and, more important, the possible life or death of four people was at stake, we would make this request of God. Since there was no time to waste, we'd ask God to do it within 10 minutes. If this sign was granted, we would proceed, but if not, we would go back to the road while we still had a chance.

Quietly, but intensely, we poured out our request to the Lord. Then we took out our watches and waited and watched. Those were some of the most thrilling moments of my life. Within about five minutes a rift appeared in the hitherto blanketed sky. The snow temporarily slackened and the sun shone through, illuminating the rock mass we had indicated. Within about seven to nine minutes, the exact situation we had asked for was perfectly granted. God's presence was unbelievably real. Just after 10 minutes the clouds closed over again and the snow became *worse,* but we went on our way rejoicing, knowing we were as safe as if we were in our warm homes, for God does not mislead those who fully trust Him.

Nine miles in at about dark, we ran head-on into an unexpected little trapper's cabin abandoned but well-stocked. According to the code of the wilderness, we helped ourselves, replacing wood used and leaving things as we found them. We had the warmest, nicest night of the trip, and my wife killed a fine specimen of a caribou. We later came out to the highway and God gave us 10 or 11 more—a fine winter's meat supply, for ourselves and others in need.

Yes, we have a God who is *real.* He will be real to you, if you will put your trust in Him.

CHAPTER FIVE

The Miracle Of Jesus

The Miracle of Jesus

Sooner or later, we must face the claims of Jesus Christ, Himself. Jesus Christ was either a monstrous liar, cruelly deceiving people who would later die in dungeons, caves, and flames for Him, or He was insane, a paranoid—or He was the Son of God, God in the flesh (John 1:14), as He claimed to be. (I Tim. 3:16) (See John 7:17)

No other view of Jesus can stand up to examination. To approach Him as a good man, for example, but less than God, is to shred logic and emasculate words of all meaning. How could such a deceiver and liar be a *good* man, if He was not God, not the only way to heaven, never coming again for us as He claimed?

As the bewildered officers who were sent by scribes and

Pharisees to arrest Jesus exclaimed, "Never man spake like this man, (John 7:46) ." Your whole life, death, eternity, heaven or hell depend upon the truth or falseness of the claims of Jesus Christ. Shouldn't you *at least consider Him?*

Never was another man born like Him. Isaiah 9:6 and Isaiah 7:14 state that the Babe to be born of a virgin would be God clothed in human flesh. The *place* of His birth, Bethlehem, was predicted some 700 years before He was born (Micah 5:2)! The tribe through which He would come, even the family line, was designated. The *time* of His birth was given (Daniel 9:25, 26) and has been carefully worked out by such scholars as Sir Robert Anderson.

Can you name one other man in history of whom this was true? A believing remnant in Israel awaited Christ's arrival. Can you name any man in history whose birthplace, family line, and time of birth were prophesied hundreds of years before he was born, and for whom, because they knew these prophecies, numerous people waited? Mary and Joseph did not even live in Bethlehem. It took a special tax enrollment, which was protested by the Jews, to bring Mary and Joseph to the little town of Bethlehem for Jesus to be born there, exactly as prophesied and exactly on God's schedule.

Never did another man live like Him. Christ's whole life was foretold in detail: His purpose, His method of death. His ministry was foretold in advance and then *perfectly fulfilled.*

All the embellishments of character of all the great men that ever walked the earth could not combine to make one Jesus. He, and He alone, was flawless, without sin. Buddha was a wife-deserter, not even professing to believe in God. Muhammad was, study shows, an ordinary man with many flaws. Christ, matchless in his perfection, was nevertheless real in His humanity.

Never did another man make such claims. Jesus Christ—creator of the universe. "All things were made by Him and without Him was not anything made that was made (John 1:3)." What holds the atoms together? Why is this intricate little world so meticulously and intelligently designed? "And He [Jesus] is before all things and by Him all things *consist* [hold together, adhere] (Colossians 1:17)."

Jesus said that He and the Father are one. He told inquiring Philip, "He that hath seen me hath seen the Father (John 14:9b)." Jesus claimed to be God. He accepted worship as God (John 20:28). Forgave sin as God! What would we think of any man alive today if he made the preposterous claim of being the "door" to heaven—if he said, "I am the way, the truth, and the life; no man cometh unto the Father but by Me?" Jesus Christ made that claim! (John 14:6) Did He *lie?* If so, *why?* Is the claim true? Is He the only way to heaven? He *claimed* to be. Who's narrow-minded, the Christian who *believes* that claim, or Jesus Christ, who made it?

If all religions lead to heaven, why did Jesus come? There were hundreds of gods, religions, and sincere worshipers already. Why did He come and make that sweeping, all-embracing claim? Why was the early world set aflame by Christians and virtually turned upside down by those who carried this claim far and near?

Never did another man die as this Man. As was foretold hundreds of years before, Jesus died *pierced* on a cross. A method unknown when the prediction was given in such descriptions as Psalm 22:16. Over 300 predictions were literally, minutely, perfectly fulfilled in His life, death, and resurrection, many on the very day He died. Some were that He would be pierced, be given vinegar, have soldiers gamble for His clothing, die with transgressors, be buried in a rich man's tomb, be mocked, thirst, and that not a bone of Him would be broken (Exodus 12:46; Psalm 34:20). The thieves' legs were broken. Had the legs of Jesus been broken, we could throw our Bibles away. But not only could the legs of Jesus *not* be broken, for God staked His reputation upon it, but neither can the Scriptures of God. Heaven and earth must have trembled and the angels crowded the ramparts of heaven as brawny soldiers raised their rod to break the legs of Jesus. All creation held its breath at the brazen challenge to God's son and His Word. But the rod was lowered, unused, the legs unbroken, for Jesus was dead already.

No one else ever died for such a purpose. He constantly and repeatedly stated, as the Old Testament had stated of Him hundreds of years before, that He came to *die* for us, to take our place, to bear our sins, to bleed in our place, because He loves us. Jesus said, by the Cross, through His tears and blood, "I love you, beloved; I love you!" No man ever loved you like that and no one ever voluntarily died in such agony to prove it. If you cannot trust Jesus who *died* for you, who *loves* you, whom can you *ever* trust?

No other man rose from the grave, conquering death. The founders of the world's religions: Buddha, Confucius, Muhammad, all are dead. Their followers do not even claim otherwise. Only Jesus Christ has power over death. He claimed, "No man taketh it [my life] from Me," He said. "but I lay it down of Myself. I have power to lay it down, and *I have power to take it again* (John 10:18)."

Jesus Christ was absolutely unique in human history because He was, as the Bible says, "God's only begotten Son" (John 3:16). He was God made known in the flesh (1 Tim. 3:16).

The Miracle of Resurrection

The Resurrection itself was Jesus' greatest and most significant miracle. Time and time again I've sat down with avowed atheists or agnostics and slowly, carefully, gone over the *facts* of the Resurrection, letting them attack it from all angles at their leisure, and then letting God, through His Book, show them the overwhelming proof of the risen Lord until suddenly, like Thomas of old, they have fallen at His wounded feet and cried out, "My Lord and My God!"

The challenges to the resurrection of Christ usually come along these lines:

"The soldiers stole the body." Absurd. What for? To risk their lives? These tormentors and persecutors of Christianity could have easily squelched Christianity and the disciples' claims by presenting the body of Christ when the disciples began to preach the resurrected Christ. *Why didn't they?* Besides, the disciples would have been telling a lie and dying for it. Why?

"The disciples stole the body." Those disconcerted, frightened disciples who fled the horrors of the cross would defy the power of Rome for a dead body? When they wouldn't even stand by Christ when He was alive! Besides, can you imagine all of the soldiers asleep, when their very lives depended on the outcome? They were to set a *sure* watch. The tomb was sealed by the imperial seal of Rome. How could the disciples break the seal and move the huge rock that sealed the tomb without awakening the soldiers? Besides, if the soldiers were asleep, as they were paid to say, how would they know the disciples came and stole the body as they were also paid to claim, according to Scripture?

Furthermore, over 500 believers saw the risen Jesus (1 Corinthians 15:1-6). He was seen at least 10 times over a period of 40 days. His disciples saw Him, ate with Him, touched Him, talked to Him. Would these men deliberately lie and then go out and suffer for that lie; losing homes, families, possessions; often being hunted and tortured to *death?* This is a psychological impossibility. The disciples did not steal the body of Jesus Christ.

"Jesus swooned, was put in the tomb while yet alive, revived, and pushed the stone away and came forth." The Roman soldiers had experience in knowing whether or not a man was dead. They easily detected life in the two thieves. Besides, medically speaking, the spear of one soldier pierced the side of Jesus. Blood and water ran forth, indicating a ruptured heart sac. How, after this excruciating experience, beaten and tortured repeatedly the night before, crucified, wounded and bleeding, could Jesus *possibly* have survived? How could He *remain* alive, pierced and bleeding, mortally wounded, and even *recover* to push aside a gargantuan rock—almost impossible for anyone, however strong—from the *inside?* Then how could He maneuver past the Roman soldiers without disturbing them, a staggering, bleeding, emaciated, specter of a man, find the disciples, and make *them* believe He had conquered death? This does not take into account the angel's appearance to the soldiers, Jesus appearing through locked doors, and the ascension. It is utterly incredible. It would take far more *faith* to believe such nonsense than to believe the truth!

"The disciples suffered from hallucinations; they wanted to see Jesus so badly that they had a vision of Him." In that case, the soldiers must have had hallucinations also. Otherwise, how can the angels and the empty tomb be explained? The *fact* remains, the *body* of Jesus Christ was *gone!* Not only that, but hallucinations for 500 people in broad daylight, repeated to some of them when Jesus ascended to heaven?

(Hallucinations usually increase in intensity and frequency.) An hallucination they could touch, eat with, talk with, that transformed their lives for good? Nor does this explain *what happened to the body!*

The fact is the disciples *saw* the risen Christ and flamed forth to tell the news; freed from doubt and fear of death; rejoicing to suffer shame for Him! Nothing can account for the dramatic, sudden change in their lives except the bodily resurrection of Christ!! They saw Him!!!

But if Jesus conquered death, then His claims are true. He *alone* knows all the facts of heaven and hell, of eternity, of life and death. What *facts,* not theories or speculations, have men to present to deny Him?

A Communist—by hearsay the leader of Communism in Southern California, a brilliant lawyer—was badly shaken at my testimony to him of the miracle-working, risen Christ. In fact, his wife said he was too upset to go to work the following day.

This man kept telling me that he believed the *teachings* of Christ, and would be willing to follow His teachings, but wasn't interested in the "foolishness" of accepting Christ, being saved, or being born again. I pointed out to him that this was the central part of the teaching of Jesus Christ!

You can't possibly be serious about believing in Christ's teachings, unless you believe that you are a sinner, as He taught; that He was God, as He taught; that He came to die for you and save you; and that you must be born again by receiving Him, as He taught!

The Miracle of Changed Lives

The Power of the Cross, of Jesus Christ to change lives instantaneously, to wash away sins, and to change hate to love, was so graphically illustrated in real life in the case of the 5 young martyrs in Ecuador. Nate Saint, Ed McCully, Jim Elliot, Roger Youderian, and Peter Fleming had flown into the domain of the savage aborigine Auca Indians to carry them the gospel of the Lord Jesus Christ. On January 8, 1956, at least five murderous Aucas; Kimo, Gikita, Nimonga, Minkayi and Dyuwi, speared and slew them bloodily and brutally, and destroyed the plane.

Frank Drown, a fellow missionary who almost went with them, told me about going to get their bodies, and how it almost broke his heart! He knew them all and loved them. Imagine the shattering news to their young wives and children, parents and families. Yet, in unbelievable love and forgiveness, God worked. All five killers became the first male Aucas to confess Christ as their Saviour.

Nate Saint was the murdered missionary pilot of the plane. Nate's sister, Rachel Saint, went in to these murderous Auca Indians, killers of her brother, and lived among them and shared the gospel with them as she mastered the language. Four of the killers received Christ and were baptized in a little over two years. The fifth was saved a little later and was baptized by the brother of Nate and Rachel Saint, Phil Saint! The wives of these Auca men also opened their hearts to the forgiving, life-changing Lord Jesus Christ, and followed Him in baptism. What a Saviour!

B. H. Carrol, an intellectual genius who had graduated from college, mastered Greek, and could actually quote much and possibly most of the Bible by age 20, came home from the Civil War crippled, cynical, and an atheist. He was compiling a book on "6000 Contradictions in the Bible."

One night, at the insistence of his mother, he attended a "brush arbor" revival meeting. He stood in the shadows in silent scorn as the ignorant Bible-believing preacher prated of Christ and the cross and salvation. Suddenly a challenge from the preacher based on John 7:17 was hurled at him. In effect, Jesus said that if anybody really wanted to do God's will, it would be revealed to that person whether or not His claims were true.

After the meeting, Carrol yielded his aching heart and life to Jesus. He rushed madly home, searched through his "6000 Contradictions in the Bible" until the break of day, trying to see them again in the Scriptures, but found to his astonishment and delight that they had all melted away, never to return! He became a great theologian and preacher of the Gospel.

Who can change the attitudes and habits of a lifetime in a moment? Only Jesus can. But He must be received by faith.

President Johnson visited Anchorage while I lived there. A 14-year-old-girl shook hands with him, and though she'd previously shaken hands with the Beatles, she said this was even better. She was *never* going to wash that hand again! But, with all due respect to the President, if this girl had serious moral problems or crippling habit patterns *before* she met the President, she still had them *after* she met him. But an encounter with Jesus Christ is life-changing.

One night in Anchorage, I dealt with Ed Perry of McRae Street. Ed was a professing agnostic, embittered somewhat by a physical tragedy in the family. He had a Roman Catholic background and was an ex-semipro football player. When I finally got him alone in the basement of his home, he was resisting hard against the Gospel.

To my surprise as much as Ed's, I abruptly interrupted our verbal sparring and said, "Ed Perry, you are going to be saved in five minutes." I marched over to his side, opened the Bible, and in five minutes Ed was a Christian, rejoicing in salvation, his bitterness gone forever, and his whole pattern of life radically changed. I *never* would have said anything like this of myself, but God laid this on my heart. Ed was saved in five minutes! What else can change a man like that but *Christ*!

If you find this story hard to swallow, ask the Rev. Ed Perry, pastor in Everett, Washington, for God soon called him into the ministry. There are many other things he would add to this story, for his life was sick with sin and shame until Jesus found him.

Christ *is* the answer. The *only* answer. I am not presenting Christianity per se. Most people have a caricature of Christianity, which they reject. Tragically, they never encounter real Christianity, which is *Christ*.

As I indicated, I have appealed both to your heart and mind. I can do nothing. I cannot possibly verbalize the glory and wonder of Jesus Christ. But if the Holy Spirit of God takes this feeble effort and reveals the reality of Christ to you so that you *want* Him, I will be happy beyond words. Only God's Spirit *can* reveal Christ to you and then only if you are *willing* to see.

An atheist was deriding a little boy because he was so happy that his alcoholic dad had accepted Christ. The atheist chided the boy for being so naive as to believe the myth of the Bible and that old-fashioned stuff about being "saved." He finished by exclaiming, "Boy, you're dreaming!"

The boy replied, "Mister, Dad used to come home and beat and kick me. I'd hide in terror when I heard him come staggering home. He cursed and beat my dear mom. We were often cold and hungry and short of clothes. Mother cried a lot. Now Dad buys nice clothes for Mother and kisses and hugs her. He takes me on his knee and tells me stories and tells me he loves me. Our home is warm and snug and we all love Jesus. Mister, if I'm dreaming, please don't wake me up!"

I've seen this miracle of Jesus happen in countless lives in many geographical areas. Jesus frees from enemies more subtle but just as deadly as alcohol: doubt, insecurity, hopelessness, dread, fear, anguish, purposelessness, uncertainty.

Time after time I've seen the light of heaven glow in dark and dying eyes; homes saved; tangled lives unraveled when people met Jesus Christ. And for the man whose life is unsullied with any cloud of circumstance, Jesus still makes life immeasurably sweeter, richer here, and offers heaven instead of hell, hereafter. My friend, with all my strength, my mind, my soul, my life, I recommend to you my Saviour and my God, the Lord Jesus Christ.

When I was in the Navy, and suicide planes were attacking us off Okinawa, I noticed a peculiar reaction, much like that of Pavlov's dog. We had a buzzer which signaled the alert for action on repeated occasions. After a while, we sailors experienced knots in the pits of our stomachs, dry mouths, and intense reactions when the buzzer sounded, usually long before the planes were sighted. We began to actually resent the buzzer! Yet had we put plugs in our ears or ignored the buzzer, we would be dead today, as many times our instant response to the buzzer got us into position to defend our ship and our lives before the enemy came.

This is exactly the way conviction works. Conviction alarms one out of his apathy; mental or moral. One can then either apply ear plugs—ignore the alarm of conviction, the nagging uneasiness—or quickly respond and honestly confront and accept the risen Christ. Christ then secures us from all enemies.

Sometimes there is but one alarm and that may be but faintly heard above the clamor of the world.

Dear friend, I love each and every one of you who may read this book. Please come now to the *Biblical* God, the

Biblical Lord Jesus Christ. Only the Biblical Christ can save you. *Trust* His Word. Trust *Him!*

Remember this, no evidence can convert you. Only God's Holy Spirit can, as you yield to Jesus. Yet as we have said, God does give objective evidence. Only the devil asks for blind faith. Consider prophecy one more time.

Sometimes when I mention the prophecies of the Word of God, I get this retort, "So what?" Jeanne Dixon [or someone else] makes prophecies also, and many of her predictions come true!"

God anticipated this objection. In the Bible He gave this test for the true prophet of God:

> 20. But the prophet, which shall presume to speak a word in my name, which I have not commanded him to speak, or that shall speak in the name of other gods, even that prophet shall die.
> 21. And if thou say in thine heart, How shall we know the word which the Lord hath not spoken?
> 22. When a prophet speaketh in the name of the Lord, if the thing follow not, nor come to pass, that is the thing which the Lord hath not spoken, but the prophet hath spoken it presumptuously: thou shalt not be afraid of him.
> —Deuteronomy 18:20-22

The test was 100% accuracy with every detail of every prophecy coming true every time. Otherwise the prophet was not of God and was stoned to death. That sort of discouraged false prophets!

There is not a "prophet," prognosticator, or predictor alive today who can pass the Biblical test. All are false, according to the Bible.

From Nostradamus to Edgar Cayce to Jeanne Dixon, however admirable they may be as people, they flunk the test as prophets of God because their predictions are hit and miss. I once counted 15 of Jeanne Dixon's predictions that failed from one book alone.

Ignoring this for the moment, suppose Jeanne Dixon predicted 100 things that would happen to you in the coming year. Many of these predictions are very detailed. One of the first is that you will stub your toe on a chair leg on January 1st at 12:35 P.M. and fall on a glass on the table, which will shatter and cut a U-shaped wound on your chin. This jagged wound will require 13 stitches. It will be sewn up by a new doctor in town named McGuire, your personal doctor being unavailable at the time. When January 1st comes, this is *exactly* what happens, right down to the most minute detail!

Then, throughout the year, 99 of these prophecies are literally, actually, perfectly fulfilled in every detail. Ninety-nine true, fulfilled perfectly; one more to go! This prophecy is for the last day of the year and says that if you drive downtown to 5th and Main at 5 P.M., you will be in a fiery car crash that will leave you blind and crippled and in excruciating pain. You will be hospitalized for six months and finally die.

Tell me, would you deliberately drive down to 5th and Main at 5 P.M. on the last day of the year? Would you consider it a safe, sane, intelligent risk, when 99 prophecies have come true without a failure, virtually impossible mathematically by chance alone?

Now for purposes of convenience let's round Bible prophecies off to a hundred, 99 of which have already been perfectly fulfilled. The 100th prophecy is that if you ignore, or refuse to accept Jesus Christ as your personal Lord and Saviour, you will die without hope and spend eternity in the lake of fire. A billion years from now your agony and despair and lostness from His love will barely have begun. Since the other Bible prophecies came true in literal and absolute fact, would it be intelligent to gamble your soul that this one will not?

We may never walk this way again together. This is no mere cold intellectual path we've trod. I confess to you that His love has stained the way with tears from my eyes as He has, I honestly believe, spoken to you through me. I'm just a voice—it's *His* heartbeat you felt. From the bloody cross, the empty tomb, and now at your heart's door, He pleads with you. "Behold, I stand at the door and knock; if any one hears My voice and opens the door, I will come in," (see Revelation 3:20). Have you invited Him in? Will you?

To invite Jesus into your heart as your Lord and Saviour, just pray this suggested prayer, or a prayer from your heart expressing this same desire.

"Lord Jesus Christ, come into my heart and life. Cleanse me from all sin by Your blood shed on the cross for me. Make me a child of God. Give me Your free gift of everlasting life. Let me KNOW that I am saved, now and forever. I now receive You as my very own personal Lord and Saviour. In Jesus name, Amen."

Jesus loves you . . . so much! He died for you, on a brutal, bloody cross. Would He, could He, turn you down when you call on Him? Never!

Jesus not only loves you and died for you, He PROMISED to save you, to enter your life, if you would invite Him in, and He CANNOT lie. Clearly then, if you invited Him in believingly, He had to save you or He had to lie. Which did He do?

God says in 1 John 5:12a, "He that hath the Son hath life." (Everlasting life, salvation.) If you invited Jesus to come into your heart and life and trusted Him to do what He died for and promised to do, where is He now? In your heart and life! What do you now have? Everlasting life! God's unbreakable Word says so!

Thank Him please, right now, for saving your soul, and giving you His free gift of eternal life!!!

Please read the instructions given in the third book of this 3-in-one book. Carefully read the chapter, "This is the Way," to review and clarify your decision. Then read the following chapter, "The Christ-Changed Life," for information on how to grow in Christ and obey Him effectively.

(Both of these chapters are in the back of this 3-in-one book, and they are the last two chapters.)

Jesus said, John 14:23a, " . . . if a man love me, he will keep my words . . ." The desire to manifest your love for Him in obedience and growth is the evidence God says will follow true conversion.

Finally, much important information on church and reading material is given at the back of the book, following the last chapter.

Whether you made a decision or not, whether you are a Christian or not, please read the entire book, including all of the three books it contains.

May God bless it to your heart in a very special way.

THE MORMON ILLUSION

Floyd C. McElveen

A Division of GL Publications
Ventura, CA U.S.A.

Contents

Preface 5
1. My Introduction to Mormonism, and to Christ 9
2. Joseph Smith and the First Vision 22
3. Joseph Smith—Prophet of God? 32
4. The Book of Mormon—
   Joseph Smith's or God's? 39
5. Joseph Smith Tested as a Translator 51
6. History, Archaeology, Anthropology
   and the Book of Mormon 58
7. The Fatal Flaw 67
8. The Truth About "Adam-God" 79
9. Contradictions Concerning the Person of God 91
10. Priesthood and Genealogies 98
11. Some Distinctive but Dubious
    Doctrines of Mormonism 110
12. The One True Church 126
13. The Final Authority 137
14. Mormon Salvation 152
15. Biblical Salvation 165
Appendix: They Way to Salvation 183
Bibliography 207

*To my much loved and understanding wife,
Virginia McElveen.
With special thanks to Bruce and Flo Walters
and the Hoy Deeters for fiancial support
and prayer to keep this project alive.*

*To Myrna Chausse for typing and encouragement;
And to all of these for their warm love
and concern for Christ, for the author
and for our Mormon friends.*

*To friends whose love and compassion
for Christ and for Mormons
led them to generously finance and advertise
this book to the salvation of souls
and the glory of Christ.*

For a simple, clear presentation of God's plan of salvation which can be used as a tract see pages 171-181.

Preface

Is it fair, is it Christian to examine Joseph Smith and to question Mormonism?

This is a question I had to pray about and settle before I wrote this book. Insofar as God has given me the light to see from His Word, the following is what I believe He has shown.

Every man has the God-given right to believe as he sees fit. America has recognized that God-given right. We may freely choose to be Christian or pagan, atheist or believer, Buddhist or Moslem, Baptist, Mormon or Catholic. Thank God for this cherished freedom. It is God, not man, who holds us responsible for the consequences of that choice.

The Authority of Love

One of the foremost badges of the true Christian is

love. John 13:35 says, "By this shall all men know that ye are my disciples, if ye have love one to another." Some people believe that this means we should never look critically at another person's religion. "Knocking somebody else's religion isn't love!" Certainly this is true if we have not first looked very critically at our own religion and compared it with God's standard, the Bible.

Another response we might get from those who question our authority to witness is "Judge not lest ye be judged." Matthew 7:1 says, "Judge not, that ye be not judged," but according to Matthew 7:5 this verse is addressed to *hypocrites*. On the other hand John 7:24 tells *Christians* to "judge righteous judgment," not according to appearance but according to the Word of God.

How tragic today that some of us Christians in the name of love have withheld the truth from those in error, lest we offend or because we did not love enough. Remember, real love warns.

It is true that we should not major on minors. It may be unnecessary to tell our neighbor that he has bad breath, or that a shingle on his roof is loose. However, it is criminal not to wake him up if he is asleep inside his house and his house is on fire. No excuse, and no empty professions of love will ever satisfy God in such cases.

The Authority of Defense

How does all of this apply to the question, "Is it fair, is it Christian, to examine Joseph Smith and question Mormonism?" It is fair because Joseph Smith first attacked all Christians and their churches. Joseph Smith declared in his "inspired" *Pearl of Great Price*, that all other churches are wrong, all their creeds are an abomination, all their professors are corrupt.

In one sweep, Joseph Smith condemns all churches, and all their beliefs, and all Christians. He is plainly saying that there was not one true Christian upon the face of the earth at the time he had his first vision, and there hadn't been for hundreds of years.

We have been challenged by Mormon leaders to examine the *Book of Mormon,* which naturally would include its author and its followers. Mormon apostle, Orson Pratt, said:

"This book must be either true or false . . . If false, it is one of the most cunning, wicked, bold, deep laid impositions ever palmed upon the world, calculated to deceive and ruin millions who will sincerely receive it as the Word of God, and will suppose themselves securely built upon the rock of truth until they are plunged with their families into hopeless despair. The nature of the message in the *Book of Mormon* is such that, if true, no one can possibly be saved and reject it; if false, no one can possibly be saved and receive it. Therefore, every soul in all the world is equally interested in ascertaining its truth or falsity . . . If, after a rigid examination, it be found an imposition, it should be extensively published to the world as such; the evidences and arguments on which the imposture was detected, should be clearly and logically stated, that those who have been sincerely yet unfortunately deceived, may perceive the nature of the deception and be reclaimed, and that those who continue to publish the delusion, may be exposed and silenced . . . by evidences adduced from Scripture and reason."[1]

We couldn't agree more! It is Christian to examine Joseph Smith and question Mormonism, because we are commanded to, both for our sake and for the sake of all Mormons.

It is both Christian and sensible to examine Joseph Smith because he claims to be a prophet of God, and we are told, "by their fruits ye shall know them." The *Book of Mormon, Pearl of Great Price, Doctrine and Covenants*, and Mormonism and the whole Mormon movement hinge entirely on this one basic question, "Is Joseph Smith truly a prophet of God?"

We wonder if a teenage boy today had a vision telling him that all Mormons were apostate, corrupt, their creeds an abomination to God, if Mormons would embrace his unwitnessed story as quickly as they did that of Joseph Smith? Why not?

With God's help, we will seek to take a fair and honest look at Joseph Smith and a few of his teachings as Scripture and the love of Christ constrain us to. God loves Mormons and non-Mormons. Christ died for each of us. There is no difference before God in that all of us are simply sinners needing a Saviour. In that sense, we are all on common ground. We need to make a firm and clear distinction between Mormonism and Mormons. We pray God will break our hearts and fill us with His love for Mormons, and we think He has. God, and perhaps others, can judge that better than we can. But loving the Mormon people is far different from loving Mormonism, just as God can love the sinner, but not his sin. Please keep that distinction in mind as we consider the claims of Joseph Smith and Mormonism.

Note

1. Orson Pratt, *Divine Authority of the Book of Mormon*, introduction, a series of pamphlets published in 1850–51. Quoted by Arthur Budvarson, *The Book of Mormon—True or False?* (Concord, Calif.: Pacific Pub. Co., 1959).

CHAPTER ONE

My Introduction to Mormonism, and to Christ

Man, was I excited! I had just moved from muggy Mississippi to the crisp, cool nights and sparkling days of LaGrande, Oregon, in July. My beautiful wife and my brand new baby boy of less than two months were sharing the adventure only a little less enthusiastically.

I loved my native south, but the heat was getting to me. I had visited Oregon while I was in the Navy, and enjoyed its cool nights, wild game, and beautiful mountains. My uncle had operated a store in Bates, Oregon. An aunt had attended Eastern Oregon College of Education at LaGrande. So after my Navy days I went back to LaGrande, enrolled in the college and played one year of football.

Many of the girls were lovely, but I wanted a girl who could bake cornbread. I found her at the University of

Southern Mississippi. Now I was back in fascinating Oregon, preparing for a deer hunt for some urgently needed meat. Not knowing the country too well and not owning a car, I had made friends with a local teenage boy and hoped to hunt the nearby Blue Mountains with him.

"Hey Mike, hurry up!" I groused at him, one scintillatingly beautiful Sunday afternoon. "If you'll quit messing around we can play a little ball and still have time to scout the mountains for deer and find out where the big bucks are before the season opens."

"O.K. I'll hurry and get—" Mike began.

"No you won't!" exploded Mike's older married brother John. As I looked at him in surprise he continued. "We are Mormons, belonging to the Latter-day Saints church and we do not believe in doing things like that on Sunday."

I was both stunned and chagrined. Back in rural Mississippi, practically everybody was a Baptist unless he'd been meddled with. We had gone to church every Sunday faithfully. I had gone forward at 12, told the evangelist I believed in Jesus, been baptized, joined the church, attended faithfully and didn't drink, smoke or curse. Hunting or fishing on Sunday was only for pagans and backsliders, and you didn't want to be too near someone like that in a lightning storm. I had been a Boy Scout leader, and a Sunday School teacher, yet here I was getting a lecture from a Mormon about God and Sunday. I was ashamed. I was also curious.

John was my local barber, and a very good friend. He was also a wheel in the local LDS church. (I didn't know the terminology then.) We ate in his house and he ate in ours. In fact, I will never forget one "squirrel banquet" we shared. We were poor, and food, especially meat, was scarce. I feel sorry for those poor unsuspecting little pine tree squirrels now, but I didn't then. One thing I will say. The survivors were a lot smarter when I left than they were when I got there.

John was such a kind and gentle man, and a good conversationalist. (That's the kind that lets you talk a lot while they mostly listen.) I was attracted to him and his wife right off, especially when he didn't scalp me when cutting my hair. We had not talked about religion up to now.

I had some serious questions about religion after viewing suicide planes, mutilated and dying buddies in the war; and again while taking courses in various colleges in psychology, evolution, comparative religions, etc. Suddenly, here it was. Here was a man who believed and practiced what he stood for. Why hadn't my church brought me to the convictions he seemed to possess? Yes, I was curious.

"May I come to your house and share with you what Mormons believe?" John asked.

"Certainly," I responded eagerly.

My wife looked somewhat askance at the arrangement, but went along with it. I did not know the difference at the time, but she was a real Christian, with Christ dwelling in her heart. I was only a professing Christian with a head belief. She thought I was a real Christian, as we attended church together, prayed together, tithed, and lived a good life.

I had gotten a little bored with church, and she felt something was not quite right, and the pastor of the Conservative Baptist Church in LaGrande, Rev. Guy Zehring, had begun to visit me periodically. I was also bored with him. He repeated things I'd heard all my life.

God loves you. Christ died for you. You ought to be faithful in church.

As John began to introduce me to Mormonism, I became intensely interested. Maybe this *was* the answer!

"Wow, John," I cried, after one session. "You mean I can really be married to my wife for all eternity?"

"It's possible," he assured me, "with some conditions that have to be met. You may even be a god on a planet and continue to have children."

This was so appealing to me. Dad died when I was four. I went to live with my grandfather. He was murdered a few months later. My grandmother got diabetes and, when I was a young teenager, she died a slow, agonizing death. I was almost afraid to fully love anything or anyone. Nothing seemed secure. Nothing was mine to keep and love really, so why break my heart to pieces?

I can still remember the rainy funerals—the cold clods of dirt falling with such dreadful finality on the casket of dad, granddad, grandmother, all so dear to my little heart. The "Old Rugged Cross," valiantly striving to drown out the sobs of loved ones.

Now I had a beautiful young wife. Miracle of miracles, she loved me and I loved her. Was there really a way I could keep her forever?

Generally happy-go-lucky on the surface, I did some serious thinking in the dark of the night. Someday, her beauty would fade. She would grow old and die soon, so soon, and it would be as if she had never been. Or accident or disease would snatch her from me or me from her. Death was an implacable ogre in ambush, ready to pounce day or night, heeding neither the peal of happy laughter, nor the cry of despair and distress.

As John continued to teach me, I became very confused. "Doesn't the Bible say somewhere that there will be no marrying, neither giving in marriage in heaven, John?"

"Sure," he agreed smoothly, "but that only concerns heaven. We can be married for eternity down here so there won't have to be any marrying or giving in marriage in heaven."

Is that really what that verse means? I wondered. Well, maybe. I sure hope so.

John said that my church had no authority to baptize, make converts, or preach the gospel. The true Church had totally vanished off the earth a century or two after Christ, and God had restored the gospel through a modern-day prophet named Joseph Smith. God and His Son had appeared to the seeking Smith when he was 14 and begun a series of visions to him concerning God, gold plates and the gospel. Joseph Smith had, by direct revelation from God, translated the inspired *Book of Mormon*. Later inspired books of Mormonism included the *Pearl of Great Price*, and *Doctrine and Covenants*.

John told me gently but firmly quoting Joseph Smith in *Pearl of Great Price* 2:19, in part, "They [the churches] were all wrong . . . all their creeds were an abomination in his sight; that those professors were corrupt."

This bothered me considerably. The Mormon creed said many of the same things other church creeds said. How could one be totally wrong and abominable and the other O.K.? I knew that many Christians down through the centuries, hundreds of years after the Mormons claimed the true church and the true gospel had totally vanished in apostasy from the earth, had sealed their love and their testimony for Christ in their blood. Were they all corrupt as Joseph Smith claimed?

John taught me that the Mormon church was the one true church on the face of the whole earth. All others were false. The only way to the highest heaven or degree of glory was to leave my church and be baptized into the Mormon church. There were three heavens, or three degrees of glory. Only Mormons could go to the highest heaven. Christ's death on the cross gave all men general salvation from hell, except some very few obstinate "sons of perdition." Personal salvation depended on one's good works. Baptism for the dead was for those who had not had the opportunity to be saved here. They could be saved after death.

I became more and more interested, but also more and more confused. I called Pastor Guy Zehring and tried to compare his answers with John's.

It really seemed to me that John was getting the best of the discussion. I prayed desperately for light. John asked me to take the *Book of Mormon*, lay my hand on it, and pray that if it were truly the Word of God and Mormonism was true to convince me of it by God's Holy Spirit. I did just that. I also prayed the same way about the Bible.

Then, in a puckish spirit, I thought the answer might be in getting John and Guy together and letting them debate the issue. Guy advised me against it, saying it probably wouldn't solve anything for me. I wondered if maybe he was afraid.

By this time I knew that I had to make a decision: become a Mormon or go back to the Christianity I knew which had never met my deepest longings; look deeper into Christianity; forget the whole mess. Each one of these options looked appealing at times.

Finally, I hovered just on the brink of becoming a Mormon. The Mormons I knew were so nice. Their youth program was attractive in the extreme. Some of their churches even had gyms! Their church-sponsored dances looked very inviting. They went out after people to share their faith with them. They were very clean and hard workers. I admired their ruggedness, and reveled in their courageous history of Western migration against impossible odds. Their strong convictions attracted me. They seemed to have such a sense of authority, and so much unity.

One last time, I went to my bedroom, fell on my knees and called out in an agony of need, "God, *please* show me the true way. I don't care which way it is, just so it's from you and the true way. Oh God, I want to be saved so badly. I thought I was when I said I accepted Christ and joined the Baptist church years ago, Lord, but now I am upset. If Mormonism is right I'll gladly accept it and follow it forever. If what I have been taught is right why hasn't it fully met my needs? Oh God, help me. Give me your light. Show me the truth about the Bible and the *Book of Mormon,* about Mormonism and Christianity, and most of all about yourself and how I can be saved and sure of heaven."

Shortly after this honest, searching prayer, I was feverishly getting ready for deer season, which opened the next day. My wife looked outside and said, "Honey, Pastor Guy Zehring just drove up."

"Oh, no," I groaned. I had work to do to prepare to leave for the hunting trip and the pastor had already talked to me five or six times saying practically the same things every time. It seemed so foolish, so unreal and empty. I had a hard time being polite. Only years later did I learn that the Bible says that "the preaching of the cross is to them that perish foolishness" (1 Cor. 1:18).

This time was different. Guy looked me in the eye and said, "Mac, you claim to be a Christian. Do you really know for sure that if you were to die this minute, you'd go to heaven to be with Jesus Christ?"

I bristled. "Nobody can know that for sure," I declared. "I believe that I would go to heaven. I believe in Jesus Christ. I have been baptized, I am religious and I lead a good life. But you said *know*."

Guy's rapier eyes pierced into my very soul. "Mac, if you died tonight, you'd go straight to hell."

"I have done everything you preachers said to do," I answered, "everything I know that the Bible says to do. Does the Bible say that you can know that you are saved?"

"It certainly does," he replied, turning to 1 John 5:13. "These things have I written unto you that believe on the name of the Son of God; that ye may know that ye have eternal life, and that ye may believe on the name of the Son of God."

I was aware of both astonishment and an intense hunger beginning to build inside of me. I had been studying chapters and books of the *Book of Mormon*, and had read the Bible for many years, but nothing had ever spoken to my heart and to my need like this. In spite of occasional doubts, I was really impressed by the Bible. I knew that many of the prophecies of the Bible concerning Jesus Christ, cities, nations and events had come true in every detail. Just the year before, 1948, after 2500 years, the Jews had reestablished the nation of Israel, and this against incredible odds, just as the Bible explicitly predicted. They had retained their identity while bigger, stronger nations had become dusty archaeological statistics hundreds of years gone by.

"How did I miss it, Guy," I asked, almost beseechingly. "Why don't I know?"

"You believed all the facts about Jesus," Guy retorted, "His death, burial, resurrection. But yours is a head belief, not a heart belief. Thousands are just like you—religious but lost. You have a historical belief like saying you believe that George Washington crossed the Delaware. But have you ever come to Jesus Christ as a lost sinner and asked Him to save you, and know that He did it?"

"I have asked Him to save me, but I never really had faith that He did it."

"Don't you see?" countered Guy. "Salvation is by faith, by trust, by believing. Ephesians 2:8,9 declares: 'For by grace are ye saved through faith; and that not of yourselves: it is the gift of God: not of works, lest any man should boast.'

"Now," he continued, "John 1:12 tells us that we are not by nature children of God. That's our big problem. We have to receive Jesus Christ by personal invitation into our hearts and lives in order to become children of God. We are thus born again into the family of God and instantly receive His free gift of everlasting life. 'But as many as received him, to them gave he power to become the sons of God, even to them that believe on his name.' Then and only then are we ready for heaven."

He added, "Jesus loves us so much He died in bloody torture for us. He promised to save us if we would believingly call on Him. When you called, and then wondered or hoped maybe He had done what He died to do and promised to do, you were in essence doubting Him and making Him a liar. Therefore He could not save you, even if you had wept and cried and pleaded to be saved every night for a hundred years, because He only saves by faith. Romans 10:9 tells us that only a heart belief, committal to Christ as the resurrected Lord (God and master) and Saviour can save us.

"Romans 10:13 makes it so clear and simple, a child can understand it, 'For whosoever shall call upon the name of the Lord shall be saved.'

"Mac," Guy said quietly but feelingly, "God loves you. Jesus shed His blood for you. If you ask Him, believing with all your heart, to save you, He will have to save you. Otherwise He would be a liar, because He promised. Will you call upon Him to save you right now?"

Oh, the battle that raged in my heart! Could it really be that simple? Was it for real? Suppose there was a burning hell, after all, and there was even the slightest chance that I might go there for eternity. Was Jesus really the eternal God, as Guy said the Bible declared Him to be? Did He rise bodily and appear to hundreds who touched Him, ate with Him and later died for Him?

Suddenly I knew. If I couldn't trust the simple clear promise of Jesus who died for me, where else was there to go? The desperate longing in me cried out for Jesus, for certainty, and I fell on my knees and poured out my heart to Him and asked Him to come into my heart and forgive me all my sins. I asked Him to make me a child of God forever, and give me everlasting life. I asked Him for a know-so salvation, and took Him as my very own personal Lord and Saviour.

I got to my feet and wiped away a tear. Guy pointed his stubby finger at me and asked, "Did Jesus save you or did He lie? He had to do one or the other."

Inside of me I knew something tremendous had happened. A burden I didn't even know I was carrying was gone; joy and peace unspeakable filled my heart. But after years of psychology, I was not about to depend just on experience, emotions or feelings. So I just said to Guy, "Well, He couldn't lie, so He must have saved me."

Guy turned to John 3:36. "He that believeth on the Son hath everlasting life." I looked very carefully at that verse, savoring every word. Then I knew, not just felt. *Knew!* Jesus had saved me! I now had, right now, everlasting life. His Word said so and He cannot lie. His Holy Spirit witnessed with my spirit that I was His child, sure of heaven with Him in accord with His written Word. Guy and I knelt again and I thanked God very simply for having saved my soul and for giving me everlasting life.

I couldn't wait to tell John! I knew instantly when I was truly saved that Mormonism was not the way. It was as if God turned a great searchlight on the whole system and revealed His answer to me. But I dearly loved John, and wanted to share my joy and utter certainty with him. I gathered up all the considerable Mormon material he had given me and hurried over to his house.

"John, John," I cried. "I've found Jesus. I've just been saved and I know I am going to heaven!"

"You've been hypnotized!" he roared, turning red in the face.

"Don't you know for sure that you have been saved, John?" I asked.

"No and you don't either," he asserted, growing more agitated by the moment.

I was shocked. Could this by my gentle, loving John. Why wasn't he rejoicing at my joy in finding Christ?

"John," I inquired seriously, "do you mean to tell me that all this time you've been talking to me about being in the one true church, about having prophets and priests, about authority, that you don't even know for sure where you are going when you die?

"Suppose I was lost in the woods with a number of other people. Suppose we were desperate with just time to get out if we chose the right trail right away, before we starved or froze to death. Suppose we bumped into you, and you declared you had an infallible map, and that you were a licensed guide for those woods and insisted that we all follow you; all other trails were wrong. Then suppose I asked you if you knew for sure that you were not lost, that you knew just where you were. And you admitted you did not, and were not even sure where you were going. John, I love you, but I know I am saved, and I cannot go your way any longer."

With that I gave John back his material on Mormonism. John and I continued to be friends. Often he visited me with Mormon leaders to try to win me back. I was touched with his obvious concern, his caring. But I knew I would never again be among those the Bible says are "ever learning but never coming to a knowledge of the truth" (see 2 Tim. 3:7).

Once you've truly met Jesus the search is over. I had read my Bible and attended church all my life, but I had missed it. I'd prayed daily, and on long, moonlit walks had often felt the warm presence of Jesus. I believed that I loved Him, but this was different, richer, sweeter by far.

Before salvation was like loving a girl and having a certain amount of communion with her before marriage, but she doesn't belong to you nor do you belong to her. Then, in the simple act of marraige, you say "I do" and she does too. There is no magic in the words, but, if it is true love, your lives are changed forever. She belongs to you and you belong to her. What you thought was love before is no comparison to what you have now. With real salvation, when you get married to Jesus in an act the Bible calls conversion, you *know* the difference. Before, I was religious but lost. Now I am saved.

John has never understood though I've prayed for him and wept for him with a real ache in my heart.

Now years later, after spending thousands of hours in Bible study and reading dozens of Mormon books and booklets—both pro and con—I want to share with other hungry hearts, in Christ's love and as God enables me, what He has shown me.

CHAPTER TWO

Joseph Smith and the First Vision

Many who read this book may well ask: Where did the Mormons get such different ideas about God and about Christ? What is the source of their doctrine? Where did their church really originate? What is the foundation on which their beliefs rest?

Very briefly, the Mormons teach that the true gospel disappeared off the earth shortly after the time of the apostolic church. They believe that *all* churches then became false, and that they had no authority from God. All the professing Christians for hundreds of years were corrupt, false, apostate. Then God *restored* the true gospel with its pristine authority through a young man named Joseph Smith. An angel appeared in a vision to young Joseph and subsequently led him to some golden plates hidden near Palmyra, New York. From these plates, God enabled Joseph Smith to produce the *Book of Mormon*, the first and foundational inspired book on which Mormonism is based.

Since Joseph Smith declared all other churches without exception to be false and all their members to be corrupt, it only seems fair to answer him. If Joseph Smith was a true prophet of God, then the First Vision should be clear and unassailable, as God is not the author of confusion. But let us hear from Mormon sources as to the importance of this First Vision.

First Vision of 1820

David O. McKay, Mormon apostle and leader, stated: "The appearing of the Father and the Son to Joseph Smith is the foundation of this Church."[1]

The Mormon apostle John A. Widtsoe said: "The First Vision of 1820 is of first importance in the history of Joseph Smith. Upon its reality rest the truth and value of his subsequent work."[2]

Obviously, the integrity of Joseph Smith and the truth of Mormonism are at stake. If the First Vision is the foundation on which Mormonism rests, let us prayerfully and carefully examine that foundation.

The Mormon church claims that Joseph Smith had a vision in 1820, when he was a 14-year-old boy. This vision occurred on the "morning of a beautiful, clear day, early in the spring of eighteen hundred and twenty." Joseph Smith had gone to the woods to pray about which of "all the sects was right." While in prayer he saw two personages standing above him in the air. One of the personages pointed to the other and said, "This is My Beloved Son. Hear Him!" Then one of the personages, whom Joseph Smith identifies as the Father and the Son, told him that all churches were wrong.

Strangely enough, there is no mention of this vision in the early Mormon church records and the *Improvement Era,* admits: "Joseph Smith's 'official' account of his first vision and the visits of the angel Moroni was . . . first published in the *Times and Seasons* in 1842."[3] This is 22 years after the event is supposed to have occurred. Yet the first vision is supposed to be the *foundation* of the Mormon church, which began in 1830! The *Book of Mormon* was published in 1830 also. Why didn't Joseph Smith give an official account of the vision before 1842?

For years, Mormons emphatically declared, "Joseph Smith lived a little more than 24 years after this first vision. During this time he told but one story!"[4] This, of course, is not true. Jerald and Sandra Tanner, in their pamphlet, *The First Vision Examined,* have shown that two versions other than his "official" version, existed in the Mormon church, but were not published until exposure by Paul Cheesman, a student at Brigham Young University, in 1965.

Yet another account of the First Vision came to light through James B. Allen, associate professor of History at BYU, in 1966, after Mormon denials for years that there were any other versions! These versions contain important discrepancies from the official version. For a detailed and scholarly explanation, get the Tanners' pamphlet, *The First Vision Examined*.

Even Brigham Young, who had 363 of his sermons

recorded in the *Journal of Discourses,* as an "inspired" apostle succeeding Joseph Smith, failed to mention the First Vision. Mormon librarian Lauritz G. Petersen in a letter dated August 31, 1959, wrote: "I have checked through the *Journal of Discourses* which records many of the sermons of Brigham Young. There is no mention there of anything by Brigham Young on the first vision of Joseph Smith."[5]

Oddly enough Oliver Cowdery, the first Mormon historian (according to *Doctrines of Salvation,* vol. 2, p. 201), did not even refer to the First Vision. Cowdery was one of the three main witnesses to the *Book of Mormon,* yet Earl E. Olsen, Mormon librarian, L.D.S. Church, wrote in a letter dated March 24, 1958, "In the records which we have on file of the writings of Oliver Cowdery, and John Whitmer, such as they are, we do not find a reference to the First Vision."[6]

First Vision of 1823

It has come to light nevertheless, that Oliver Cowdery, assisted for accuracy by Joseph Smith himself, did publish an account of the First Vision in the Mormon *Messenger and Advocate,* in September, 1834, and in February, 1835, differing in important respects from the later "official" 1842 version. Actually, the first reports in the Mormon church of Joseph Smith's First Vision claimed that he was 17 years old, not 14.

(Good Mormon friends, in honest puzzlement over the clear contradictions and confusion we are about to present, have told us we had Joseph Smith's First Vision confused with another vision or visions that he had. We sympathize with their heartbreak over what the following facts will reveal. However, we have read many of Joseph

Smith's visions and we are well aware of them, as numbers of other students of Mormonism are. The vision we are discussing was plainly declared, by Joseph Smith himself and other Mormon authorities, to be the First Vision. We must face reality, gently, but firmly.)

Orville Spencer, a leading Mormon in the early church, wrote a letter from Nauvoo, Illinois, in 1842, stating: "Joseph Smith, when the great designs of heaven were first made known to him, was not far from the age of seventeen."[7]

Now this is in accord with the account of Smith's age, *17 years old in 1823,* when first reports of a vision were given, as proven from the *Messenger and Advocate,* volume 1, pages 78, 79, referring to a revival that is supposed to have taken place in and around Palmyra, New York, at about the time of Joseph Smith's vision. "While this excitement continued, he continued to call upon the Lord in secret for a full manifestation of divine approbation and for, to him, the all important information, *if a supreme being did exist,* to have an assurance that he was accepted of Him . . . On the evening of the 21st of September, 1823, previous to retiring to rest, our brother's mind was unusually wrought upon the subject which had so long agitated his mind—his heart was drawn out in fervent prayer . . . while continuing in prayer for a manifestation in some way that his sins were forgiven; endeavoring to exercise faith in the Scriptures, on a sudden a light like that of day, only of a purer and far more glorious appearance and brightness, burst into the room . . . and in a moment a personage stood before him . . . he heard him declare himself to be a messenger sent by the commandment of the Lord, to deliver a special message, and to witness to him that his sins were forgiven."[8]

Notice please, this is a Mormon source, and an official Mormon account admitting that *Joseph Smith at 17, in 1823,* did not even know whether or not there was a Surpeme Being, even though later Mormons claim he had a vision of the *Father* and the *Son* at *age 14, in 1820!* In fact, Mormon leader and apostle David O. McKay declared that this First Vision, which Joseph Smith claimed he had at age 14, was the *foundation* of the Mormon church! Why then, did Joseph Smith not even know if a Supreme Being existed when he was 17 years old in 1823?

First Vision and Angels

Furthermore, in the *Deseret News,* May 29, 1852, Joseph Smith was quoted as having said, "I received the first visitation of angels, which was when I was about fourteen years old." This points out another discrepancy from many Mormon sources. The early accounts of the vision list an *angel* appearing to Joseph Smith, not the Father and the Son.

Apostle Orson Pratt stated: "By and by an obscure individual, a young man, rose up, and, in the midst of all Christendom, proclaimed the startling news that God had sent an angel to him . . . This occurred before this young man was fifteen years of age."[9] This is obviously referring to Smith's First Vision.

John Taylor, the third president of the Mormon church, stated; "How did this state of things called Mormonism *originate*? We read that an *angel* came down and revealed himself to Joseph Smith and manifested unto him in vision the true position of the world in a religious point of view."[10]

In spite of this irrefutable evidence from Mormon apostles themselves, the story of the First Vision *grew* and was *changed* until today's version: that Joseph Smith saw the Father and the Son. According to the current version, in 1820, when he was 14 years old, Joseph Smith saw a pillar of light. "It no sooner appeared than I found myself delivered from the enemy which held me bound. When the light rested upon me I saw two Personages, whose brightness and glory defy all description, standing above me in the air. One of them spake unto me, calling me by name and said, pointing to the other, *This is my Beloved Son. Hear Him!*"[11]

Neither Joseph Smith, nor inspired Mormon apostles quoting him, stuck to the original story about *the year, Joseph's age, or the content of the vision.*

First Vision and the Priesthood

Joseph Smith himself gave positive evidence that he did *not* see the Father and the Son in 1820. In 1832 Joseph Smith claimed to have a revelation from God which stated that a man could *not* see God without the priesthood. By Joseph Smith's own admission, he was not a priest in 1820, nor did he even claim to be granted this office until sometime in the early 1830s![12]

Joseph Smith's 1832 revelation concerning the priesthood is recorded in section 84 of *Doctrine and Covenants*, verses 21,22, "And without the ordinances thereof, and the Authority of the Priesthood, the power of godliness is not manifest unto men in the flesh, for without this no man can see the face of God, even the Father, and live."

Mormon apostle Parley P. Pratt declared, "The truth is this: that without the Priesthood of Melchisedek, 'no man can see God and live!' "[13] Joseph Smith was *not* a priest in *1820*. If his revelation that no man could see God without the priesthood were true, then Joseph Smith had never seen God, and his claim in 1842 of having seen God in 1820 was not true. If his 1820 claim were true, then his revelation from God in 1832 that no man could see God without the priesthood was false. Either way this would label Joseph Smith as one who was not the prophet of God some people thought he was.

Moroni or Nephi

Another problem worth mentioning in this connection is that the angel who is supposed to have appeared to Joseph Smith is almost always named Moroni, both by Joseph Smith and other Mormon writers. Nonetheless, in the 1851 first edition of the *Pearl of Great Price*, page 41, the angel's name was Nephi, not Moroni. Further proof of this may be found in *Times and Seasons*, volume 3, pages 749 and 753, *and* in the writings of the mother of Joseph Smith, Lucy Mack Smith, in her *Biographical Sketches*, 1853.

In Summary

Some observations about Joseph Smith and the First Vision seem in order. Former president and inspired Mormon apostle David O. McKay declared that the First Vision is the foundation of the Mormon church. On this all the authority that Mormons claim they have ultimately rests.

We ask why so many Mormon leaders, apostles, presidents, and writers are so *confused* about what Joseph Smith saw or didn't see? Why did Joseph Smith himself give several utterly irreconcilable accounts of the First Vision? Why did Joseph Smith's and the Mormon's official version not come out until 1842 if this vision is so important to Mormonism? The church began in 1830, and the *Book of Mormon* was published in 1830, yet the 1820 vision upon which the church is *founded,* is not officially given until 1842!

Why do we have contradictory "revelations" from God to His inspired apostle? God never contradicts Himself. When any word, or revelation, is contradictory, it cannot be from God. Did Joseph Smith really have a vision? If so, when? At what age? What did he really see? Was it a good angel or an evil angel, if he had a vision? Was it from God or from one of Satan's spirits appearing as an angel of light? "And no marvel; for Satan himself is transformed into an angel of light. Therefore it is no great thing if his ministers also be transformed as the ministers of righteousness" (2 Cor. 11:14,15).

Think again about the contradictions as to the *time* of the vision, the *age* of Joseph Smith, and the *content* of the vision. Think about Joseph getting a revelation in 1832 revealing that only those ordained to the priesthood could see God and live, yet he was supposed to have seen God in 1820, many years before he was made a priest by his own testimony. First Corinthians 14:33: "For God is not the author of confusion, but of peace, as in all churches of the saints."

It can be little comfort to know that many cults began with a vision or claims of a vision because they would not believe the Word of God, or because they believed the Word of God was not enough. God therefore sent them "strong delusion" that they should believe a lie (see 2 Thess. 2:10-12).

Finally, Mormons need to seriously consider Galatians 1:8. "But though we, or an angel from heaven, preach any other gospel unto you than that which we have preached unto you, let him be accursed."

If this First Vision is the foundation, let's see what Joseph Smith built on it.

Notes

1. David O. McKay, *Gospel Ideals* (Salt Lake City: The Church of Jesus Christ of Latter-day Saints, 1953), p. 85.
2. John A. Widtsoe, *Joseph Smith—Seeker After Truth* (Salt Lake City: Deseret Book Co., 1951), p. 19.
3. *Improvement Era*, July 1961, p. 490. (A monthly periodical published by The Church of Jesus Christ of Latter-day Saints.)
4. *Joseph Smith, the Prophet*, 1944, p. 30. Quoted in Jerald and Sandra Tanner, *The First Vision Examined* (Salt Lake City: Modern Microfilm Co., 1969), p. 2.
5. Jerald Tanner, *Mormonism:* A Study of Mormon History and Doctrine (Clearfield, Utah: Utah Evangel Press, 1962), p. 79.
6. Tanner, *Mormonism*, p. 8.
7. *Millenial Star*, vol. 4, p. 37.
8. *Messenger and Advocate*, vol. 1, pp. 78,79. Quoted in Tanner, *The First Vision Examined* (Salt lake City: Modern Microfilm Co., 1969), p. 15.
9. *Journal of Discourses* (Liverpool, England: F.D. and S.W. Richards, Pub; 1854. Reprinted edition, Salt lake City, 1966), vol. 13, pp. 65,66. The *Journal of Discourses* is a collection of sermons by Brigham Young, Orson Pratt, Heber Kimball and others from 1854 to 1886.
10. *Journal of Discourses*, vol. 10, p. 127.
11. Joseph Smith, *Pearl of Great Price* (Salt lake City: The Church of Jesus Christ of Latter-day Saints, 1958), p. 48, #17.
12. Bruce R. McConkie, ed. *Doctrines of Salvation* (Salt Lake City: Bookcraft, Inc., 1954). vol. 1, p. 4.
13. Parley P. Pratt. *Writings of Parley P. Pratt*, p. 306. Quoted by Jerald and Sandra Tanner, *Mormonism, Shadow or Reality* (Salt Lake City: Modern Microfilm Co., 1972). p. 144.

CHAPTER THREE

Joseph Smith— Prophet of God?

Was Joseph Smith a prophet of God? I am so thankful that God did not leave such important decisions up to the opinions or whims of men. He gave an absolutely infallible test so that the simplest Christian could determine whether or not a professed prophet was true or false. It is so clear that even those who are not Christians can apply it and not be led astray in their search for truth.

Here is God's test for a prophet: "But the prophet, which shall presume to speak a word in my name, which I have not commanded him to speak, or that shall speak in the name of other gods, even that prophet shall die. And if thou say in thine heart, How shall we know the word which the Lord hath not spoken? When a prophet speaketh in the name of the Lord, if the thing follow not, nor come to pass, that is the thing which the Lord hath not spoken, but the prophet hath spoken it presumptuously: thou shalt not be afraid of him" (Deut. 18:20-22).

From this as well as numerous other Bible passages we know that God spoke through His true prophets, as they prophesied, word for word. Since God cannot lie or be mistaken, His *true* prophets were *always* accurate in fulfillment. Any prophet not meeting this test of fulfilled prophecy was a false prophet. (See Deut. 13:1-5; Isa. 9:13-16; Jer. 14:13-16; Ezek. 13:1-9.)

One false prophecy would forever disqualify a man as a prophet of God. According to the Scriptures a false prophet would have been killed for presuming to speak that which God had not spoken, under Old Testament law.

Following are a few of Joseph Smith's prophecies that did not meet God's simple test of accuracy:

1. Concerning the New Jerusalem and its Temple (Rev. 21:22). According to this prophecy in *Doctrine and Covenants* 84:1-5, given September 1832, the city and temple are to be built in Missouri in *this* (the current) generation. The apostles of the Mormon church knew about this prophecy and declared in the *Journal of Discourses* (vol. 9, p. 71; vol. 10, p. 344; vol. 13, p. 362), their certainty that this prophecy would come to pass within the generation encompassing the 1832 prophecy by Smith. In fact, on May 5, 1870, apostle Orson Pratt staunchly declared: "The Latter-day Saints just as much expect to receive a fulfillment of that promise during the generation that was in existence in 1832 as they expect that the sun will rise and set tomorrow. Why? Because God cannot lie. He will fulfill all His promises."[1]

The city was *not* built; the temple was *not* built in *this* generation. The prophecy was false.

2. Zion, Missouri cannot fall or be moved, *Doctrine and Covenants*, section 97. Joseph Smith was in Kirtland, Ohio at the time he made this prediction and was unaware that Zion was moved—two weeks prior to the so-called revelation.

3. Nauvoo House is to belong to the Smith family forever, *Doctrine and Covenants* 124:56-60. Joseph Smith was killed in 1844. The Mormons were driven from Nauvoo and the house no longer belonged to the Smith family. This prophecy was false. Joseph Smith was a false prophet.

4. Joseph Smith's enemies will be confounded when they seek to destroy him, 2 Nephi 3:14, The *Book of Mormon*. Smith was shot in jail in Carthage, Illinois on June 27, 1844.

5. Jesus Christ was to be born "at Jerusalem, which is the land of our forefathers," Alma 7:10, The *Book of Mormon*. God's Word says that Jesus would be born in Bethlehem (Mic. 5:2), which prophecy was fulfilled (Matt. 2:1).

6. The coming of the Lord, *History of the Church*, volume 2, page 182. In 1835 prophet-president Joseph Smith predicted "the coming of the Lord, which was nigh . . . even fifty-six years should wind up the scene."[2]

7. Concerning "moon inhabitants," *Journal of Oliver B. Huntington*, volume 2, page 166. This devout and dedicated Mormon associate of Joseph Smith quoted Joseph Smith describing his revelation concerning the moon and its inhabitants: "The inhabitants of the moon are more of a uniform size than the inhabitants of the earth, being about six feet in height. They dress very much like the Quaker style and are quite general in style, or the one fashion of dress. They live to be very old;

coming generally near a thousand years."[3]

Joseph Smith undoubtedly never dreamed that men from the earth would one day walk on the moon. He probably felt quite safe in giving this "revelation."

8. A most revealing prophecy is related by David Whitmer, one of the Three Witnesses to the *Book of Mormon*. In his book, *An Address to All Believers in Christ* (Richmond, Missouri, 1887), Whitmer said that Joseph Smith received a revelation that the brethren should go to Toronto, Canada, and that they would sell the copyright to the *Book of Mormon*. They went, but could not sell the book, and called Joseph Smith to account. The ever agile Smith told them, "Some revelations are of God; some are of men, and some are of the devil."

No biblical prophet ever used such an excuse, for no true prophet of God ever had a failure. Smith would have been immediately stoned to death, during Old Testament times, for posing as a prophet of God. If Smith could not tell whether a prophecy was of God, of man or of the Devil, he could not be trusted for his revelations of the *Book of Mormon* as well as other writings. What a man to trust with one's eternal destiny!

Mormons would like to denounce Whitmer's book as "apostate writing," but still claim that he is one of the sacred Three Witnesses, who "never denied his testimony," in which case he certainly was not an apostate.

9. On another occasion the wily Smith declared: 'Verily thus saith the Lord: It is wisdom in my servant David W. Patten that he settle up all his business as soon as he possibly can, and make a disposition of his merchandise, that he may perform a mission unto me next spring, in company with others, even twelve including

himself, to testify of my name and bear glad tidings unto all the world."[4]

The date on which this prophecy was given was April 17, 1838. David Patten died of gunshot wounds on October 25, 1838. He did not live to go on a mission in the spring. God, who knows the future, would not call a man to go on a mission and have it predicted and recorded if He knew the man would die before the time of the mission. This would make God appear to be an ignorant fool, unprepared or unknowing of the future. His revelations and prophecies would certainly not be the "sure word of God."

Mormons try pathetically to defend this prophecy of Smith's by saying that David Patten may have been called on a mission to some other world (after death). If that is true, there is no record that the other eleven men also died to accompany Patten on this mission to which they were all called to fulfill. How strange that God did not even bother to mention such a stupendous thing as death in a man's life, leaving Himself wide open to a false prophecy charge. God does not trifle with His Word or His prophets. This prophecy of Joseph Smith was a false prophecy, not one from God.

God's test for a prophet is very simple. God's test for a prophet is very clear. Joseph Smith cannot pass the test. His prophecies failed. Joseph Smith was a false prophet.

Mormon friends that I have confronted with this evidence have had various reactions as might be expected. Some have been shaken. They have admitted that Joseph Smith was a false prophet and have turned with all their heart to Jesus Christ alone, much to their joy and mine.

One lovely Mormon lady had labored indefatigably in the Mormon church and had become quite prominent in the women's work in a nearby state. She read this material, talked to me personally and was wonderfully delivered from Mormonism to Christ. She dearly loves the Mormon people and has a tremendous burden for them. Later, I had the inexpressible joy of leading her Mormon husband to Christ. How he wept for joy when Jesus took his sins away and gave him the free gift of everlasting life! Such sure and lasting peace he never found in Mormonism.

Other Mormons, in defense of the *Book of Mormon* and the Mormon church, and in fear of the awesome implications to themselves and their families, refuse to admit the obvious—Joseph Smith was a false prophet. They try desperately or valiantly, depending on your viewpoint, to rescue him from his inextricable dilemma.

"You've taken what he said out of context!" some have declared.

"Maybe he meant something else," was one forlorn rejoinder.

"People in the Bible had faults," several remarked, which has nothing whatever to do with God's test for a prophet.

"I just don't believe Joseph Smith was a false prophet!"

"It's just a bunch of lies!" one dear Mormon soul cried, ignoring the fact that the quotations are almost exclusively from Mormon books, sources, and apostles, and are well documented so that she can check for herself and draw her own conclusions.

Surely all true Christian hearts go out in compassion to Mormons, if there is an ounce of the love of Christ in us. To see and feel the anguish of those who begin to recognize that they have been misled is not pleasant. However, the anguish of a lost eternity without Christ is infinitely more horrible. Real love cannot evade our responsibility. We may feel very much like a doctor who must steel himself to tell a dear friend he has cancer.

The test has been given. Joseph Smith was not a prophet of God. He was a false prophet.

Notes

1. Pratt, *Journal of Discourses*, vol. 9, p. 71.
2. Joseph Smith, *History of the Church* (Salt Lake City: The Church of Jesus Christ of Latter-day Saints, 1902–1912), vol. 2, p. 182.
3. Huntington Library, San Marino, California, from the *Journal of Oliver B. Huntington*, vol. 2, p. 166.
4. *Doctrine and Covenants* 114:1.

CHAPTER FOUR

The Book of Mormon—Joseph Smith's or God's?

God is just as able to preserve His Word, which He promised to do, as He was able to give it in the first place. He has inculcated a fervent fidelity to His Word in the hearts of many godly scholars and translators. Through the centuries, many of His true people have given their lives to preserve the purity of His Word.

Accuracy and Harmony of the Bible

Over 5,000 manuscripts, and bits and pieces of manuscripts, of the Word of God have been found virtually all over Europe and Asia. So, we do not have to depend on just one translation from one manuscript. The harmony and accuracy of these manuscripts are amazing.

The writings of the church fathers, some of them contemporary with the apostle John, contain the text of practically the entire New Testament. These writings match accurately with the New Testament manuscripts we use. The Dead Sea Scrolls also harmonize with our later versions. This is further corroboration that we have the Word of God as it was originally given.

The accuracy of the Scriptures is attested to by many erudite biblical scholars. One of these is the former Princetonian scholar and genius Robert Dick Wilson. A devout Christian and a linguist who was coversant with 26 languages, Robert Dick Wilson claimed that he doubted that even one word in a thousand had been changed or carried any different meaning from the original God gave.

Robert Dick Wilson spent a lifetime in careful study of God's Word in the original languages. He was a professor of Semitic Philology at Princeton and indubitably one of the world's great scholars. In reference to the Bible, Robert Dick Wilson summed up his convictions in his book, *A Scientific Investigation of the Old Testament:* "In conclusion, let me reiterate my conviction that no one knows enough to show that the true text of the Old Testament in its true interpretation is not true."[1]

Robert Dick Wilson is only one of many dedicated biblical scholars who has attested to the accuracy of the Bible as we now have it. These people have proven by research what Jesus declared: "Heaven and earth shall pass away, but my words shall not pass away" (Matt. 24:35). And the infallible Son of God is not mistaken, nor does He lie.

We often read of Socrates, and his story is widely accepted without question. However, the proof that Socrates ever lived comes from *one* manuscript by *one* person, Plato! The only other account of this Greek philosopher is in the manuscript of a comical play by a

Greek writer named Aristophanes. Yet no one doubts the existence of Socrates.

Much of history that we commonly accept as true, comes to us from very early sources. The story of Julius Caesar and the Gallic wars is recorded in several manuscripts but the oldest is dated 900 years after Caesar's day. Yet we accept, as incontrovertible fact, the verification of this history.

On the other hand we have thousands of manuscripts and portions of manuscripts from widely differing places concerning Jesus Christ and His Word. This means that no scribe, even if God had allowed it, could have changed something in the translation without its being caught by another biblical scholar. For these manuscripts have been compared assiduously again and again by both the enemies and friends of Jesus Christ.

The Mormon's Acceptance of the Bible

In spite of the overwhelming evidence as to the accuracy and harmony of the Bible, the Mormons profess to believe the Bible, "insofar as it is translated correctly."[2] However they do not add any such qualification to their acceptance of the *Book of Mormon* which they declare to be the very Word of God.

To question the Bible is to question the authority and truthfulness of the Lord Jesus Christ. To show how far some Mormons have used this loophole in their "Articles of Faith" to deny the Bible as the infallible Word of God, read what LDS apostle Orson Pratt says in his comments about the Bible: "Who knows that even *one verse* of the Bible has escaped pollution, so as to convey the same sense now that it did in the original?"[3]

We hope we may be pardoned for pointing out that this

logic seems just a little suspect. Pratt was writing to prove that the *Book of Mormon* is the inspired Word of God, without error. Since hundreds of verses of the "polluted" Bible were copied verbatim from the much maligned *King James Version* into the *Book of Mormon*, this hardly seems to help his argument! You do not introduce water from a polluted stream into a pure, clear stream and continue to call the one polluted and the other pure!

Joseph Smith copied verses and chapters from all over the Bible. Second Nephi, chapters 12 through 24 in the *Book of Mormon*, is copied mostly word for word from the *King James Version* of Isaiah, chapters 2 through 14.

Revelation for the Book of Mormon

In the *Pearl of Great Price*, pages 50-54, Joseph Smith gives an account of a vision he had in 1823. The "messenger sent from the presence of God," Moroni, told him that God had work for him to do. He was to find some gold plates on which was written a book that Joseph Smith was to translate. The messenger told him where the plates were hidden and gave him instructions concerning them.

Also preserved, with the gold plates, were the Urim and Thummim mentioned in the Old Testament (see Exod. 28:30; Num. 27:21; Ezra 2:63). According to Joseph Smith, the Urim and Thummim was a kind of divine spectacles (two stones in silver bows) God kept for thousands of years and put in a box with the gold plates to help him interpret and translate the language in which the book was written. This language was reformed Egyptian. According to *Doctrine and Covenants*, Joseph Smith declared that God gave him the power to translate the reformed Egyptian hieroglyphics into English and produce the *Book of Mormon*.

Joseph Smith would put on the Urim and Thummim and be able to translate the message on the gold tablets. After Smith translated the first 116 pages of the *Book of Mormon,* which got lost or stolen, an "angel" apparently took these spectacles away. Then Joseph used the "seer stone" or treasure-hunting stone, which was common property in that day of many fortune-tellers and treasure seekers, to translate the reformed Egyptian hieroglyphics. This stone is also called the Urim and Thummim by Mormon writers. I wonder why God bothered to provide the spectacles, after preserving them for so many centuries for Joseph Smith to use, when they were so litle used and so easily replaced by something else.

According to the three witnesses of the *Book of Mormon,* David Whitmer, Oliver Cowdery and Martin Harris, Smith would put the stone into a hat, and then put his face into the hat as he started to translate from the gold plates. The gold plates were seldom, if ever, present! How odd! They seem as superfluous as the Urim and Thummim spectacles. Again, I wonder why Joseph Smith even bothered to dig them up.

David Whitmer, in *Address to All Believers in Christ,* says that as Joseph Smith put his face into his hat with the seer stone, "something resembling parchment would appear."[4] The hieroglyphics would appear, one character at a time, with the English interpretation underneath. Joseph Smith would read it and Oliver Cowdery, or whoever was the amanuensis or secretary at that time would write it. If correctly written, the character or sentence would disappear. If not, it would remain until corrected. This means that every letter, every character, was exactly what God said, letter-by-letter and word-for-word. There could be no mistake because the character or word would not go away until 100 percent accuracy was achieved.

The written word was perfect. And when this 1830 publication of the *Book of Mormon* was printed, Joseph Smith pronounced that book perfect or "correct" also. He should know if he were a true prophet of God.

Some Problems with the Book of Mormon

Joseph Smith said this reformed Egyptian was a language known to no man, but was the language that Mormon (the father of Moroni) wrote on the gold plates somewhere around A.D. 384 to 421, just before he died. *It is a problem to many that this language was reproduced in the* Book of Mormon *in the same words of the 1611 King James Bible in hundreds and thousands of instances.*

It doesn't seem likely that reformed Egyptian, a language which was known to no man and which perished from the earth over 1,000 years before 1611, the year the King James Bible was published, would contain thousands of the same words and phrases, in the exact order in which they are found in the *King James Version* of the Bible. *Even the italicized words in the* King James Version *appear in the* Book of Mormon. Joseph Smith did not italicize them but included them into the *Book of Mormon* text as if they were the words of God.

The scholars who translated the *King James Version* italicized certain words to warn the reader that they were not in the original Hebrew or Greek text but were added for smoother reading or explanation. A few of the many examples of italicized words which are in the *King James Version* and the *Book of Mormon* can be seen by comparing Isaiah 53:2,3,4 with Mosiah 14:2,3,5.

Another problem we find with the Book of Mormon *is in the poor grammar in which some of it is written.* Now, some of the sweetest saints I have ever known use poor grammar. That, in itself, is not the point; blaming God for poor grammar is. Even when God gave His inspired word through such vessels as the unlearned and ignorant Peter, He did not use poor grammar.

Joseph F. Smith, sixth president of the Mormon church declared, "Joseph did not render the writing on the gold plates into the English language in his own style of language as many people believe, but every word and every letter was given to him by the gift and power of God."[5]

Joseph Smith himself declared, as late as 1841, in *History of the Church*, "I told the brethren that the Book of Mormon was the most correct of any book on earth."[6]

If the translated word was perfect, and if the 1830 *Book of Mormon* was perfect, why have the Mormons made some 4,000 changes in grammar, punctuation and word structure in the perfect *Book of Mormon*? These later Mormons, who were better educated, became increasingly embarrassed over grammatical errors in the *Book of Mormon;* so they made changes in later editions.

We have both a reproduction of the 1830 *Book of Mormon* and the current *Book of Mormon* and we can see the changes with our own eyes. Several students of Mormonism have made a count of the changes and the results have been noted in books, particularly by Arthur Budvarson, Marvin Cowan, and Jerald Tanner, as well as others.

Following are just a few examples of changes that have been made since the 1830 *Book of Mormon* (italics added):

1830 edition, page 52, "And are come forth out of the waters of Judah, which swear by the name of the Lord."

1963 edition, 1 Nephi 20:1, "And are come forth out of the waters of Judah, *or out of the waters of Baptism,* who swear by the name of the Lord."

1830 edition, page 303, "Yea, I know that he allotteth unto men, *yea, Decreeth unto them Decrees which are unalterable,* according to their wills." 1963 edition, Alma 29:4, "Yea, I know that he allotteth unto men according to their wills."

1830 edition, page 31, "Neither will the Lord God suffer that the Gentiles shall forever remain in the *state of awful woundedness.*" 1963 edition, 1 Nephi 13:32, "Neither will the Lord God suffer that the Gentiles shall forever remain in that *awful state of Blindness.*"

1830 edition, page 555, " . . . his sons and to his daughters, *which were not, or which* did not seek his destruction." 1963 edition, Ether 9:2, " . . . his sons and to his daughters *who* did not seek his destruction."

1830 edition, page 262, "And *it came to pass* that he began to plead for them, from that time forth; but it reviled him, saying: Art thou also possessed with the Devil? And *it came to pass* that they spit upon him." 1963 edition, Alma 14:7, "And he began to plead for them from that time forth; but they reviled him, saying: Art thou also possessed with the devil? And they spit upon him."

Another change from the 1830 *Book of Mormon* concerns Mosiah 21:28. King Benjamin had already died (Mosiah 6:5; p. 168) in the 1830 edition of the *Book of Mormon.* Apparently, Smith forgot this and in Mosiah 21:28, listed King Benjamin as being *alive*! Later, embarrassed Mormons changed the king's name to *King Mosiah* to remove the obvious contradiction!

One night I was sharing these facts with a fine, intelligent young graduate of Brigham Young University. This young man is something of a linguist having studied four or five languages. He served as a Mormon missionary to Lebanon and also in Switzerland. He now teaches Mormon priests in the Aaronic priesthood.

His answer? After groping for some time with various attempts which he saw fell far short, he said, "You know the difficulty of translating from one language to another. Then we have to take into account Joseph Smith's poor grammar and somewhat limited vocabulary. This may explain some of the problems."

As we can easily see, this in no way is an answer or solution to the problem. I was greatly surprised that this was the strongest answer my learned Mormon friend could come up with. If God did give Joseph Smith a letter-by-letter, word-for-word translation of His pure and perfect Word, surely He would have given it with correct grammar.

Interestingly enough, Joseph Smith's grammar was excellent as long as he copied verbatim from the King James. Why wouldn't it be excellent if he copied from "God's parchment" as he claimed?

Is the *Book of Mormon* a revelation from God or did Joseph Smith copy verses and chapters from the King James Bible and add material from his own imagination and from other available sources? Who really wrote the *Book of Mormon?*

If the Mormons claim that God directed Joseph Smith in translating the *Book of Mormon* they accuse God of using faulty grammar and of making other mistakes that later needed to be corrected. It does not seem wise, to say the least, to make this accusation about the Omniscient God of the Universe.

If we say Joseph Smith wrote the book, with its

grammatical errors and other mistakes, we deny what Joseph Smith claimed, what the three witnesses claimed and what president Joseph F. Smith claimed. This would mean that Joseph Smith's testimony that the *Book of Mormon* is a letter-by-letter, word-by-word inerrant translation by the power of God is false. This accusation would irreparably jeopardize his claim that he was a prophet of God.

The Witnesses

In the front pages of the *Book of Mormon* is "The Testimony of Three Witnesses." The three witnesses, Oliver Cowdery, David Whitmer and Martin Harris, are said to have "seen the plates which contain the record . . . and . . . the engravings which are upon the plates." However, when questioned closely the witnesses said they never really saw the gold plates except when they were wrapped up or covered. They used terms like "vision," or "I saw them with the eye of faith."

Also, on the same page as the names of the three witnesses, is "The Testimony of Eight Witnesses." These witnesses were: Christian Whitmer, Jacob Whitmer, Peter Whitmer, Jr., John Whitmer, Hiram Page, Joseph Smith, Sen., Hyrum Smith and Samuel H. Smith. Of these eleven total witnesses, over half apostatized from the Mormon church. When I say *apostatized,* I don't mean they denied the church such as Peter, in a weak moment of fear, denied Christ, had his heart broken as any true Christian would, wept bitterly and within a few short hours sought his Saviour again. These witnesses departed from the Mormon church. Included were Cowdery, Whitmer and Harris and five of the eight witnesses. The three who remained were Smiths.

(Even one or two of Joseph Smith's sons eventually left the LDS and affiliated with the Reorganized Church of Latter Day Saints.) Mormons claim that some of these witnesses came back to the church. And this is partly true.

Some of these who apostatized even claimed they had revelations from God that Mormonism was false and that they should get out. Of course, Mormons don't accept their revelations, even though their visions sound as believable as those of Joseph Smith. We wonder why Mormons so readily accept the vision of a 14-year-old boy and so quickly reject the visions of several of these men.

David Whitmer, one of the original three witnesses, said God spoke to him in His own voice and told him to "separate myself from among the Latter-day Saints."[7]

According to *Doctrines of Salvation*, Cowdery and Harris returned to the church in their latter years and died in full fellowship.

Joseph Smith and other Mormon officials are on record as calling his three main witnesses "thieves and liars."[8] In *History of the Church* Joseph Smith said, "Such characters as . . . David Whitmer, Oliver Cowdery, and Martin Harris, are too mean to mention, and we would like to have forgotten them."[9]

According to *Doctrines of Salvation*, Cowdery and Harris returned to the church in their latter years and died in full fellowship.

Can you *imagine* Jesus Christ calling His witnesses, Matthew, Mark, Luke, John and Paul, a bunch of liars and yet asking us to *believe* them as Joseph Smith has asked us to believe his witnesses to the *Book of Mormon*? Can you imagine Jesus Christ saying He'd like to forget the Gospel writers and Paul as Joseph Smith said he'd like to forget his main witnesses to the truth of the *Book of Mormon*?

There is one additional fact we feel we must include. Joseph Smith was tried and convicted of being a "glass-looker" (crystal-gazing fortune-teller and treasure hunter) by a justice of the peace in Bainbridge, New York in 1826, six years after he was supposed to have had his first vision in 1820. The charge was made, according to the record of the trial, by one Peter G. Bridgemen, who said that Josiah Stowell had been deceived by Smith concerning finding lost property and gold treasures. He said Smith claimed to have powers by looking through a *stone*— the same process whereby Joseph Smith was able to translate the *Book of Mormon*, according to the three witnesses. A photograph of the original court record can be found in Jerald and Sandra Tanner's *Joseph Smith's 1826 Trial*.[10]

R. Hugh Nibley, on page 142 of *The Myth Makers*, admitted that if such a record could be found it would be a "devastating blow" to Joseph Smith. It *was* found—by Wesley P. Walters on July 28, 1971.

Notes

1. Robert Dick Wilson, *A Scientific Investigation of the Old Testament* (Chicago: Moody Press). Quoted by John R. Rice, *Our God-Breathed Book—The Bible* (Murfreesboro, Tenn.: Sword of the Lord Pub., 1969).
2. "Articles of Faith," *Pearl of Great Price*, Article #8, p. 60.
3. Orson Pratt, *Divine Authenticity of the Book of Mormon*, pp. 45-47. Quoted by Marvin Cowan, *Mormon Claims Answered* (Salt Lake City: Marvin Cowan Pub., 1975), p. 21,22.
4. David Whitmer, *An Address to All Believers in Christ* (Richmond, Mo., 1887), p. 12; reprinted by Bales Bookstore, Searcy, Ark., 1960.
5. *Journal of Oliver B. Huntington*, p. 168. Typed copy at Utah State Historical Society.
6. Smith, *History of the Church*, vol. 4, p. 461.
7. Whitmer, *An Address to All Believers in Christ*, p. 27.
8. *Times and Seasons, vol. 1, p. 81; Elders Journal, p. 59; Senate Document 189*, pp. 6,9.
9. Smith, *History of the Church*, vol. 3, p. 232.
10. Jerald and Sandra Tanner, *Joseph Smith's 1826 Trial* (Salt Lake City: Modern Microfilm Company, 1971).

CHAPTER FIVE

Joseph Smith Tested as a Translator

Martin Harris was one of the "three witnesses" to the *Book of Mormon*. He had been asked to mortgage his farm to help publish and distribute the *Book of Mormon*. As a precaution, Harris slipped off with a page or two of "reformed Egyptian" characters to Professor Charles Anthon, a renowned scholar of Columbia Univerity.

After examining the material, Anthon warned Harris that he was the victim of a fraud. The characters were not Egyptian hieroglyphics. However, Joseph Smith claimed in his revelation, *Pearl of Great Price,* that Anthon stated "that the translation was correct, more so than any he had before seen translated from the Egyptian. I then showed him those which were not yet translated, and he said that they were Egyptian, Chaldaic, Assyric, and Arabic; and he said they were true characters" (*Pearl of Great Price* 2:64).

Even if Anthon had not, in a letter, refuted the testimony of Joseph Smith, Smith's claim raises several problems. *First* the reformed Egyptian was supposed to be a completely lost language "known to no man." Yet here is a man without any "divine revelation" who could read it! Not even Joseph Smith could do that! And Anthon did it without a Urim and Thummim!

Second, why did the papers have Chaldaic, Assyric and Arabic characters, if the gold plates were written only in reformed Egyptian?

Third, since this would have been the first and only translation from reformed Egyptian in over a thousand years, how could Anthon have said that it was the most correct translation from the Egyptian he had ever seen? How on earth could he have known if the translation into English was correct or not?

Fourth, Mormons claim this incident with Anthon fulfilled Isaiah 29:11,12: "And the vision of all is become unto you as the words of a book that is sealed, which men deliver to one that is learned, saying, Read this, I pray thee: and he saith, I cannot; for it is sealed: and the book is delivered to him that is not learned, saying, Read this, I pray thee: and he saith, I am not learned." If you read the passage carefully, you will see that the main subject is regarding the condition of the people at *that* time. It does not refer to a book at some future time.

Even so, Anthon never got hold of the complete book, only a paper or so with some characters on it. But Harris, according to Joseph Smith in *Pearl of Great Price*, said that Anthon claimed the translation was correct. He could only say this if he was able to *read* it. But Isaiah said the "learned man could *not* read the book because it was sealed."

There are several other problems, but this should be enough. God *never* contradicts Himself, not even in the *slightest detail* in fulfilling prophecy. This is how God told us to test the true from the false. And to refuse to make such a test would be to disobey God who told us to "believe not every spirit, but try [test] the spirits whether they are of God: because many false prophets are gone out into the world" (1 John 4:1). We are told that false prophets can perform miracles (lying wonders). We are also told that they appear as angels of light, ministers of righteousness.

Matthew 7:15 tells us, "Beware of false prophets, which come to you in sheep's clothing, but inwardly they are ravening wolves." If we love Jesus and His Word we can do no less than obey Him and apply the test to those who claim to be prophets of God. Terrible eternal loss will be the result to ourselves and countless others if we do not. If Joseph Smith could pass the test, we would be happy to accept him as a prophet of God. Unfortunately, he cannot.

The capstone to this whole story is a letter Professor Anthon wrote seven years later to E.D. Howe, February 17, 1834. "The whole story about my having pronounced the Mormon inscription to be reformed Egyptian hieroglyphics is *perfectly false* . . . . I soon came to the conclusion that *it was all a trick—perhaps a hoax.* . . . *The paper contained anything else but Egyptian hieroglyphics.*"[1]

Perhaps the most damaging blow of all to Joseph Smith's credibility as a translator or prophet receiving revelations from God was an episode dating back to 1835. Joseph Smith purchased some Egyptian mummies and rolls of papyrus from Michael H. Chandler. Joseph Smith received revelations from God as to the meaning of the characters and sketches on the papyri. This translation, along with three drawings from the Egyptian papyri, he published as the "Book of Abraham" in the *Pearl of Great Price*. He claimed the first drawing, or "Facsimile no. 1," showed the idolatrous priest of Elkenah attempting to offer Abraham upon the altar as a sacrifice. The four jars underneath were idolatrous gods, etc. The bird pictured was the "Angel of the Lord."

Unfortunately for Joseph Smith, *this* time a scientific, analytical test could be made of his claims. Egyptian was a known language to Egyptologists, while "reformed Egyptian" was not.

Bishop F.S. Spalding sent copies of this and several other facsimiles that Smith drew and translated from the Egyptian papyri to several of the foremost Egyptologists in the world.[2] They *all agreed* "embalming the dead" was the subject of the picture. *All* of them said that Joseph Smith's interpretation was *false*, and not a true translation of the facsimile or Egyptian hieroglyphics.

Then in 1967, a manuscript formerly believed to have been destroyed in the Chicago fire was unearthed. This was positively identified by the Mormons as the *original manuscript* from which Joseph Smith "translated" the information in the "Book of Abraham." It appeared to settle the matter.

The "original manuscript" for the "Book of Abraham" actually is an Egyptian funeral text from a few centuries before the birth of Christ, giving instruction to the embalmers. Joseph Smith's translation had this same text telling about Abraham and his life in Mesopotamia some 2,000 years earlier. Facsimiles nos.

1, 2, and 3, as well as other material from which Joseph Smith claimed to translate the "Book of Abraham" have been examined and shown to be mistranslations by leading Egyptologists. As we reported in earlier editions of this book, one purported Mormon Egyptologist, Dee Jay Nelson also pronounced the book a false translation.[3] For awhile, Dee Jay Nelson was quite friendly with Dr. Nibley, who seemed to have some confidence in him as an Egyptologist. He was addressed as Professor Nelson by Dr. Hugh Nibley in a note to N. Eldon Tanner advising Mr. Tanner, a member of the First Presidency, that it would be 'a good idea to let Prof. Dee Jay Nelson have copies,' referring to the papyri. Later, Nelson left the Mormon church. Somewhere along the line, apparently about May 1978, Nelson ostensibly purchased a doctor's degree from a diploma mill, Pacific Northwestern University. Nelson undoubtedly had acquired some knowledge of Egyptology, but increasing evidence seems to indicate that he deceived both Mormons and non-Mormons as to the authenticity of his credentials. Jerald and Sandra Tanner uncovered the fact that Mr. Nelson seems not to have an earned doctorate, nor is he legitimately a professor. We occasionally referred to him as 'Professor Nelson,' as Dr. Hugh Nibley did, but I do not recall referring to him as Dr. Nelson. We do feel sorry for him, however, and for those who may have been temporarily misled by his claims. Since we too quoted him, we felt that we owed our readers and our Mormon friends this explanation.

However, this has no real bearing whatsoever on the false translation by Joseph Smith of the "Book of Abraham." World renowned Egyptologists with impeccable credentials have declared the 'translation' of the "Book of Abraham" and its facsimiles to be a false translation. Not one Egyptologist has supported it, all have spoken with one voice against it, as they have examined the manuscript and Joseph Smith's translation. (Joseph Smith got 1,125 words from 46 characters, a mathematical impossibility, and these words were all wrong!)

Marvin Cowan got replies from Professor John A. Wilson of the University of Chicago, and Richard A. Parker of Brown University supporting the fact that Joseph Smith could not translate Egyptian into English. Parker had also examined Joseph Smith's Egyptian Alphabet and Grammar and found it to be false, with no resemblence to the meanings ascribed to them by Egyptologists.

Actually, a number of Egyptologists have agreed that the "Book of Abraham" papyri and its facsimiles are taken from an Egyptian 'Book of Breathings' which is a part of, or an outgrowth of the Egyptian 'Book of the Dead,' and has nothing whatsoever to do with Abraham! Besides Professors Wilson and Parker, another Egyptologist who has uncovered these facts is Klaus Baer, Associate Professor of Egyptology, University of Chicago's Oriental Institute.

For those seriously interested in the replies Marvin Cowan got from Wilson and Parker, and for probably the most thorough documentation and blow by blow description of the "Fall of the Book of Abraham," in print we suggest this to you. Get "Mormonism, Shadow or Reality," Jerald and Sandra Tanner, and read carefully this fascinating chapter, "Fall of the Book of

Abraham." Order from Utah Lighthouse Ministries, Box 1884, Salt Lake City, Utah 84110.

Perhaps at this time we should ask our Mormon friends if they can honestly and with all their hearts repose their eternal destiny on the credibility of Joseph Smith. As Mormons, this is what they are doing.

Any court in the country would accept as conclusive the evidence which these Egyptologists have presented. Joseph Smith lied about "translating" the Egyptian text. "The Book of Abraham" is undeniably false.

Notes

1. Letter from Professor Charles Anthon to E.D. Howe, February 17, 1834. Quoted by Tanner in *Mormonism, Shadow or Reality* (Salt Lake City: Modern Microfilm Company, 1972), p. 105.
2. The Egyptologists were: Dr. A.H. Sayce, Oxford University; Dr. William M.F. Petrie, London University; Dr. A.C. Mace, Department of Egyptology, Metropolitan Museum of Art, New York; Dr. J. Peters, Director of the Babylonian Expedition of the University of Pennsylvania, 1888-1895; Dr. S.A.B. Mercer, Western Theological Seminary, Chicago; Dr. E. Meyer, University of Berlin; Dr. Baron V. Bissing, University of Munich.
3. Dee Jay Nelson, *The Joseph Smith Papyri*, Part 2, and *The Eye of Ra*. See also Tanner, *Mormonism, Shadow or Reality*, in their chaper "The Fall of the Book of Abraham."
4. From a photocopy of the original letter sent by Dee Jay Nelson.

CHAPTER SIX

History, Archaeology, Anthropology and the Book of Mormon

It seems conclusive that any book truly inspired by God will be accurate historically and archaeologically. Following is a very brief synopsis of the history of the *Book of Mormon* in this context.

History of the Book of Mormon

The *Book of Mormon* claims that a people called the Jaredites, refugees from the Tower of Babel, migrated to America about 2247 B.C. They occupied Central America until they were wiped out by internal strife. One survivor, the prophet Ether, recorded the history of the Jaredites on 24 metallic plates.

About 600 B.C. the two families of Lehi and Ishmael left Jerusalem, crossed the Pacific Ocean and landed in South America. Two sons of Lehi, Laman and Nephi, got in a fight and the people took sides and divided into two warring camps—the Lamanites and the Nephites. The Lamanites were cursed by the Lord because they were rebellious and against His commandments. Part of their curse included dark skins, which supposedly accounts for the origin of the American Indians.

God favored the Nephites who migrated to Central America about the time of Christ. Just after His crucifixion, Christ came to America and instituted baptism by immersion, the sacrament of bread and wine, the priesthood and gave many other teachings. Both Lamanites and Nephites were converted. Things were fairly smooth for about 200 years, then apostasy came. The term "Lamanite" then was placed on everyone who left the faith.

One hundred and fifty years later, the religious Nephites and irreligious Lamanites went to war again. In about A.D. 421 the Nephites were all killed, and the infidel Lamanites were left in control of the land. Columbus discovered them when he landed in 1492.

The commander in chief of the Nephites was a prophet and priest named Mormon. When he saw that they were defeated, he gathered the record of his predecessors and made an abbreviated history which he wrote on gold plates. He gave these gold plates to his son Moroni. Moroni hid them in a hill near Palmyra, New York, and about 1400 years later appeared as an angel to Joseph Smith and told him where to find the plates. In the box that held the plates was a large pair of spectacles, one glass called Urim, and the other Thummim. According to the three witnesses, by the help of these spectacles, Urim and Thummim or "interpreters," plus a "seerstone," Joseph Smith translated the hieroglyphics into English. The hieroglyphics were "reformed Egyptian," according to

Joseph Smith, a language now "known to no man." In this fashion, the *Book of Mormon* was supposedly revealed.

Why were the plates buried in Palmyra, New York, aside from the fact that Joseph Smith lived in that area?

Well, as war began between the Lamanites and the Nephites, Mormon wrote a letter to the king of the Lamanites requesting him to meet the Nephites in the land of Cumorah, by a hill called Cumorah, "and there we would give him battle!" According to the story, Mormon hoped thereby to gain a military advantage, and apparently the Lamanite king and his forces were happy to oblige him! So men, women and children marched over formidable mountains and through steaming jungles and across swift rivers for thousands of miles, by the hundreds of thousands, to fight a battle to the death in a place by a small insignificant hill most of them had never heard of!

One must admit this is quite a story. We cannot help but entertain the notion that this may have been the only way Joseph could think of to get the "gold plates" to his vicinity near Palmyra, New York.

Several remarkable problems need to be noted about this history.

The first problem concerns the rapid increase in population. According to the *Book of Mormon* in 30 years two *nations* grew from 28 people or less (see 1 Nephi; 2 Nephi 5:5,6,28). In this time the two nations (which at the greatest possible rate of increase could have numbered only several hundred, with the majority being women and children) divided and became fierce enemies called the Nephites and the Lamanites.

Nephites and Lamanites at various times "multiplied exceedingly, and spread upon the face of the land, and became exceeding rich" (Jarom 8), and "did multiply and spread. . . began to cover the face of the whole earth, from the sea south to the sea north, from the sea west to the sea east" (Helaman 3:8). They were "numerous almost, as it were the sands of the sea" (Mormon 1:7).

The second problem concerns the mighty cities the Nephites and Jaredites built. They "did build many mighty cities" (Ether 9:23; see also Alma 50,15). There are at least 38 names of cities mentioned in the *Book of Mormon:* Ammonihah, Bountiful, Gideon, Jacobugath, Jerusalem, Manti, Shem, Zarahemla, etc., all in the New World. However, not one of these city sites has ever been found in South or Central America.

By contrast a great amount of evidence has been uncovered concerning the ancient cities of the Mayas and Incas who occupied these areas! The historical or archaeological support, which should be virtually overwhelming for such a civilization as the Mormons claim, simply does not exist. In fact, the opposite is true.

The third problem with the history of the Book of Mormon *is in the languages of the early people.* It is impossible that the languages of reformed Egyptian and Hebrew could have so completely disappeared if they were used so extensively in the Americas for hundreds of years.

Archaeology and the Book of Mormon

I have before me now, as I type this manuscript, a beautiful 1961 edition of the *Book of Mormon*. Among the lovely pictures in the front of the book, is a picture of some murals depicting people, very un-Egyptian huts, water, boats, rowers, etc. The caption under the picture says, "Egyptian-like murals found on temple walls in

Mexico." This is probably supposed to convey to the unwary reader's mind that this is a link in the chain of evidence for the background of the *Book of Mormon*, as it relates to the origin of the *Book of Mormon* people and their alleged presence in South and Central America. Actually this mural does not look any more Egyptian than it does Peruvian or African or Indian.

I have personally seen lavish, beautifully-illustrated books on archaeology concerning South or Central America, which ardent Mormon missionaries sometimes use to *infer* archaeological proof for the *Book of Mormon*, and so for Mormonism. Yet, there is not one knowledgeable archeologist, Mormon or non-Mormon, who will claim that there is any archaeological proof to support the *Book of Mormon*. There is no evidence to support the existence of any of the cities Joseph Smith claims covered the Americas, apart from Joseph Smith's imagination.

Mormon authority John L. Sorenson, assistant professor of anthropology and sociology at Brigham Young University, commented, "We are of the opinion that Latter-day Saints ought to be satisfied with the truth and not try to improve upon it by gratuitous 'proofs' which are themselves based on untruth."[1] Professor Sorenson made his comments in rebutting *Book of Mormon Evidences in Ancient America,* by Dewey Farnsworth, one of the books seeking to establish evidence for the *Book of Mormon*.

Dr. Ross T. Christensen, a Mormon anthropologist, said, "The statement that the Book of Mormon has already been proved by archaeology is misleading."[2] Remember, these statements are from *Mormon authorities* in the field of archaeology.

In all of my research on Mormonism, I have not found one non-Mormon archaeologist who gives any credence to the *Book of Mormon* history whatsoever. None of them uses it as a guide in archaeological research in South and Central America. If any of my readers know of a bona fide, accredited, knowledgeable non-Mormon archaeologist who does use the *Book of Mormon* as a guide, please send me his name and address.

A member of the Smithsonian Institution in Washington has commented, "The Smithsonian Institution has never used the *Book of Mormon* in any way as a scientific guide. Smithsonian archaeologists see no connection between the archaeology of the New World and the subject matter of the Book."[3]

On the other hand, archaeologists frequently discover proof which utterly contradicts and demolishes the claims of the *Book of Mormon*. Though scientific research has demonstrated that the American continent was devoid of many domestic animals such as cattle, swine, horses, asses and certain other animals until the Europeans came to America, the *Book of Mormon* claims these were all here long before Christ.

With the exception of Brigham Young University the institutions of higher learning in America agree with the Smithsonian Institution that, "There is no evidence whatever of any migration from Israel to America, and likewise no evidence that pre-Columbian Indians had any knowledge of Christianity or the Bible."[4]

Anthropology and the Book of Mormon

Not only is there no archaeological proof to support the *Book of Mormon* history of the vast civilization that supposedly covered all of South and Central America, but anthropologists also deny the claims in the *Book of Mormon*.

Those who specialize in anthropology and genetics refute Joseph Smith's claim that the American Indians are descendants of the Israelites. Rather they say that the Indians resemble and are more closely related to peoples of eastern, central and northeastern Asia. These Asian people have a "Mongoloid Spot," a blue or blue-gray spot on their tailbones at birth. The American Indians also have a Mongoloid Spot. The Israelites, who are Semites, do not have it! American Indians are not Lamanite descendants of Israelites who migrated to America.

If the Indians are not descendants of the Israelites as the Mormons claim, then Joseph Smith and the *Book of Mormon* are in error, and certainly not inspired of God.

Faith and the Book of Mormon

Mormons must deal honestly with hard evidence such as we have been pointing out. So many times I, as well as others, have brought these weighty and serious problems to the attention of Mormons only to be given a "testimony" about believing by faith. But there is never any attempt on their part to face or solve the problem with factual evidence.

Those of us who know the biblical Christ have a tremendous testimony as to the joy, new life, certainty and inner transformation our wonderful Saviour has given us. We have been saved, converted, born again, washed clean from our sins by the blood of Christ. We have been made children of God, given eternal life at a definite point in time and we *know* it. However, if strong evidence were produced that Christ had been born in Athens instead of Bethlehem, or that the Bible was totally false on a number of historical and archaeological points or that many of the biblical prophecies had failed, then we would be foolish to answer with our "testimony" as to how the Holy Spirit had convinced us of the truth of the Bible.

Faith cannot operate without some intellectual content. God never asks for blind faith, only the devil does that. The God of biblical truth is also the God of historical and archaeological truth, and the one never contradicts the other in fact.

God says, "Faith cometh by hearing, and hearing by the word of God" (Rom. 10:17). But for this to be valid, one must first have confidence that the Bible really is the Word of God. True, this confidence is established in the willing heart by the Holy Spirit. He also reveals to the seeker the desolate fact that he is a *lost* sinner, and the sublime and wonderful fact that Christ is the one and only Saviour. However, even the Holy Spirit does not do this without some factual intellectual content. This is why Jesus and the disciples often said, referring to prophecies made centuries before, "This is that which the prophet said. . ." Fulfilled prophecy, historical and archaeological trustworthiness, the resurrection of Christ, and other evidence, all furnish a solid foundation from which true faith can be launched. One is not bludgeoned into believing by fact alone, much room is left for faith.

Mormon friends question that the Bible teaches that we can be saved by faith alone without works; however, they hastily retreat into a faith-alone shelter when facts threaten to destroy the very fabric of Mormonism. There is no way that "testimony" can clear up contradictions or turn that which is false into that which is true.

In Summary

God asks for faith which rests on solid facts and proven promises.

Take another look at the Mormon cities that supposedly flourished in South and Central America. Scores of Bible cities have been verified easily. Some of these were as old as, and others much older than, many of the Mormon cities named in the *Book of Mormon*—cities and city-states like Ur of the Chaldees, Jerusalem, Nineveh, the Hittite city-kingdom, etc. Archaeologists continue to unearth cities the Scriptures tell about.

The Bible has been found, even by unbelievers, to be geographically and archaeologically accurate. Archaeologists—believers and unbelievers—use the Bible as a guide and find it extremely reliable in research in Bible lands.

If we are supposed to trust a book to guide us in truths about a world we have not yet seen, we would surely expect to find it accurate and trustworthy, historically and geographically, in matters about the world we have seen. The Bible meets this requirement. The *Book of Mormon* does not.

Notes

1. John L. Sorenson in a review of the Dewey Farnsworth book.
2. Ross T. Christensen, Mormon Anthropologist, U.A.S. *Newsletter*, No. 64 (Provo, Utah: University Archeological Society, January 30, 1960), p. 3.
3. Quoted from Tanner, *Mormonism, Shadow or Reality* (Salt Lake City: Modern Microfilm Co., 1975), p. 97.
4. Dr. Frank H.H. Roberts, Jr. Director of the Bureau of American Ethnology at the Smithsonian Institution. Quoted by Marvin W. Cowan, *Mormon Claims Answered*, published by Marvin W. Cowan, 1975.

CHAPTER SEVEN

The Fatal Flaw

Is the God of Mormonism the God of the Bible? Is the Christ of Mormonism the Christ of the Bible?

Ephesians 4:15 cautions us to be "speaking the truth in love," and I will endeavor, as God enables, to do just that. God loves Mormons and non-Mormons and Christ died for both. He is looking for honest, searching hearts wherever He may find them.

The very heart of any position claiming to be Christian is what it teaches about God and about Jesus Christ. If one has wrong views about God, then it is easy for wrong doctrine to flow from this fatal flaw.

Let us then kindly and objectively see what Mormonism teaches about God and what the Bible teaches about God. Is the God of Mormonism the God of the Bible?

The God of the Mormons

The heart, the very quintessence of Mormon doctrine, the embryo from which Mormonism was spawned, the sustenance which nourishes it, and the goal for which earnest Mormons strive is their belief in God:

"We believe in a God who is Himself progressive, whose majesty is intelligence; whose perfection consists in eternal advancement—a Being who has *attained* His exalted state by a path which now His children are permitted to follow, whose glory it is their heritage to share. In spite of the opposition of the sects, in face of direct charges of blasphemy, the Church proclaims the eternal truth, '*As man is, God once was: as God is, man may be*'[1] (italics added).

Here, in the *Articles of Faith*, one of Mormonism's most treasured books, we have the hub of their teaching. What is it? God was once a man and He earned or attained or progressed His way to being God. Man, in turn, may also earn, attain or progress his way into being a God. This is one of the fundamental reasons for the good works Mormons do, for their church and temple work.

Lest someone still thinks this is not what Mormonism teaches, let me again quote—from their own sources—none other than prophet Joseph Smith: "God himself was once as we are now, and is an exalted man, and sits enthroned in yonder heavens! . . . I am going to tell you *how God came to be God*. We have imagined and supposed that God was God from all eternity. I will refute that idea, and take away the veil, so that you may see."[2]

From still another Mormon source: "Mormon prophets have continuously taught the sublime truth that God the Eternal Father was once a mortal man who passed through a school of earth life similar to that through which we are now passing. Remember that God our Heavenly Father was perhaps once a child, and mortal like we are, and rose step by step in the scale of progress in the school of advancement."[3]

Do we now understand clearly what Mormonism teaches about God and about man? Prophet Smith and his followers teach that God was not always God, and that He had to earn, progress, work, attain His way into being God. He was once a man just like us before He ever became God. We too may work, progress, earn and attain our way to being a god. "As man is, God once was; as God is, man may be."

The God of the Bible

The Bible is the original revelation about God, preceding the *Book of Mormon* by many long centuries. In any conflict of views the Bible must have precedence over the *Book of Mormon* as well as any other of the sacred books or teachings of Mormonism.

Now let's compare the God of the Bible with the God of Mormonism. First of all, there has never been, there is not now, and there never will be any but the one true and only God.

God's Word declares in 1 Corinthians 8:5,6, "For though there be that are *called* gods, whether in heaven or in earth, (as there be gods many, and lords many) but to us there is but *one God*" (italics added). In this verse the apostle Paul is referring to pagan polytheism, which included many gods and idols. He declares emphatically that there is only one God, the God known to us true believers in Christ.

Even more devastating to Mormonism, however, is the word of God in Isaiah 43:10, "Ye are my witnesses, saith the Lord, and my servant whom I have chosen; that ye may know and believe me, and understand that I am he: *before me there was no God formed, neither shall there be after me!"* (italics added).

Look carefully also, at Isaiah 44:6. "Thus saith the Lord the King of Israel, and his redeemer the Lord of hosts; I am the *first,* and I am the *last;* and beside me there is *no* God" (italics added).

Continue on to Isaiah 46:9. "Remember the former things of old: for I am God, and there is *none else*; I am God, and there is *none like me"* (italics added).

Now it is clear that God declares that He is the *one* and *only* true God, in this universe or any other, in this world or any other, on this planet or any other. There *is* no other God. This is the very same God of Genesis 1:1, "In the beginning God created the heaven and the earth." Genesis 1:16 tells us He made the stars and Genesis 2:1 declares, "Thus the heavens and the earth were finished, and all the host of them."

God made all possible worlds, universes, planets, stars and He is the one and only God of them all. There are *no* other Gods in existence anywhere. He *alone* is the one and only true God. There was no God before Him, there is no other God now, and *there never will be any other God.* He is the first and the last.

One of the primary names of God, *Jehovah,* means in essence, self-existent one; one who has life originally, permanently, and forever, within Himself.

God, then, was *never* a man, *never* mortal, but was *always* God. He is not now an "exalted man," as Mormonism claims. God explicitly declares, "For I am God, and not man" (Hos. 11:9).

Because God plainly declared in Isaiah 43:10 that there would be no God after Him, *no man will ever now, or in the future, or in eternity, become a god*. Therefore the Mormon creed, their main thrust, "As man is, God once was; as God is, man may be," is totally untrue to the Bible. It is not of God. "*Before* me there was no God formed, neither shall there be *after* me" (Isa. 43:10; italics added).

God did not attain His way to being God and He was never a man. He always was God. Psalm 90:2 says, "Before the mountains were brought forth, or ever thou hadst formed the earth and the world, even from everlasting to everlasting, thou art God."

Now we all know that everlasting means without end, enduring forever. Then what does "*from* everlasting," mean? Exactly the same, but applied to the past. God was God from everlasting past, just as He alone is God now, and just as He alone will be God in the everlasting, non-ending future!

This is utterly contrary to the Mormon teaching that "as man is, God once was; as God is, man may be." We cannot have it both ways. Either we believe this or we believe the Bible.

Mormonism says God was once man. God's Word says God was always God, never man, from everlasting, eternity past.

Mormonism says God had a beginning. God's Word says He did not.

Mormonism says there are many Gods and will be

more. God's Word says there never has been, is not now and never will be any other God.

Mormonism says man can become a god. God's Word says there will never be any other God. Christianity, biblically and historically, has always been monotheistic, believing in one God. Paganism, biblically and historically, has always been polytheistic, believing in more than one God. Neither the Old Testament nor the New Testament, nor Jesus, nor His disciples, nor early Christians, as can be proven from church history, ever taught that there was more than one God.

Thus far in this chapter, we have contrasted the God of Mormonism with the God of the Bible. We have discovered that the God of the Mormons and the God of the Bible seem to have little in common. To be sure, Mormons refer to God in some biblical terms which cloak the glaring and fatal differences from the unwary; but when they call their God "eternal" they have a totally different meaning than the Bible does. When Mormon writings give glowing accounts of "the eternal God, mighty Creator, everlasting Father," and so on, these wonderful words do not mean what they seem to say. They have no true relation to the one true God of the Bible whose very name as revealed to Moses is "I AM," underlying the fact that God always was, is now, and forever shall be the one and only God!

In the second part of this discussion on the fatal flaw we ask another question: *Is the Christ of Mormonism the Christ of the Bible?*

The Christ

As the Mormons have done with God, so have they done with Jesus Christ. The Bible teaches that Jesus

Christ is God the Son. God came down to earth in human flesh to shed His blood for our sins and conquer death for us by His bodily resurrection.

The Mormons teach that Jesus Christ is a God named *Jehovah*, another God, different from God the Father whose name is *Elohim*. The Bible uses these names interchangeably as applied to the one true God and Jesus Christ, as indicated in Deuteronomy 6:4, "The Lord [Jehovah] our God [Elohim] is one Lord [Jehovah]." However, the Mormons' teaching concerning Jesus Christ is that "Christ the Word, the Firstborn, had of course *attained* unto the status of Godhood while yet in pre-existence."[4]

Contrary to Mormon teaching, Christ always was, is now and forever shall be, God. He did *not attain* to being God for there was *never* a time when He was *not* God.

Of course, Christ had a human beginning insofar as becoming a man through the virgin birth. However, consider Isaiah 9:6: "For unto us a child is born, unto us a son is given [a clear and universally acknowledged prophecy of the coming Christ]: and the government shall be upon his shoulder: and his name shall be called Wonderful, Counsellor, *The mighty God, The everlasting Father,* The Prince of Peace" (italics added). Here God's Word calls Jesus Christ "God, The everlasting Father." (See also Jer. 32:18.)

That's right, Jesus Christ is that one, true and eternal God, manifested in the flesh (see John 1:1; 1 Tim. 3:16). Christ is called God numerous times: "My Lord and my God" (John 20:28); "But unto the Son he saith, Thy throne, O God, is for ever and ever" (Heb. 1:8). Since God declared in Isaiah 43:10 (and in numerous other places) that He is the one and *only* God, and that there will *never* be another, Jesus Christ, then, is either a false god and no god at all, or He is that one true God revealed in the flesh as the Son of God.

Another prophecy concerning Jesus Christ the God-man, Micah 5:2, "But thou, Bethlehem Ephratah, though thou be little among the thousands of Judah, yet out of thee shall he come forth unto me that is to be ruler in Israel; whose goings forth have been from of old, from everlasting." This "from everlasting" definitely means from all eternity past, without any beginning, as we have already discovered.

John 1:1 states, "In the beginning was the Word, and the Word was with God, and the Word was God." (Later in John 1:14 we see that "The Word was made flesh and dwelt among us," making Christ and the Word synonymous.) John 1:1 teaches us that Christ was the Word and that He was with God and that He *was* (not became) God. Again, here in the first verse of John's Gospel, we see that God was God from the beginning (which here has the sense of meaning "from all time") and so Jesus Christ was God from the beginning, from all time!

Jesus Christ accepted worship as God on many occasions because He was God. For example, "And as they went to tell his disciples, behold Jesus met them, saying, All hail. And they came and held him by the feet, and worshipped Him" (Matt. 28:9).

Now God has absolutely forbidden the worship of any other god, in biblical passages such as Exodus 34:14, "For thou shalt worship no other god; for the Lord, whose name is Jealous, is a jealous God." The fact that Jesus permitted, encouraged and accepted worship identified Him as God, and there is only one God who has been and will be God, "from everlasting to everlasting."

Not only is the God of Mormonism not the God of the Bible, but we also have to affirm that the Christ of Mormonism is not the Christ of the Bible. The Mormon's teaching about God and Jesus Christ lead us to still more error in doctrine—the doctrine of salvation.

The Way to Salvation

The Mormon belief that "as man is, God once was: as God is, man may be" lends itself to unsaved man's deception that he can somehow earn his salvation, or help earn it. This belief fosters the idea that man can become one of God's sheep by ignoring his sin nature and acting like a sheep, which is as futile as a pig acting like a sheep in order to become a sheep.

We need to have our nature changed by the new birth, and thus receive a new nature: "For all have sinned, and come short of the glory of God" (Rom. 3:23). No church, baptism or great amount of good works can change our nature or pay for past sins. We must turn to Jesus *alone* for salvation, knowing that His shed blood will cleanse us from all sin. Simultaneously, as we call believingly on Him, He will enter our life to change our nature from within. This makes us true children of God. "Nothing in our hands we bring, simply to His Cross we cling."

Salvation is ours through the grace of God: "For by grace are ye saved through faith; and that not of yourselves: it is the gift of God: not of works, lest any man should boast" (Eph. 2:8,9).

The *grace of God* of which Mormons sometimes write is far removed from the grace of God of which the Bible speaks. The Mormon concept of grace consists in part of doing church, temple and religious good works and so making oneself *worthy* of the grace of God. Biblical grace is extended freely to the *totally undeserving,* as in the case of the thief on the cross (see Luke 23:39-43). As we call on Christ, undeservingly but believingly, He responds with instant salvation. Then as He enters our lives and makes us children of God, our lives are changed by Christ from within. We receive a new nature, new desires, new love and new power. Behold the mad murderer, Saul, who became the magnificent missionary, Paul, after one vital encounter with the risen Christ on the road to Damascus.

In Summary

One of the most puzzling things for Christians to understand and accept is that Mormon friends will use the same terminology but mean something entirely different.

So many Christians, tragically, never look behind the words of sincere Mormon friends who declare to them that they have accepted Christ as their Saviour, and love Him. They say they are depending on Him for their salvation. Of course, they may add, they have a little more light, truth, or a higher salvation, since they are Mormons and in the Mormon church!

Mormons use the name "Christ," but in using the word they are thinking of someone or something entirely different, unless they don't know Mormon doctrine. In that case he is not a Mormon at all, except in name. If he truly accepts the Christ of the Bible, he will soon thirst for an oasis of true Christians, and will leave the Mormon church.

In any event, if you have a Mormon friend, love him and be patient with him as you would want him to be with you and as Christ is with us. However, probe gently but carefully into his testimony until you discover which

Christ he is trusting, and whether or not he believes there is more than one God.

A true Mormon must believe Mormon scriptures such as Joseph Smith's *Pearl of Great Price:* "And the Gods ordered, saying: Let the waters under the heaven be gathered together unto one place, and let the earth come up dry; and it was so as they ordered; And the Gods pronounced the dry land, earth; and the gathering together of the waters, pronounced they, great waters; and the Gods saw that they were obeyed" (Abraham 4:9,10).

To believe that other *gods* even exist is polytheistic paganism, not Christianity. It is a denial of the Word of God. We really must choose, as must our Mormon friends, to believe either the biblical God or Mormonism's gods. They are mutually exclusive.

The intensely religious, but lost, Pharisees made a fatal error. They worshiped God under His correct name, did many good works for Him, belonged to the worship system God had established, prayed much, gave much, prospered much, were extremely religious, and had priests in their church. The Pharisees appeared as angels of light and ministers of righteousness and really believed themselves to be right, to be in the one true "church" serving God, but they were tragically wrong. They never truly accepted Jesus Christ as God and remained forever lost, with the exception of a few who trusted Jesus.

In Matthew 24:23,24, our Lord spoke the awesome words: "Then if any man shall say unto you, Lo, here is Christ, or, there; believe it not. For there shall arise false Christs, and false prophets, and shall show great signs and wonders; insomuch that, if it were possible, they shall deceive the very elect."

Facts alone can never open eyes. However the Holy

Spirit does use facts, and this is written in the love of Christ that He may, through these facts, open many eyes to deliverance and salvation.

Notes

1. James E. Talmage, A Study of the *Articles of Faith* (Salt Lake City: The Church of Jesus Christ of Latter-day Saints, 1952), p. 430.
2. Joseph Fielding Smith, comp., *Teachings of Prophet Joseph Smith* (Salt Lake City: Deseret News Press, 1958), p. 345.
3. Milton R. Hunter, *The Gospel Through the Ages* (Salt Lake City: Deseret Book Co., 1945), p. 104.
4. B.R. McConkie, *What the Mormons Think of Christ* (tract) (Salt Lake City: Deseret News Press). p. 36.

CHAPTER EIGHT

The Truth About "Adam-God"

The Adam-God doctrine is a thorn in the side of the LDS church that they wish would go away. Brigham Young taught that Adam was God. He taught this doctrine for over 20 years in many different sermons. The Mormon church believed it, accepted it, and taught it for at least 50 years. Present-day Mormons usually deny this doctrine.

"Living Prophet" and present LDS president, Spencer W. Kimball, now calls this Adam-God doctrine "false doctrine." If Mormons follow Brigham Young in this heretical doctrine about Adam being God, they reveal the LDS church to be false, undeniably. The Adam-God doctrine contradicts the *Book of Mormon*. It contradicts the Bible. Not only that, it is sheer, unadulterated nonsense. However, it is an inescapable fact that Brigham Young taught this doctrine! To abandon the doctrine and preserve the integrity of the "prophet" is impossible. This would shred logic, emasculate honesty, and denude truth.

Let me boil this down. To believe that Brigham Young was a prophet of God and accept his Adam-God revelation, is to admit that the present-day "prophet" Spencer W. Kimball and the LDS church are false. To *deny* the Adam-God doctrine is to deny the "prophet" who gave it—Brigham Young—and to admit that he was a false prophet. This doctrinal contradiction proves that the LDS church is a false church, led for years by a false prophet.

Let us now take a brief but honest look at the evidence. Notice the dates as we proceed.

The Adam-God Doctrine

Brigham Young apparently introduced this doctrine in a sermon he gave on April 9, 1852. Read it *in context* for yourself in the *Journal of Discourses:* "Now hear it, O inhabitants of earth, Jew and Gentile, Saint and sinner! When our father Adam came into the Garden of Eden, he came into it with a celestial body, and brought Eve, one of his wives, with him. He helped to make and organize this world. He is Michael, the Archangel, the Ancient of Days! about whom holy men have written and spoken— He is our *father* and our God, and the *only God with whom we have to do*" (vol. 1, p. 50,51, italics added).

Brigham Young taught that Adam was God over and over again. This was no isolated, one-time shot.

Now read the clear contradiction by the Mormon's present president and living prophet, Spencer W. Kimball: "We warn you against the dissemination of doctrines which are not according to the scriptures and which are *alleged* to have been taught by some of the General Authorities of past generations. Such, for instance, is the Adam-God *theory*. We denounce that theory and hope that everyone will be cautioned against this and other kinds of *false doctrine*"[1] (italics added).

Mormons would have their people and others believe that Brigham Young was misquoted or misunderstood. They would like to think that this Adam-God doctrine is an attempt by anti-Mormons to defame their prophet.

Nevertheless, any honest Mormon who is willing to face the facts can find out for himself exactly what Brigham Young gave on the subject in the *Journal of Discourses* and other Mormon writings. For those who do not have access to the *Journal of Discourses*, Melaine Layton, Jerald and Sandra Tanner, and Bob Witte all have photo-reprints of Brigham Young's sermons on Adam being God in their respective books.

Adam, Who Is He?

Mark E. Peterson, Mormon apostle, wrote a book, *Adam, Who Is He?* He claimed that Mormon apostle Charles C. Rich listened to the April 9, 1852 sermon that Brigham Young preached on the Adam-God doctrine and heard Brigham say something different on one point than that which was actually recorded. According to apostle Rich, Brigham Young said: "What a learned idea! Jesus, our elder brother, was begotten in the flesh by the same character that was in the Garden of Eden, and who talked with our Father in heaven." Let us check this claim and verify historical accuracy and honesty.

The Mormon church historian, Leonard J. Arrington, wrote a book, *Charles G. Rich, Mormon General and Western Frontiersman*. In it Arrington tells us about a trip that Rich made. He says Rich left San Bernardino, California on March 24, 1852, bound for Salt Lake Valley, with a wagon load of supplies. He returned to San Bernardino from Salt Lake City, arriving at San Bernardino August 20, 1852, in 22 days, "the quickest trip on record," according to Arrington.[2] Obviously, if it took Rich 22 days to travel from Salt Lake City to San Bernardino—and that was "the quickest trip on record," it would have taken him at least 22 days to travel from San Bernardino to Salt Lake Valley. So if he left San Bernardino March 24, it would have been impossible for Charles C. Rich to have arrived in Salt Lake City on April 9, in time to have heard Brigham Young's sermon. Mormon writers cannot even get together on evasions of truth!

Brigham Young said that when his sermons were corrected, they were *scripture*.[3] He spoke as the official "living prophet" of the LDS church, giving his people, ostensibly, God's revelation to them. One year after he preached this sermon, the gist of the Adam-God sermon was printed in the Mormon *Millenial Star,* emphasizing what Brigham Young had taught about Adam being God. The sermon was soon reproduced in the *Journal of Discourses,* where Brigham Young had to approve of it. He did not change it or deny it any way ever. From 1852 until Brigham Young died in 1877, the sermon remained intact as he permitted it to be reproduced in the *Journal of Discourses*. It is still there today.

Mark Petersen's claim was just one of many attempts to cover up Brigham Young's Adam-God teaching. We ask honest Mormons to face the truth. We have presented some of the evidence to the fact that Brigham Young undeniably taught the heretical doctrine that Adam was

God, and added that he was "the only God with whom we had to do." This eliminates Jesus, Elohim and all other Mormon gods.

We deny that Brigham Young was misquoted or misunderstood in his April 9, 1852 message. We call attention to the fact that Brigham Young was still teaching the same Adam-God doctrine 21 years later! In a quote from the Mormon paper, *The Deseret News*, June 18, 1873, 21 years after Brigham Young's first Adam-God sermon of April 9, 1852, Young said: "How much unbelief exists in the minds of the Latter-day Saints in regard to one particular doctrine which I revealed to them, and which God revealed to me. . . namely that Adam is our Father and God. . . . Our Father Adam helped to make this earth, it was created expressly for him and after it was made he and his companions came here. He brought one of his wives with him, and she was called Eve, because she was the first woman upon this earth. Our Father Adam is the man who stands at the gate and holds the keys to everlasting life and salvation to all his children who have or who ever will come upon the earth. . . . 'Well,' says one 'Why was Adam called Adam'? He was the first man on earth, and its framer and maker. He, with the help of his brethren, brought it into existence. Then he said, 'I want my children who are in the spirit world to come and live here. I once dwelt upon an earth something like this, in a mortal state. I was faithful, I received my crown and exaltation [became a "God" according to Mormon teaching]. I have the privilege of extending my work, and to its increase there will be no end. I want my children that were born to me in the spirit world to come and take tabernacles of flesh, that their spirits may have a house, a tabernacle or a dwelling place as mine has, and where is the mystery?'"[4].

God's Creation

It would be difficult to get more contradictions of the Bible in one short statement than this. Read the simple account in Genesis 1—2 stating that God created man, breathed the breath of life into him—which if he had already been alive would have been unnecessary. This creation then became the first man, Adam, a living soul. Eve was created by God, here on this earth, from Adam; she obviously was not brought here by Adam as "one of his wives." Adam had absolutely nothing to do with creating the earth. He was a mere insignificant creature created by God after the earth was created.

(Incidentally, God gave one wife to Adam, not more than one. Man broke this pattern of monogamy later, both to his sorrow and God's. In the New Testament God clearly affirmed His plan for marriage in such passages as Matthew 19:5. Speaking of a man leaving his father and mother and cleaving to his wife, He said, they two shall be one flesh. No Christian in the entire New Testament is ever said to have had more than one wife at a time; and bishops, elders and deacons, as proven Christians, were absolutely forbidden to be the husband of more than one wife [see 1 Tim. 2—3; Titus 1]. Under the new covenant —the New Testament—with greater light and the Holy Spirit indwelling His people, God forbids completely the practice of taking more than one wife, which He "overlooked" back in the Old Testament [Acts 17:30].

Historically, Mormon leaders have ignored and shattered God's explicit command in regard to marriage. Many Mormon founders—Joseph Smith and Brigham Young, and their bishops and elders—had more than one wife. This means that they were not qualified for the offices they held, and that all their claims of authority were spurious in the eyes of God!)

Not only did Brigham Young, in 1852, introduce the Adam-God doctrine, he continued to preach it down through the years, as another of his sermons from 1857 prove;[5] and he was still preaching it in 1873. Other Mormon sources also substantiate this fact. Brigham Young's Adam-God doctrine was quoted in Mormon publications accurately and widely for many years. Brigham Young saw many, if not all, of these quotations, such as the sermons he gave to the *Journal of Discourses*. He had years and years of opportunity to correct any misquotations in them. He did not do so. This effectively proves that he taught and meant that Adam is God, and "the only God with whom we have to do"! Woe to the Mormon who does not believe the "living prophet" and his "revelation"! And woe to the Mormon who does!

F.D. Richards, a prominent Mormon, said: "Concerning the doctrine that Adam is our Father and God . . . the prophet and Apostle Brigham has declared it, and that is the word of the Lord."[6]

And then in the *Diary of Hosea Stout:* "Another meeting this evening. President B. Young taught that Adam was the Father of Jesus and the only God to us."[7]

Mormon leader George Q. Cannon taught that "Jesus Christ is Jehovah," and that "Adam is his Father and our God."[8]

A very interesting comment is made by Mormon A.F. MacDonald in "Minutes of the School of the Prophets, Provo, Utah, 1868-1871" (pp. 38,39) many years after the first Brigham Young Adam-God sermon in 1852. "The doctrine preached by Prest Young for a few years back wherein he says that Adam is our God—the God we worship—that most of the people believe it . . . Orson

Pratt has said he does not believe it, . . . if the President makes a statement it is not our prerogative to dispute it . . . when I first heard the doctrine of Adam being our Father and God, I was favorably impressed—enjoyed and hailed it as a new Revelation—it appeared reasonable to me as the father of our spirits, that he should introduce us here.''

Mormon Edward W. Tullidge wrote, ''Adam is our Father and God. He is the God of the earth. So says Brigham Young.''[9]

The point is established as a fact: Brigham Young did indeed teach that Adam was God, ''the only God with whom we have to do.'' As Melaine Layton, a knowledgeable ex-Mormon says in her fine unpublished book, ''Mormonism,'' concerning the Adam-God doctrine: ''It is true that Mormons today do not believe this; however, I have had a number of Mormon people tell me that they themselves believe it. Most others have never heard of the idea and say that it is simply not true. However, facts are: For more than 50 years (1852-1903), Mormonism's official writers taught without hesitation that Adam is our God, and the major share of the people believed it!''

The Contradicting Prophet

Consider again the incredible contradiction by President and ''living prophet,'' Spencer W. Kimball: ''We warn you against the dissemination of doctrines which are not according to the scriptures and which are *alleged* to have been taught by some of the General Authorities of past generations. Such, for instance, is the Adam-God *theory*. We denounce that theory and hope that everyone will be cautioned against this and other kinds of *false doctrine*'' (italics added). As Wally Tope says so cogently concerning this statement, "Either Spencer W. Kimball is lying; hasn't done his homework; or refuses to believe plain English; all of which are inexcusable."[10]

There is simply no way out. It is impossible and utterly dishonest to pretend that Brigham Young was misquoted and misunderstood for over 50 years by Mormon leaders and thousands of Mormons. If his "revelations" are contradicted at a later date, why have a "living prophet"? How do Mormons know they are not now misunderstanding their current Mormon prophet? The Adam-God doctrine is false doctrine, by a false prophet, in a false church.

This false doctrine led to other blasphemous doctrines which Brigham also taught. Among these is that Adam was the literal father of Jesus, as a result of sex relations with the virgin Mary, so that Jesus was really not born of a virgin as the Bible declares in Matthew 1:18-20. Brigham Young flatly declared that "Jesus Christ was not begotten by the Holy Ghost."[11]

The Bible says, "That which is conceived in her is of the Holy Ghost."

The Mormon Jesus

The Mormon Jesus is not virgin born, is a spirit-brother of Satan, was not God from eternity, is not one in nature, essence and substance with God the Father and the Holy Spirit. The Mormon Jesus is a false Jesus, a Jesus who does not exist except as part of the Mormon illusion. No matter how much a Mormon loves or pays homage to the Jesus he knows, it is a futile and fatal folly. And Brigham Young's Adam-God doctrine played a large part in the forming of this false Jesus of Mormon myth.

Mormons sometimes say that Brigham Young did not

mean that Adam was *Elohim*, but a man who achieved godhood on some other planet. They may also add that it was *Elohim* who was pictured as being the God who had sex relations in his physical body with the "virgin" Mary, not Adam. Brigham Young himself unmistakably and forever clarified what he meant. On February 19, 1854, two years after his initial Adam-God sermon, Brigham Young said, speaking of Christ: "Who did beget him? His Father, and his father is our God, and the Father of our spirits, and he is the framer of the body, the God and Father of our Lord Jesus Christ. Who is he? He is Father Adam"[12]

Here Brigham Young identifies Adam as the heavenly Father, God, the "Father of our spirits," and the Father of the Lord Jesus Christ. Clearly and irrefutably, Brigham Young taught that Adam directly, physically, in sex relations with Mary, begat Jesus Christ. Thus Brigham Young violated Scripture, denied the virgin birth, and identified the God of Mormonism as Adam!

Early Mormons had strong "testimonies" of the truth of Brigham Young's Adam-God doctrine, just as Mormons today have strong "testimonies" that it is a false doctrine. This illustrates the fallacy of "testimony" as compared with the sure Word of God. Spencer Kimball and today's Mormons would be excommunicated from the church as apostates for denying the Adam-God doctrine if they had lived in Brigham Young's time. Conversely, those Mormons who would accept and teach Brigham Young's Adam-God doctrine today would be in danger of excommunication as apostates! How can a Mormon know who is teaching truth when today's revelations by a living prophet may be false tomorrow.

There is no doubt that Brigham Young taught that

Adam was God, and the direct, literal, physical father of the Lord Jesus Christ.

But even if Young did really mean that *Elohim,* a God of flesh and blood, had physical sex relations with the "virgin" Mary, it is still a blasphemous statement. This would mean that Mary was not a virgin when Jesus was born, as the Bible says she was. God violated the marriage rights of Joseph in an adulterous relationship—the very thing He forbids—with Mary. God does not violate His own commandments! God have mercy on those who dare to stoop so low in dishonoring Him and His Word to rescue Brigham Young! Jesus was born by the miracle of the Holy Spirit enabling the virgin Mary to conceive, not by physical sex relations with a philandering God!

Incidentally, Adam did not exist before he was created. As God plainly says, the natural comes first, then the spiritual (see 1 Cor. 15:46). When Jesus said, "Before Abraham was, I AM," He was declaring that before Abraham existed, Jesus was the Eternal God! Certainly Abraham existed physically before the man Jesus. Jesus as God has existed from eternity.

God loves Mormons and so do I. I can only pray that the knife of truth will have the anesthesia of His love upon it as He uses these facts to operate on the hearts of Mormons who honestly want to know the truth.

With genuine sorrow, but with absolute certainty, we repeat: for the Mormon church to deny the Adam-God doctrine brands Brigham Young as a false prophet. This means that the LDS church is false. To accept the doctrine denies the Bible, not to mention common sense. It also denies prophet and President, Spencer W. Kimball.

These facts have Mormon followers boxed in. God does *not* want Mormons to despair, but He *does* want them to have their eyes opened to the biblical Lord Jesus Christ. He loves them and wants them saved from sin and hell and from the delusion of Mormonism and its false Christ before it is forever too late. Satan always has an answer, which is why most cults basically never change, exposed. However, God will reveal Himself to those honest, seeking Mormons who will face the facts and not try to elude the truth by hiding behind their "testimony" or their "burning in the bosom" (see chap. 13) or some of Satan's clever but dishonest answers.

Mormon "revelation" has led its "prophets" and people into an impossible maze of contradiction, confusion and cover-up. Please don't despair. Turn to the Lord Jesus Christ and He will save you and heal your broken heart. The biblical Lord Jesus Christ, Himself eternally God, will give you something a thousand times sweeter than Mormonism or the Mormon Jesus ever could. His salvation (the Mormon's exaltation) is a gift (see Rom. 6:23). Call on the Lord Jesus Christ to save you (see Rom. 10:13), believe Him that He did, and you can be certain that you are saved *now* (see 1 John 5:13).

Notes

1. *Church News*, October 9, 1976.
2. Leonard J. Arrington, *Charles G. Rich, Mormon General and Western Frontiersman* (Salt Lake: BYU Press, nd.), p. 173.
3. *Journal of Discourses*, vol. 13, p. 95.
4. *The Deseret News*, June 18, 1873.
5. *Journal of Discourses*, 1857, vol. 5, p. 331.
6. *Millenial Star*, August 26, 1954, vol. 16, p.534.
7. *Diary of Hosea Stout*, April 9, 1852, vol. 2, p. 435.
8. *Diary Journal of Abraham H. Cannon*, June 23, 1889, vol. 11, p. 39.
9. *The Women of Mormondom*, 1877, pp. 79, 179, 196, 197.
10. Wally Tope, "Maximizing Your Witness to Mormons," p. 20.
11. *Journal of Discourses*, vol. 1, pp. 50,51.
12. Brigham Young Papers, February 19, 1854, call number Ms F 219 #81, Church Historians' Office, Salt Lake City. Quoted from Chris A. Vlachos, *Adam Is God???* (Clearwater, FL: Ex-Mormons for Jesus, 1979), p. 9.

CHAPTER NINE

Contradictions Concerning the Person of God

The Bible is the foundation of what God had to say to man. When there is a contradiction between what the Bible teaches and what the *Book of Mormon* or any Mormon book teaches, the Bible must be given preeminence.

We do not intend to try to give in this book an exhaustive exploitation of the many contradictions between the Bible and the various books of Mormon doctrine. If you are anxious to pursue the subject we recommend *Mormonism, Shadow or Reality*, by Jerald and Sandra Tanner. This 600-page volume contains an open challenge to any scholar or group of scholars to try to answer, point by point, the contradictions it reveals.

However, we do want to take a close look at some of the contradictions between the Bible and Mormon teachings concerning the doctrine of God. We also will reveal contradictions between "inspired" Mormon books written by Joseph Smith and the *Book of Mormon* concerning the person of God.

Mormons Believe There Are Many Gods

Mormonism denies that there is *one* God. While the *Book of Mormon* seems to teach the doctrine of the trinity as Christians believe it, other teachings of Joseph Smith say there are many gods.

The Scriptures say: "But to us there is but one God" (1 Cor. 8:6; see also vv. 4,5); "Before me there was no God formed, neither shall there be after me" (Isa. 43:10); "I am God, and there is none else" (Isa. 45:22). (See also Deut. 4:35; 32:39; 2 Sam. 7:22; Ps. 86:10.)

The *Book of Mormon* says: ". . . of the Father, and of the Son, and of the Holy Ghost, which is one God, without end" (2 Nephi 31:21). Alma 11:26-31 quotes Amulek as answering Zeezrom that there is only *one* God, and Amulek is described as a man filled with the Spirit of the Lord. Alma 11:22 and Mosiah 15:4,5, also speak of the Father and Son as being one God.

However, in *Doctrine and Covenants*, we read that Abraham, Isaac and Jacob "have entered into their exaltation, according to the promises, and sit upon thrones, and are not angels but are gods" (132:37). In the *Pearl of Great Price*, Joseph Smith wrote, "So the Gods went down to organize man in their own image, in the image of the Gods to form they him, male and female, to form they them" (Abraham 4:27). The Bible and the *Book of Mormon* both declare that there is *one* God but *Doctrine and Covenants* and the *Pearl of Great Price* declare that there are many gods.

The statement of the three witnesses in the front of the *Book of Mormon* includes this sentence: "And the honor be to the Father, and to the Son, and to the Holy Ghost, which is one God." Contrast this with a statement from the *Teachings of Prophet Joseph Smith* in which Joseph Smith says, "In the beginning, the head of the gods called a council of the gods." Also in one version of his first vision he claims that the Father and Son appeared to him as two different beings with two different literal bodies. Some Mormon friends of mine use this as a basis for their belief that God the Father and God the Son are two different Gods. This belief is contrary to the Bible and the *Book of Mormon*.

Still more confusing to anyone studying the doctrine of God in Mormon teachings are contradictions that can be found *in the same book*. For one example, the *Pearl of Great Price* says in Moses 2:9,10: "And I, God, said: Let the waters under the heaven be gathered together unto one place, and it was so; and I, God, said: Let there be dry land; and it was so. And I, God, called the dry land Earth; and the gathering together of the waters, called I the Sea; and I God saw that all things which I had made were good." But in Abraham 4:9,10 the *Pearl of Great Price* reads: "And the Gods ordered, saying: Let the waters under the heaven be gathered together unto one place, and let the earth come up dry; and it was so as they ordered; and the Gods pronounced the dry land, earth; and the gathering together of the waters, pronounced they, great waters; and the Gods saw that they were obeyed."

Mormons Believe God Is an Exalted Man

We have mentioned that Mormons teach that God was once a man before He progressed to being God. According to their teaching, God is now an exalted man, and man himself may become a God.

The Scriptures teach us: "Before the mountains were brought forth, or ever thou hadst formed the earth and the world, even from everlasting to everlasting [that's forever past, forever future], thou art God" (Ps. 90:2); there is "no variableness, neither shadow of turning" with God (Jas. 1:17); "For I am the Lord, I change not" (Mal. 3:6); "In the beginning God . . ." (Gen. 1:1); "Now unto the King eternal, immortal, invisible . . ." (1 Tim. 1:17).

The *Book of Mormon* says, "For do we not read that God is the same yesterday, today, and forever, and in him there is no variableness neither shadow of changing?" (Mormon 9:9); "For I know that God is not a partial God, neither a changeable being, but he is unchangeable from all eternity to all eternity" (Moroni 8:18); "God . . . being from everlasting to everlasting" (Moroni 7:22).

The *Pearl of Great Price* says, "Behold, I am the Lord God Almighty, and Endless is my name, for I am without beginning of days or end of years" (Moses 1:3).

With these definite, clear assertions from the Bible, the *Book of Mormon* and the *Pearl of Great Price*, that God had no beginning, that He was always God, and that He is an unchangeable being, what a shock it is to encounter the following in James Talmage, *The Articles of Faith:* "As man is, God once was; as God is, man may be."[1]

God's answer to this untruth is, "For I am God, and not man" (Hos. 11:9).

One of the problems Mormons have with the claim that God was once a man is this: If God was once a man *before* He became God then man, in effect, becomes the creator or at least the evolving forerunner of God, instead of God creating man. In conversations with Mormon friends, I have pointed this out and they have quickly denied that such is the case. Yet it is an obvious fact. If we follow this line of reasoning Mormons often say that this man who became God really had another God for a Father, and perhaps even a Mother God. The Mormons usually get increasingly vague at this point.

Mormons Believe God Has a Physical Body

In keeping with their doctrine that God is an exalted man, Mormons and Mormon teaching claim that God has a visible, material body. Biblical verses like Exodus 33:11 are used in support of this doctrine, "And the Lord spake unto Moses, face to face, as a man speaketh unto his friend."

God has been seen in anthropomorphic or theophanic appearances, as a man, angel, etc., and as incarnate in Christ. He has never been seen in His divine essence. Exodus 33 continues in verse 20, "And he said, Thou canst not see my face: for there shall no man see me, and live." John 1:18 adds, "No man hath seen God at any time; the only begotten Son, which is in the bosom of the Father, he hath declared him."

After His resurrection, Jesus appeared to His disciples and said, "Behold my hands and my feet, that it is myself: handle me and see; for a spirit hath not flesh and bones, as ye see me have" (Luke 24:39). Jesus here confirmed that a spirit cannot be seen or touched.

"God is a Spirit" (John 4:24)—not *has* a Spirit, but *is* a Spirit. A Spirit is invisible as the Bible says God is, and does not have a body of flesh and bone. It is true that we find in Scripture, references to the mouth, arms, eyes, ears, face and hands of God. However, these references are symbolic, not literal. God uses them to communicate truth to us that we can understand.

If our Mormon friends insist on taking every description of God as literal they may wind up with a very strange God. Deuteronomy 4:24 says, "For the Lord thy God is a consuming fire," the blast-furnace God. Jeremiah 23:24 says, "Do not I fill heaven and earth? saith the Lord." If God were flesh and bone, this might make it a little uncomfortable for the rest of us! In Jeremiah 2:13, God calls Himself the "fountain of living waters." Psalm 91:4, "He shall cover thee with his feathers, and under his wings shalt thou trust." Surely this verse cannot be taken literally, for our wonderful God is not a chicken or a bird.

The Mormon claim that God is an exalted man and has a physical body has carried the Mormons to the brink of blasphemy. Brigham Young, in *Journal of Discourses,* says, "Adam . . . is our father and our God and the only God with whom we have to do." Again he says, "Jesus Christ was not begotten by the Holy Ghost."[2]

Brigham Young went on to say that the Father of Jesus was the first of the human family—Adam, the same character that was in the Garden of Eden!

The Bible says, "For that which is conceived in her is of the Holy Ghost" (Matt. 1:20).

Certainly, the fact that man has a body of flesh and bone does not mean that God is made of the same material, especially when He clearly teaches that He is not. To believe literally that man is made in the image of God could be most confusing. Would God look like a man or a woman? Which race would He resemble in facial characteristics? We are made in the image of God in that we have self-awareness, abstract reasoning power, a spiritual nature and a God-awareness.

In Summary

It seems undeniable that there really are contradictions between the teachings of the Bible and the teachings of the *Book of Mormon* and Mormon prophets and teachers. It also seems undeniable that Mormon books and prophets contradict each other.

Mormon friends have often said to us, "You are taking what Joseph Smith (or whoever) said out of context!"

Of course, taking things out of context is a problem for all of us, isn't it? Obviously I cannot quote entire passages, chapters or volumes; there would not be enough space. That is why I have carefully listed the quotations, pages, etc., and quoted mostly from the Mormons' own teachings, so that they may read what is said in context for themselves. I want them to see that the portions I have quoted accurately reflect the teaching of the context as a whole.

Any book that claims to be the Word of God must be tested by the Bible. There is no other book inspired by the Holy Spirit. The Bible is the one and only Word of God and it is enough.

Notes

1. James Talmage, *The Articles of Faith*, p. 430.
2. Young, *Journal of Discourses*, vol. 1, pp. 50, 51.

CHAPTER TEN

Priesthood and Genealogies

The Mormons have done exactly what Jesus Christ said *not* to do. They have put "new wine in old bottles!" They have wed grace to law and made Christianity into a Jewish sect. They have resurrected what Christ buried. They have figuratively "sewn up" the veil that Christ, as our High Priest, rent forever to provide for us free access into the Holy of Holies.

How have they done this? Why have they done this? In their attempt to justify their existence and lend authority to their beliefs, and in their attempt to prove that they are the "one true church" they have restored the distinctively Jewish, Old Testament priesthood, and have turned again to the study and preserving of genealogies. The Mormon church claims that only those who hold the priesthood in the Mormon church have the authority to administer the ordinances of the gospel. Therefore, they believe there is no true salvation, no access to the "highest" heaven outside of the Mormon church. All ordinances performed by any other church are in vain.

Genealogies once had a firm connection with the priesthood as to verifying qualifications for the priesthood. Mormons have built up the most elaborate genealogical system in the world.

The Aaronic Priesthood

The lesser of the two priesthood organizations in the Mormon church is the Aaronic or Levitical priesthood. This Aaronic priesthood was supposedly restored when John the Baptist appeared to Joseph Smith and Oliver Cowdery May 15, 1829, and conferred the Aaronic priesthood on them. Read the account in *Pearl of Great Price*, Joseph Smith 2:68-73.

(Mormons love to deny other churches' authority and assert their own, by quoting Hebrews 5:4, "And no man taketh this honour unto himself, but he that is called of God, as was Aaron." Exodus 28, 29 tell us exactly how Aaron and his sons were called and consecrated and not one Mormon on earth is called and consecrated in that way today! Read it and see!)

Since Oliver Cowdery later defected from the LDS church and was even called a liar by Joseph Smith and others, I would say that his testimony of the restoration of the Aaronic priesthood is a little suspect, to say the least. (Both Marvin Cowan and Jerald Tanner in their respective books, *Mormon Claims Answered* and *Mormonism, Shadow or Reality*, quote several Mormon writers who totally contradict the claims of the restored Aaronic priesthood.)

The order of the Aaronic priesthood in the Mormon church includes *deacons*, boys 12 and 13 years of age; *teachers*, boys 14 and 15; and *priests*, boys 16 and 17 years of age.

The Melchizedek Priesthood

According to Talmage, sometime after the Aaronic priesthood was conferred in 1829, Peter, James and John also conferred the Melchizedek priesthood on Joseph Smith and Oliver Cowdery.[1] Mormon historian B.H. Roberts admits that "there is no definite account of the event [the conferring of the Melchizedek priesthood on Joseph Smith and Oliver Cowdery] in the history of the prophet Joseph, or, for matter of that, in any of our annals."[2]

This higher order of the two Mormon priesthoods is "called the Melchizedek Priesthood . . . because Melchizedek was such a great high priest" (*Doctrine and Covenants* 107:2). (See Gen. 14:18; Ps. 110:4; Heb. 5:6; 6:20; 7:1.) The officers of this priesthood include *elders*, *seventies*, and *high priests*. The Mormons believe that, "like God himself, the Melchizedek Priesthood is eternal and everlasting in nature." It is "an everlasting principle, and existed with God from eternity, and will to eternity, without beginning of days or end of years."[3]

Long years before God ever established the priesthood as a continuing office through Aaron, the Scriptures tell of a man named Melchizedek (Gen. 14). Melchizedek was without recorded beginning or ending and was a high priest and king. In these things he was a picture of the Lord Jesus Christ, our everlasting God (Isa. 9:6), High Priest, and King of kings.

After the introduction of this one man, Melchizedek,

there was no other Melchizedek priesthood ordained of God for centuries. No man, after Melchizedek, held this office until Jesus came and fulfilled the picture that Melchizedek and his priesthood portrayed. When Jesus came He alone was declared to be a "priest for ever after the order of Melchizedek" (Heb. 7:21). Jesus, "because he continueth ever, hath an unchangeable priesthood" (Heb. 7:24). According to Greek scholars like Robertson and Thayer, *unchangeable* means "untransferable." Jesus alone, for all time, is our Melchizedek priest. For anyone to claim to be a Melchizedek priest today seems exceedingly unwise. Read Hebrews 7.

One look at the Mormon church with its restored Aaronic and Melchizedek priesthoods should convince anyone who is at all acquainted with the New Testament church that the Mormons have restored too much! They restored what was never there! There were no officers such as Aaronic or Melchizedek priests, seventies, high priests, etc., in the New Testament church. Nevertheless, this is the structure upon which the LDS church is built—the authority of the restored Aaronic and Melchizedek priesthoods, found only in the Mormon church.

The office of deacon, as the New Testament describes it, should be sought by those who are "the husbands of one wife, ruling their children and their own houses well" (1 Tim. 3:12). Can a 12-year-old boy qualify for deacon under this description?

God commanded that the priests were to come through the tribe of Levi, and directly through Aaron and his sons and descendants. Yet most Mormons claim to be either from the tribes of Ephraim or Manasseh—the wrong tribes!

One of the highest duties of the priests in the Old

Testament was to offer blood sacrifices. Mormon priests do not. If this is a restoration of the priesthood, why don't they?

Genealogies

The real purpose of all Mormon genealogical work is to provide information for baptizing for the dead, proxy sealing ordinances (an ordinance whereby husbands and wives are sealed together in the marriage union for time and eternity), and ordination and endowments for dead relatives to help save or exalt them. Thus Mormons search out the names of the dead through genealogical research and proceed to be baptized in their behalf. President Joseph Fielding Smith said, "The greatest commandment given us, and made obligatory, is the temple work in our own behalf and in behalf of our dead."[4]

The Mormon church keeps microfilms of all this genealogical work in large tunnels drilled in a granite mountain in Little Cottonwood Canyon, southeast of Salt Lake City. These genealogies go back for centuries. Forty-five million people have already been baptized by proxy. In 1975 alone more than three million were baptized in 16 Mormon temples. Thirteen camera crews in this country and 67 other camera crews around the world labor to add microfilmed information about the dead to this mass. Over 120 million dollars have been spent in this effort.

In 1966 "The total microfilm load included 579,679,800 pages of documents. There were more than 5 billion names in the files—the church puts about 4 million dollars a year into the Genealogical Society. It has 575 employees and is run by a board which includes two Apostles."[5]

Friends, all of you who are bound by priests and genealogies, read carefully and joyfully. I have good news for you!

Good-bye Sacrifices, Priests and Genealogies

Good news! Wonderful news! No more sacrifice has to be offered for our sins. Jesus offered "one sacrifice for sins forever" (Heb. 10:12), and thereby did away with the need for any other sacrifice.

Old Testament priests had as their chief function the offering of blood sacrifices as an atonement for sin (see Lev. 9:1,2). All their sacrifices symbolized the day when Christ, the Lamb of God, would shed His blood for our sins. When Jesus died on the cross the picture was fulfilled and the need for sacrifices, and therefore the need for priests, was done away with.

When my friend John was sharing his Mormon doctrine with me, he frequently claimed that all churches were false except the Mormon church. One reason for this is that we had no authority because we had no official priesthood, no apostles or prophets. What does God say about this?

Every Christian is now declared to be a priest. "But ye are a chosen generation, a royal priesthood, an holy nation, a peculiar people; that ye should show forth the praises of him who hath called you out of darkness into his marvelous light" (1 Pet. 2:9). "John to the seven churches which are in Asia: Grace be unto you, and peace, from him which is, and which was, and which is to come; and from the seven Spirits which are before his throne; and from Jesus Christ, who is the faithful witness, and the first begotten of the dead, and the prince of the kings of the earth. Unto him that loved us, and washed us from our sins in his own blood, and hath made us kings and priests unto God and his Father; to him be glory and dominion for ever and ever. Amen" (Rev. 1:4-6).

The death of Christ eliminated the formal Jewish priesthood. The veil in the Temple which symbolized the separation of mankind from God, was torn "from the top to the bottom" when He died and He became our High Priest and opened direct access to God (Heb. 10:18-21). Now we can enter into the presence of God through His sacrifice. Jesus is our High Priest, our Sacrifice and our Mediator. We need no other.

Everyone who accepts the Sacrificial Lamb of God as his atonement for sin, *everyone* who becomes a Christian is part of this chosen generation and is included in this royal priesthood, including women and Negroes. We have the authority of the Word of God and the indwelling Holy Spirit who has promised to guide us in His truth, the Word of God. We are *all* appointed His ambassadors, which gives us immense and certain authority (see 2 Cor. 5:17-21). This is not true of the Mormon "priesthood."

Genealogical records were completely destroyed by the Romans. These genealogical records were kept meticulously by the Jews because of family lines and tribal inheritance. Both Matthew and Luke record the genealogy of Christ. God allowed this to be included in His Word so that the Messiahship of Jesus Christ could be proven. Hundreds of years before Jesus Christ, prophets told that He would come from a certain people, from a certain tribe, from a certain family line, from a certain individual within a family. This was part of God's magnificent proof that Jesus Christ was God in the flesh as He claimed to be.

After Jesus was crucified, Titus, in A.D. 70 destroyed

all the genealogical records in Jerusalem. All that remained were those recorded in God's Word. God was saying, "The Messiah has come and He has been genealogically verified. It is finished."

Genealogical records were the means of proving the qualifications of priests. Their bloodlines could be traced all the way back to Aaron. When God instituted the Jewish priesthood He chose only one of the 12 tribes of Israel, the Levites, to be priests. Within the tribe of Levi He chose one man, Aaron, as His high priest. All true priests were descendants of Aaron (see Exod. 28:1; 31:10; Lev. 8:2; 9; Num. 3:1-4). Anyone other than a blood descendent of Aaron, who claimed to be a priest, was a false priest, regardless of how many voices they heard or visions they saw claiming that God had given them the authority of the priesthood. Aaronic descent had to be proven.

When God allowed these genealogical records to be totally destroyed, after having miraculously preserved them for centuries, He made it impossible for anyone to trace bloodline descent back to Aaron and thus claim to be an Aaronic priest! Anyone who claims to be an Aaronic priest today is a false priest.

Furthermore, God warns against giving "heed to fables and endless genealogies, which minister questions, rather than godly edifying which is in faith" (1 Tim. 1:4). Again His Word says, "Avoid foolish questions, and genealogies, and contentions, and strivings about the law; for they are unprofitable and vain" (Titus 3:9). The Jewish system is discarded by God in this age of grace. Only those who would out-Hebrew the Hebrews, would cling to a system long set aside by God. This is why we find *no* priests listed—Aaronic, Melchizedek or any other kind—in the church Jesus established! There is no such office today. The New Testament church had no need for them and any church that has an official order of priests is not a New Testament church. It is not a Christian church, whatever else it may be.

The Latter-day Saints make much ado about their Aaronic and Melchizedek priesthood. In the love of Christ we beg them to reconsider. Do not build up what God has torn down. There are not, there cannot be, any priests today. We do not doubt the integrity and sincerity of many who claim to be priests or of those who believe them to be. But to try to restore what God has done away with and put men at least partly back under works instead of wholly under the blood of Christ for full and complete salvation is tragic, both now and eternally, to them and to those who follow them.

Not even Paul or Peter claimed to be priests, except in the sense that every Christian is. As priests, those of us who have accepted the biblical Christ can approach God for ourselves through the blood of the Lord Jesus Christ. We became priests when we obtained His full, free and forever salvation.

Not long ago a dedicated Mormon assured me that he was depending on Jesus alone for his salvation. I said, "Suppose someone not in the Mormon church accepted Christ and depended on Him alone to get him into the 'highest heaven.' Would that person make it?"

The Mormon was suddenly silent, mute evidence that consciously or unconsciously he is depending on Christ plus the Mormon church. According to the Scripture, the only way to salvation is by accepting Jesus Christ as *all-sufficient*, plus nothing (see Eph. 2:8,9).

Consider the parable Jesus told about the Pharisee and

the publican in Luke 18:9-14. The Pharisee undeniably belonged to the "one true church" in the sense that he belonged to the worship system God established in the Old Testament. His system still retained priests, men like Caiaphas, and they were still legitimate as this came before the cross. Therefore, the Pharisee could boast that he was in the one true church that God established, and his church contained the one and only authoritative priesthood. He was very religious and, apparently by man's standards, very good. He prayed, "God, I thank thee, that I am not as other men are, extortioners, unjust, adulterers, or even as this publican. I fast twice in the week, I give tithes of all that I possess" (Luke 18:11,12). He was faithful in church, he believed in God, he tithed every cent, he was fair in business and did not get money by force or dishonesty. He treated his neighbor right, paid his debts and was true to his wife.

The publican on the other hand was a mess. He was a Jew who was considered to have sold out to the Roman conquerors. He collected taxes from the Jews for the Romans. One way such despised publicans made their way was by collecting more tax than the Romans levied and pocketing the difference. Some became rich by this means. The publican had *no good works* to commend him to God whatsoever. It is significant that he said nothing to God about prayers, tithe, or not being an adulterer. He was a sinful, hopeless, dishonest wretch. Mormon friends, *which* of these two men would you let into heaven?

The publican prayed, not even lifting his eyes toward heaven, beating on his breast in his agony of need and conviction of sin, "God be *merciful* to me, a sinner."

Which man went home "justified" free from sin,

saved? God said, of the publican, "This man went down to his house justified, [saved, forgiven, made right with God] *rather* than the other."

Many Mormon friends say to me with great vehemence, "Do you mean to say that a man who went to church, lived right, paid his debts, etc. could die and miss heaven, and that a man who lied, stole, cheated, and lived a wicked life, could say, 'Jesus save me,' and be saved in the last days or hours of his life? Nonsense!" Yes, that is exactly what I mean to say and the Bible verifies it (see Jesus' encounter with the thief on the cross, Luke 23:39-43; also the parable of the laborers in the vineyard, Matt. 20:1-16). Mormons cannot understand how God's grace can apply to those who have not worked for salvation, who have not earned it.

We all have a sin nature. No amount of works can ever change that, only Jesus can. At whatever point in life you accept Christ as your personal Saviour, it is then that you become a *new creation* in Christ. Then good works will flow from you, not to buy your salvation, but in love and gratitude, proof that you have been saved. The blood of the Lord Jesus Christ can wash anyone clean whenever he comes honestly, with all his heart to Him. Nothing else will satisfy God.

My good friend, Marvin Cowan, for years a dedicated Mormon and converter of others to Mormonism, told me poignantly how earnestly he believed in and labored for the Mormon church before he met the Lord Jesus Christ and was freed from this system. Now he is a Baptist missionary to Mormons whom he loves and for whom his heart aches. He is another of many who has said hello to Jesus and good-bye to priests. His heart's desire, and mine, is to win Mormons to Jesus Christ. Mormon or non-

Mormon, any hungry heart reading this, won't you say hello, once and for all, to Jesus right now?

"Behold, I stand at the door, and knock: if any man hear my voice, and open the door, I will come in to him, and will sup with him and he with me" (Rev. 3:20).

Notes

1. Talmage, *Articles of Faith*, pp. 204–211.
2. B.H. Roberts, *A Comprehensive History of The Church of Jesus Christ of Latter-day Saints* (Salt Lake City: Deseret News Press, 1930), vol. 1, p. 40.
3. Bruce R. McConkie, *Mormon Doctrine* (Salt Lake City: Bookcraft Inc., 1966), p. 477.
4. Joseph Fielding Smith, *Doctrines of Salvation*, vol. 2, p. 149.
5. Wallace Turner, *The Mormon Establishment* (Boston: Houghton Mifflin Co., 1966), pp. 81,82.

CHAPTER ELEVEN

Some Distinctive but Dubious Doctrines of Mormonism

Some of the most distinctive doctrines of the Mormon church are not found in the *Book of Mormon* but in some of their other sacred writings. In this chapter we will discuss the Mormon's view on plural marriage, hell, baptism for the dead, the three heavens, pre-existence and Negroes.

Polygamy

In the beginning, God provided one wife for Adam. (See Gen. 2:18-25.) Here we again are not dealing with speculation or theory, but with biblical fact.

God instituted marriage with one wife for one man. After sin began to darken the heart of man, he often took more than one wife. More often than not, this was to man's sorrow as well as God's.

Under grace in the New Testament God definitely limited man to one wife. Anything else was adultery. "A bishop then must be blameless, the husband of one wife, vigilant, sober, of good behavior, given to hospitality, apt to teach" (1 Tim. 3:2). God did not and does not have one standard for bishops (pastors) and another for other Christians. This merely means that a bishop had to be a proven, practicing Christian, the husband of only one wife.

The *Book of Mormon* agrees with the Bible on this: "Behold, David and Solomon truly had many wives and concubines, which thing was abominable before me, saith the Lord" (Jacob 2:24). Jacob 3:5 also states that the commandment of the Lord was to have one wife. Yet the prophet Joseph Smith later had a revelation recorded in *Doctrine and Covenants* 132:4. "For behold, I reveal unto you a new and an everlasting [*mark* that word!] covenant; and if ye abide not that covenant, then are ye damned."

Smith then proceeded to elaborate on the doctrine of man being allowed more than one wife. In fact, if a man did not keep this covenant he would be damned. Smith went on to say in *Doctrine and Covenants* 132:38,39 that God had in fact *given* David and Solomon their wives. Finally, Joseph Smith even concludes that the Lord even *justified* his servants David and Solomon in having many wives!

Now Joseph Smith received this convenient revelation on July 12, 1843. He was killed in 1844. Several Mormon writers claim that Smith had as many as 48 wives. Even the most charitable view could hardly avoid the strong implication that Joseph Smith was living in adultery long before he got his "revelation."

It is interesting to notice that included in Joseph

Smith's revelation was a warning for his wife, Emma Smith, to receive the other wives. Check the tense also. "Receive all those that *have been given* unto my servant Joseph. . ." (*Doctrine and Covenants* 132:52).

This doctrine was against the law of the land, and accounted for a great deal of the persecution Mormons received.

Perhaps in an attempt to buoy up the revelation of Joseph Smith, other Mormon leaders went even farther in trying to make this doctrine valid. In speaking of the marriage in Cana, Orson Hyde states that Jesus Christ was married at Cana of Galilee; Mary, Martha and others were His wives.[1] This is ridiculous if not blasphemous. Obviously the eternal Creator, which Jesus is, would not marry a creature. In John 2:2 we are told that Jesus "was called [invited], and his disciples, to the marriage." It is not customary for one to get an invitation to one's own wedding. In John 2:8-10 the *bridegroom* not *Jesus*, is congratulated by the ruler of the feast for the quality of the wine. The ruler of the feast was not aware of the miracle Jesus performed. Orson Pratt, another Mormon leader, in the *Seer*, page 159, claimed that Jesus had wives.

This polygamous teaching of the Mormons is one more indication that Mormons believe in a Christ who is totally different than the one taught in the Bible. They mean another Christ. Another Jesus or a false Christ, the Bible warns, can never save no matter how sincerely one accepts him. The non-eternal Christ of the Mormons who had to "attain" His way to being God, who was a polygamist, and, as the Mormons also teach, a created being and a brother of the devil, can save no one. The name may be the same, the terms the Mormons use may be similar, but the Person is entirely different.

The Mormons clung tenaciously to the doctrine of polygamy as espoused by their prophet Joseph Smith until the pressure of the law became so great that they had to give up the open practice. President Wilford Woodruff got a convenient "revelation" from God in time to avoid increasing government pressure and prosecution against polygamy. On September 25, 1890, he issued a manifesto declaring the Mormons' intentions of obeying the law of the land to have only one wife. Mormons pledged their honor to keep this law, but many of the Mormon leaders later admitted in public that they had broken the pledge and taken other wives.

The Mormons are in a dilemma. Brigham Young, the Mormon inspired prophet said, "The only men who become Gods, even the Sons of God, are those who enter into polygamy.[2] Joseph Smith had said that those who did not fully accept this doctrine would be damned. The *Book of Mormon* says one wife only, anything else is an abomination to God. President Woodruff said God told him (decide for yourself if by revelation as he claimed or by government pressure) that the everlasting covenant was nullified! Back to one wife!

It seems to us that Mormons are damned if they do and damned if they don't, insofar as plural marriage is concerned. Remember please, God said He is not the author of confusion.

It is rather difficult to understand if Joseph Smith's revelation was *everlasting* how it could be annulled even temporarily. Does this not make the word "everlasting" almost meaningless?

Hell

Jesus Christ taught much about hell. Of the 24 times

hell is mentioned in the New Testament, 22 of those times Jesus, the lover of our souls, is the speaker. His description of hades in Luke 16 is very graphic.

Jesus told about a man named Lazarus who died and was "carried into Abraham's bosom." A rich man in this actual, factual account also died and went to hell. It does not in the least matter whether or not we agree that there is a hell as far as the truth of this account is concerned. Jesus does not lie and He said there is an eternal hell for the lost. The Bible definitely, plainly teaches that there is a hell, and describes the final form of it in Revelation 20:15: "And whosoever was not found written in the book of life was cast into the lake of fire."

The *Book of Mormon* pretty well agrees with the Bible about hell. "And behold, others he [the devil] flattereth away, and telleth them there is no hell; and he saith unto them: I am no devil, for there is none—and thus he whispereth in their ears, until he grasps them with his awful chains, from whence there is no deliverance. Yea, they are grasped with death, and hell; and death, and hell, and the devil, and all that have been seized therewith must stand before the throne of God, and be judged according to their works, from whence they must go into the place prepared for them, even a lake of fire and brimstone, which is endless torment" (2 Nephi 28:22,23).

In spite of these plain declarations in the Bible and the *Book of Mormon*, John A. Widtsoe, a noted Mormon authority and writer and an apostle of the Mormon church, states, "In the Church of Jesus Christ of Latter-day Saints, there is no Hell. . ."[3]

Other Mormon authorities teach that hell is not eternal; it will have an end—a sort of limited, one-thousand-year or so purgatory for the lost. In trying to research what the Mormons teach on hell we run the gamut from apostles, teachers and inspired books that teach an endless hell, others that teach a limited hell, and still others that teach no hell at all. *As it is on so many other Mormon beliefs, Mormon leaders, their books and their church members are hopelessly divided and do not seem to know what they really believe.*

If you think this is an unfair exaggeration, check the writings of 10 or so Mormon apostles on the subject of hell, read about hell in the three inspired Mormon books, then ask 10 dedicated Mormons what they believe about hell.

Some Mormon leaders, in an attempt to evade the awful horror of hell, try to explain it away by saying that any punishment from God is eternal because God is eternal. Therefore, only one moment of punishment from God would seem like an eternity. Conversely, however, they do not like to consider that one minute's blessing would be the same as an eternal blessing. Would heaven last only one minute? When Jesus said, "These shall go away into everlasting punishment but the righteous into life eternal" (Matt. 25:46), did He indicate that everlasting life and heaven itself are temporary or fleeting? If God's eternal blessings mean forever, so do His eternal condemnations.

The same Greek word, *aionios,* that is used to describe the eternal continuance of hell is also used to describe the eternal continuance of God and the eternal continuance of heaven! So if God is eternal or everlasting, and if heaven is everlasting, then hell also is everlasting.

Even when the Bible refers to the "second death" (Rev. 2:11; 20:14), in speaking of those who go to hell, it does not mean they cease to exist. Revelation 14:11 and numerous other verses tell us about the eternal anguish and torment of those in hell. When God says that all men are "dead in trespasses and sins"(Eph. 2:1) before they personally come to Christ He does not mean they cease to exist. Even though they feel, think, eat, breathe, etc., God says they are dead. "Dead" in these instances, like "perish" and "destroy," refers not to loss of being, but loss of well-being; it doesn't mean extinction, but ruin.

In the *Book of Mormon* we read: "For behold, if ye have procrastinated the day of your repentance even unto death, behold, ye have become subjected to the spirit of the devil, and he doth seal you his; therefore, the Spirit of the Lord hath withdrawn from you, and hath no place in you, and the devil hath all power over you; and this is the final state of the wicked" (Alma 34:35).

The Bible and the *Book of Mormon* both teach an eternal hell. When Mormon apostles and writers deny the existence of an eternal hell, they hopelessly contradict the Bible and the *Book of Mormon*.

Baptism

If the final state of the wicked is sealed with the devil in hell, as the *Book of Mormon* teaches, it seems futile that Mormons would be baptized as substitutes for those who have already died.

Mormons believe that baptism is one of the essentials for salvation. Those who never heard the gospel or were never baptized, or lived and died before the restored gospel, cannot be saved unless someone living is baptized for them. This doctrine was not taught in the *Book of Mormon* but was the result of later revelations of Joseph Smith. Accounts of these are found in *Doctrines and Covenants*, sections 124 and 128.

In all the Bible, covering many centuries, there is not one command that we should be baptized by proxy for the dead. In *Doctrines and Covenants* 128:16, Joseph Smith refers to 1 Corinthians 15:29 to support his doctrine of baptizing for the dead: "Else what shall they do which are baptized for the dead, if the dead rise not at all? Why are they then baptized for the dead?" Here is one example where Mormons take a verse out of context.

The subject of the passage in 1 Corinthians is *resurrection*, not baptism. The whole of 1 Corinthians 15 gives God's beautiful picture of the resurrection of Christ and of our own resurrection if we are Christians. (The resurrection of the ungodly is covered in other references, i.e. Rev. 20.) Paul is answering many questions about the resurrection. He says that even those pagans who baptize for their dead, do so because they believe that there is a resurrection of the dead. "Else what shall *they* do who are baptized for the dead, if the dead rise not at all? Why are *they* then baptized for the dead? (italics added). His comments do not identify himself or any other Christian with those who baptize for the dead. He is simply acknowledging the fact that even pagans believe in the resurrection of the dead; how much more should Christians.

We know of two heretical groups just after Paul's time that baptized for the dead, the Cerinthians (not Corinthians!) and the Marcionites. Christians did not and do not now baptize for the dead. This single reference to baptism for the dead makes no comment of approval or disapproval; it does not say that the dead are helped or saved. Paul used this as an illustration.

The Bible unmistakably teaches that there is no chance whatsoever for men to be saved after death. The fate of the lost is then sealed immediately and forever once and for all. That is why missionaries of the cross go forth with such urgency in obedience to the command of Christ. That is why they sacrifice and die, that others may hear the gospel. What is the use if, after the lost die, Christ Himself will preach the gospel to them?

As a missionary to Alaska, I faced threats of death; I saw my beautiful little daughter ill with rheumatic fever as we lived in a bitterly cold and uninsulated cabin, without electricity or running water. I suffered the beating of my children and saw my lovely wife fight for her health as we sought to spread the gospel to the lost. Yet ours was a picnic compared to what many godly missionaries endure for a lifetime, not just for a couple of quick years, for Jesus Christ and His precious gospel. These missionaries are willing to bury their lives, their ambitions, and leave their families to risk hardship and death all because they know men are lost without Christ! These lost people have *no hope* if they are not reached while they are *alive*!

There is no chance after death. "Now is the accepted time, now is the day of salvation" (see 2 Cor. 6:2). "As it is appointed unto men once to die, but after this the judgment" (Heb. 9:27). There is no salvation for those without Christ, "He that believeth on the Son hath everlasting life: and he that believeth not the Son shall not see life; but the wrath of God abideth on him" (John 3:36).

All men are resurrected: the saved to life, everlasting life (see John 6:40) and the unsaved unto damnation (see John 5:29; Rev. 20:3-6). Revelation 20:15 adds the final word on the unsaved: "And whosoever was not found written in the book of life was cast into the lake of fire."

Heaven

In *Doctrine and Covenants* 76, Joseph Smith taught

that there are three heavens or three degrees of glory. The first heaven is the *telestial* glory where even unbelievers go. The *terrestrial* or second heaven is for good and religious folks who aren't Mormons, and also those Mormons who have not measured up to all the Mormon requirements for celestial glory. The third heaven is the *celestial* glory which is for Mormons only!

Biblically, Mormons attempt to base this doctrine on 1 Corinthians 15:35-54. Part of this passage reads, "All flesh is not the same flesh: but there is one kind of flesh of men, another flesh of beasts, another of fishes, and another of birds. There are also celestial bodies, and bodies terrestrial: but the glory of the celestial is one, and the glory of the terrestrial is another. There is one glory of the sun, and another glory of the moon, and another glory of the stars: for one star differeth from another star in glory" (1 Cor. 15:39-41).

In this glorious resurrection passage, the subject is definitely bodies, not heaven or heavens per se. In verses 35-38, Paul uses grain as an illustration of the difference in our bodies after the resurrection. He then illustrates his point with a reference to the different flesh of humans, animals, fish and birds (v. 39). Then he refers to the difference in human and possibly angel or celestial bodies (v. 40). Finally, he refers to the different glory of the sun, moon and stars in their individual, personally identifiable kinds of glory (v. 41).

Then in verse 43 Paul says our earthly bodies, which die and decay, are different from our resurrection bodies. Our resurrection bodies are glorified bodies, yet retain their human and their personal identity. Here Paul simply emphasizes the fact that there is a vast difference in the glory of bodies in heaven and bodies on earth. "There is one glory of the sun, and another glory of the moon, and another glory of the stars: for one star differeth from another star in glory" (v. 41). The subject is still resurrection *bodies*, not three different heavens.

Now Paul swings right back into the point of his illustration in verse 42, "So also is the resurrection of the dead. It [the body] is sown in corruption; it is raised in incorruption" (v. 42). The main difference in glory that Paul is talking about is the difference between the body we now have, our natural body, and, if we are Christians, the glorious, resurrection, spiritual body we shall have.

Again, the subject of this passage is *bodies* not heavens. This passage does not teach three heavens as Joseph Smith and the Mormons claim. The context gives no support to such a claim. Indeed, the same context talks about one star differing from another star in glory. To be consistent then, Mormons should teach millions of different heavens or degrees of glory, because there are millions of stars that differ from one another in glory.

Marvin Cowan, CBHMS missionary to the Mormons says, "Paul mentions *four* kinds of flesh. Does this verse teach there are four heavens? That reasoning is just as valid as what the LDS do with the next two verses."[4]

The thief on the cross cried out to Jesus and was instantly saved and assured he would be that very day with Christ in paradise. Paul, the mightiest missionary this world has ever seen, a tremendous apostle, and one of the Holy men through whom God gave His Word, was caught up to the third heaven. (According to the Mormons, that is the highest heaven there is.) Guess who was already there? That's right, the thief who was unbaptized, had no good works, temple works or religion whatsoever to recommend him! He was saved by the blood of the Lord

Jesus Christ. He was saved instantly and forever because he called believingly on Jesus Christ and had his sins washed away and his nature changed by Jesus. Proof? The third heaven is also called paradise! Read it for yourself! "I knew a man in Christ above fourteen years ago, (whether in the body, I cannot tell; or whether out of the body, I cannot tell; God knoweth;) such an one caught up to the *third heaven*. And I knew such a man, (whether in the body, or out of the body, I cannot tell: God knoweth;) How that he was caught up into *paradise*, and heard unspeakable words, which it is not lawful for a man to utter" (2 Cor. 12:2-4, italics added).

This clearly and totally contradicts what the Mormons teach about heaven and how to get there. Paul goes on in the passage to reveal that it was himself who was caught up into paradise, the third heaven, where Jesus took the saved thief.

In actual fact, there is but *one heaven of God*. Both in Scripture and Hebrew usage, three heavens are spoken of, but the first is the heaven of the clouds, the second is the heaven of the sun, moon and stars, and the third is the *one and only* heaven of God.

The heaven of clouds and atmosphere. "The Lord shall open unto thee his good treasure, the heaven to give the rain unto thy land in his season" (Deut. 28:12). "Who covereth the heaven with clouds, who prepareth rain for the earth" (Ps. 147:8).

The heaven of sun, moon and stars. Genesis 1:17, speaking of the sun and moon, "God set them in the firmament of the heaven to give light upon the earth."

The heaven of God. "Thus saith the Lord, The heaven is my throne" (Isa. 66:1).

There is not one indication in all the Bible that there is

more than one heaven of God. On the contrary consider this: "And if I go and prepare *a* place for you, [one only, not three] I will come again, and receive you unto myself; that where I am, there ye may be also!" (John 14:3). Jesus is here speaking to all Christians and assuring them that He will come back for *all* of them and that they will *all be together* with Him (and surely Jesus will be in the "highest heaven," the only heaven of God) in one place forever!

"And then shall he send his angels, and shall *gather together* his elect from the four winds, from the uttermost part of the earth to the uttermost part of heaven" (Mark 13:27).

"For the Lord Himself shall descend from heaven with a shout, with the voice of the archangel, and with the trump of God: and the dead in Christ shall rise first: Then we which are alive and remain shall be caught up together with them in the clouds, to meet the Lord in the air; and so shall we ever be with the Lord" (1 Thess. 4:16,17).

There is *one heaven*, and *one hell*, and we go to either the one or the other, depending on what we do with Jesus Christ.

Preexistence

Though this is a complicated doctrine from the Mormon standpoint, we want to mention only a few simple facts.

Basically, Mormons teach that men were eternally existing intelligences, then men entered the pre-mortal spirit world by birth as God had sexual relations with one of His wives.[5] Oddly enough, this God whom Mormons believe has a body of flesh and bone, had children that are spirits only.

Such verses as Jeremiah 1:5 are called upon by the Mormons in support of the doctrine that we existed as spirits before we were born as humans: "Before I formed thee in the [womb] I knew thee; and before thou camest forth out of the womb I sanctified thee, and I ordained thee a prophet unto the nations."

As is customary, a tremendous superstructure has been built on this exceedingly skimpy and ambiguous foundation.

A Mormon lady, wife of a local Mormon leader, considerably shaken by some of the facts I had been sharing with her, phoned several nights ago concerning this text. "Doesn't this prove we existed before we were born if God knew us before we were formed in the womb?" she asked.

Absolutely not! Not any more than Matthew 7:23, "And then will I profess unto them, I *never knew* you: depart from me, ye that work iniquity" would prove that there were people existing whom God was not aware of!

There are two possibilities. We do not know the exact moment that life enters a fetus. This reference in Jeremiah could conceivably refer to that time before the fetus was fully developed in the womb and yet had life. The second and most plausible from my viewpoint, is that this is merely speaking of God's foreknowledge. Surely Mormons do not believe that Jeremiah was actually ordained as a prophet in the spirit world before he had a body! Yet if we claim that God literally knew Jeremiah before he was born, to be consistent we also have to literally accept what God said about ordaining him as a prophet before he had a body, while he was yet in the spirit world! Even more of a problem for the Mormons is that this verse not only says that God knew Jeremiah and ordained him as a prophet before he was formed in the womb, but that He also sanctified him. To Mormons, this whole life is a probationary period, but this interpretation would indicate that Jeremiah had it made before he was even born!

Now look closely at Acts 15:18: "Known unto God are all his works from the beginning of the world." This speaks of God's foreknowledge of all things. It most certainly does not mean that His works existed before He made them! If God knew His works from the beginning of the world, that certainly includes the earth. It does not mean that the earth existed before He made it! Jeremiah is one of God's works. It certainly does not mean that Jeremiah existed before he was born. God's works included the creation of Adam. It emphatically does not mean that Adam existed before he was created any more than it means that the earth existed before it was created. Romans 8:28-30 gives highlights of God's wonderful foreknowledge, without which He would not be God, and all of our security for eternity would be gone.

God said in Genesis 2:7, "And the Lord God formed man out of the dust of the ground, and breathed into his nostrils the breath of life; and man became a living soul." That is when man's life started. He had no life before, anywhere at any time. Notice that God did not put into Adam one of His pre-existent spirit children which only exist in Mormon literature. Man got life for the first time direct from God.

The Negro

The changing Mormon position on the Negro in the church is still another contradiction that greatly weakens the validity of the "one true church."

In June, 1978, President Spencer Kimball announced that by divine revelation the Mormon church is now free to accept the black man into the priesthood. However for many years this was not the church's position. According to Mormon doctrine, because of some pre-existent sin, the Negro was cursed with black skin. This curse was perpetuated through Ham. Because of this, the black man *forever* (according to some Mormon books and authorities) was forbidden the priesthood, the highest heaven, etc.

Mormon writer, Arthur M. Richardson, declares, "The Church of Jesus Christ of Latter-day Saints has no call to carry the gospel to the Negro, and it does not do so."[6] Richardson's view clearly contradicted Mark 16:15: "Go ye into all the world, and preach the gospel to every creature"; (black, red, white or whatever). It also contradicted the *Book of Mormon,* 2 Nephi 26:28: "Behold, hath the Lord commanded any that they should not partake of his goodness? Behold, I say unto you, Nay; but *all* men are privileged the one like unto the other, and none are forbidden" (italics added).[7]

Notes

1. Orson Hyde, *Journal of Discourses*, vol. 2, p. 210.
2. Brigham Young, *Journal of Discourses*, vol. 11, p. 269. (See also vol. 3, p. 266.)
3. John A. Widtsoe, *Evidences and Reconciliation* (Salt Lake City: Bookcraft, 1960), p. 216.
4. Marvin W. Cowan, *Mormon Claims Answered*, p. 101.
5. Milton R. Hunter, *Gospel Through the Ages* (Salt Lake City: Deseret Books, 1945), pp. 98, 126-129.
6. Arthur M. Richardson, *That Ye May Not Be Deceived*, p. 13. Quoted by Tanner, *Mormonism, Shadow or Reality*, p. 274.
7. See my book which deals with this subject, *The Mormon Revelations of Convenience* (Minneapolis: Bethany Fellowship, Inc., 1978).

CHAPTER TWELVE

The One True Church

There is a very curious thing about the claims of Mormonism. At one time they can convey the idea that they are a legitimate Christian body, whose doctrines, except in a few particulars, are not very different from the usual Christian statement of faith. Yet, at the same time they subscribe to a church whose inspired books proclaim that all other churches are wrong, all their creeds are an abomination, and all their professors are corrupt!

Concerning the Mormon creed, the "Articles of Faith" which can be found in the *Pearl of Great Price*, it is confusing to consider why *all other creeds* are an abomination to God, but when the tenets of these creeds are transferred verbatim to the Mormon "creed" they suddenly become holy and acceptable to God!

If all our creeds are an abomination, as Joseph Smith

proclaimed by revelation, "all their creeds were an abomination in his sight" (Joseph Smith 2:19, *Pearl of Great Price*), we would hardly expect the Mormon "Articles of Faith" to adapt the fundamental beliefs contained in them as their own.

More confusing still is the inspired teaching by Smith in the *Book of Mormon* and by divinely guided Mormon apostles who declare, "All will be damned who are not Latter-day Saints.[1] Again, we read, "Both Catholics and Protestants are nothing less than the 'whore of Babylon' whom the Lord denounces by the mouth of John the Revelator as having corrupted all the earth by their fornications and wickedness. Any person who shall be so wicked as to receive a holy ordinance of the Gospel from the ministers of any of these apostate churches will be sent down to hell with them, unless they repent of the unholy and impious act."[2] (Yet in other Mormon books we are told that we will be in one of the two lowest heavens or degrees of glory.)

The Mormons claim to be the one true church in a number of their books, but we will quote *Doctrine and Covenants* 1:30. Here the Mormon church is called, "the only true and living church upon the face of the whole earth."

What the Mormon church really teaches is, "There is no salvation outside . . . the Church [of Jesus Christ of Latter-day Saints]."[3]

In the *Book of Mormon*, 1 Nephi 13:26, Joseph Smith wrote, "A great and abominable church. . . [has] taken away from the gospel of the Lamb many parts which are plain and most precious; and also many covenants of the Lord have they taken away." This reference is to the churches that supposedly apostatized. Now the *Book of*

Mormon dates this writing around 600 B.C., 600 years *before* Christ came, before there was any gospel of the Lamb, and certainly before there were any Christian churches to which Smith refers.

This is one of the reasons, nevertheless, that Smith uses to show the need for the *Book of Mormon* and the one true church. *All* other churches became false, and all the Christians were corrupt and the true gospel disappeared from off the earth. The gospel had to be "restored" and a new revelation given.

Jesus said explicitly, in Matthew 24:35, "Heaven and earth shall pass away, but my words shall not pass away!"

Again, Jesus declared in Matthew 28:20 that He would be with His church and His people "Alway, *even* to the end of the world." *Alway. Continuously.* Just who was Jesus going to be with if there were not any church or Christians left on earth a short while after He died? And Jesus further claimed, in Matthew 16:18, "I will build my church; and the gates of hell shall not prevail against it."

If Mormonism is true, what Jesus said was untrue. For Mormons say the gates of hell *did* prevail against His church, and total apostasy eliminated His true church, His true people, and His true Word off the earth for over a thousand years, to be "restored" by Prophet Smith!

This Mormon doctrine is not only untrue to the Bible, it is utterly untrue to church history. Thousands, indeed even millions scattered around the world, were living for Jesus Christ even during the Dark Ages. The formal Catholic church did get far away from God, but Luther and many others were saved even in its corrupt embrace. *Foxe's Book of Martyrs* tells how hundreds of thousands died for Jesus Christ, were burned at the stake, tortured unspeakably, and torn apart by wild beasts, all the while proclaiming their undying love for Jesus Christ.

Many other books of church history record how, during these hundreds of years Joseph Smith would have us believe no true believers and no true church was on earth, Christians died rejoicing in their salvation and praising their wonderful Saviour.

One striking example from among thousands that can be given, were the martyrs of the Theban Legion. A group of Roman soldiers numbering 6,666 men who had accepted Christ, the Theban Legion, in A.D., 286 refused to deny Christ and make pagan sacrifices. They were cut to pieces with the sword.

There were various Christian groups meeting down through the centuries, long before, during and after the Protestant Reformation, who never were a part of the "Mother" church. *Trail of Blood* and many other books of history have preserved the names of these churches for us: Paulicans, Brethren of the Common Lot, Montanist, Paterins, Novations, Arnoldist, Cathari, Albigenses, Waldenses, Henricans, Anabaptists, Baptists, and the well-known names of those churches springing out of the Protestant Reformation such as Lutheran, Presbyterian, Congregational, Methodist, etc. (See 'Special Comment' at end of chapter.)

In 1536, after years of faithfully serving the Lord Jesus Christ and translating the Bible into the language of the people, William Tyndale was burned at the stake, near Antwerp, England, praying until his last breath for those who tortured him. In 1415, John Huss, a precious, faithful Christian was burned at the stake because of his love and faithfulness to Jesus Christ, and actually sang praises to Jesus until the crackling of the flames drowned out his voice. Please remember, this and thousands of like events happened during the centuries when Joseph Smith says God's true church and true gospel, and His true people had vanished from the earth (later to be restored in 1830 by Prophet Smith!). Millions died for their faith in faithfulness to Jesus Christ during this period of over a thousand years when Joseph Smith claimed that all true Christians, the true church and the true gospel had disappeared from the earth.

According to Joseph Smith and Mormon teaching, no one during this time and no one today is in the one true church except a relatively small group of people called Mormons. Mormons must either believe this teaching, which is contrary to the Bible and church history, or deny the Prophet Joseph Smith.

Some Mormon parents sacrifice a great deal to send their sons out as missionaries. So do these fine, but misled, young men who give two years of their lives to the Mormon cause. According to the August, 1961 *Mormon Missionary Handbook*, Mormon missionaries must lead potential converts to say about their own churches and all other churches, "They are false." In the new, modified and somewhat more subtle and sophisticated *Mormon Missionary Handbook*, this terminology was softened. No change, however, was made in the *Pearl of Great Price* or in Mormon doctrine, that all other churches are false.

Apostles in the Mormon Church

One of the reasons Mormons give to show that their church is the one true church is that they have "apostles" in their church. These apostles are called the Twelve, and it is believed that they hold the restored office of the original apostles. An ordained apostle is "one who is ordained to the office of apostle in the Melchizedek Priesthood. . . . This apostleship carries the responsibility of proclaiming the gospel in all the world and also of administering the affairs of the Church. . . . The original Twelve in latter-days were selected by revelation to the three Witnesses to the *Book of Mormon*."[4]

There are several problems with this claim. In the first place, if we use "apostle" in the narrow sense of an office or as a gift given to certain men chosen of God, the LDS church has too many apostles. Revelation 21:14 says that the wall of God's heavenly "city had twelve foundations, and in them the names of the twelve apostles of the Lamb." The Twelve were personally called by Christ. They were among those who witnessed the living Jesus in His ministry, death and resurrection. As a special sign of their apostleship they worked miracles. (See Matt. 10:7,8; Acts 3:6-8; 5:12-16; 9:37-40; 2 Cor. 12:12.)

The LDS church, up to now, has appointed 80 apostles. Today they have 12 apostles plus three men in the First Presidency who are also apostles. It is true that others were called apostles in the Bible, but only 12 form the *historical foundation* of the church (Rev. 21:14); Christ is now and forever the *theological foundation* of the church (1 Cor. 3:11).

In the second place, if we use "apostle" in the wider sense, the word means "one sent forth" or "sent one." This applies to every Christian who is a true child of God. We are all sent ones, sent out to share Christ. This wider use of apostle was used of Barnabas, Andronicus, Epaphroditus, Junia, etc.

Paul says he was "called to be an apostle, separated unto the gospel of God" (Rom. 1:1). He did not accompany Jesus but was specially chosen by God. (See Acts 22:12-15 for an account of Paul's calling; see also 1 Cor. 9:1.) Other apostles founded many of the early churches.

If the title of "apostle" were meant to be a perpetual office in the church, God surely would have left us with a definite list of qualifications, directions as to their duties, authority, purpose and responsibilities. He gave us such directions and qualifications for the offices of bishop (1 Tim. 3:1-7), deacon (1 Tim. 3:8-13), and elder (1 Tim. 5:1-21), but none is given for apostle.

There is still another problem with the Mormon claim that theirs is the only true church because it is founded on the apostles. The Mormon church began in 1830, and the "foundation," the Twelve Apostles, were not chosen until February 14, 1835. What was the status of the Mormon organization during the years before the Twelve Apostles?

The New Testament speaks of "false apostles," "I know thy works, and thy labour, and thy patience, and how thou canst not bear them which are evil: and thou hast tried them which say they are apostles, and are not, and hast found them liars." (Rev. 2:2).

Prophets in the Mormon Church

In a previous chapter we discussed the role of prophets as foretellers of the future, under the guidance of God. We discussed the test for a prophet as given in the Scriptures. We cited many cases where Joseph Smith did not meet the prophet test, neither have any of his successors which proves beyond doubt that they were false prophets.

Prophets of God, though undoubtedly students of the Scriptures, did not get their message by study but by direct revelation from God. True prophets, those who foretold future events under God's guidance with 100 percent accuracy all the time, and those who received direct revelations foretelling the future, have passed away.

Now that we have the completed Word of God, the foretelling of future events is unnecessary. God's written Word is sufficient. Since the New Testament prophets passed from the scene no so-called prophet, in this sense, has passed the prophet-test. All are false prophets.

Unfortunately, this often did not deter their followers who failed to heed or apply God's test for a true prophet. So, a multitude of cults have been founded by so-called prophets of God that delude precious men and women and lead to a lost eternity.

Hebrews 1:1,2 aptly sums it up for us: "God, who at sundry times and in divers manners spake in time past unto the fathers by the prophets, hath in these last days spoken unto us by his Son, whom he hath appointed heir of all things, by whom also he made the worlds."

Another biblical meaning of the title "prophet" has to do with "forth-telling" of God's Word. Many good men from many different churches still do that when they preach and teach the Word of God.

The One True Church

There is only one "true church" mentioned in the Bible and every true believer—Baptist, Methodist, Lutheran, Presbyterian, whatever—belongs to that church the moment he receives Christ. There are those who are members of the one true church who never belonged to any denominational church, the thief on the cross for example! He too now belongs to the one true church!

First Corinthians 12:13 says that *all* Christians are baptized by the Holy Spirit into the body of Christ. (This is not speaking of water baptism. The Spirit does not baptize us in water.) Ephesians 5:29-32 and other passages tell us that Christ's body in this sense is His church, and His church is His body! First Corinthians 12:13, "For by one Spirit are we all baptized into one body, whether we be Jews or Gentiles, whether we be bond or free; and have been all made to drink into one Spirit."

So every Christian is in the one true church, placed there by the Holy Spirit the moment he is saved! We might add that this unity among true Christians does not extend to groups that doubt portions of the Word of God, substitute ritual for reality and social change for the new birth. These have a form of godliness, but deny the power thereof (see 2 Tim. 3:5), and are nominal Christians or Christians in name only.

Being in a good local church is vitally important. Hebrews 10:25 cautions us not to forsake the "assembling of ourselves together." There are hundreds of churches and denominations, and some with no denomination, that teach basically the same thing about Jesus Christ and His wonderful salvation, and also all major, fundamental doctrines of the Bible. That is why hundreds of different churches and denominations can get together happily to hold city-wide evangelistic meetings, or to reach an area for Jesus Christ. Actually, we have far fewer differences on the whole among true Christians of different denominations than Mormons have among themselves. We have a spiritual unity in Christ far greater than any artificial unity of a physical nature.

We do have some differences that are important to us individually. We have different ways of governing our churches where the Bible does not spell out clearly and specifically how it should be done; differences in approach, outreach and doctrines of less than a fundamental nature. Serious Christians seek a church that presents Christ most clearly to them and makes His salvation clear, that reaches the lost, stresses that only the blood of Jesus Christ can cleanse us from our sins; a church that sticks as close to the Word of God as it possibly can.

In Summary

How did the Mormons get so far afield from the truth of the Word of God, so far that "inspired" Prophet Brigham Young could say, "No man or woman in this dispensation will ever enter the celestial Kingdom of God without the consent of Joseph Smith!"[5] This is a direct challenge to the Word of God and to the Lord Jesus Christ, "For there is one God, and one mediator between God and men, the man Christ Jesus" (1 Tim. 2:5). "Neither is there salvation in any other: for there is none other name under heaven given among men, whereby we must be saved" (Acts 4:12). *This name is Jesus*.

Joseph Smith is the man who led the Mormons astray, and still does because they refuse to consider or accept the clear evidence from God in Deuteronomy 18:20-22, and other passages, that he was a false prophet.

Mormons would do well, every time some unfavorable report of Joseph Smith appears, not to shove it under the rug and proclaim that it is the work of anti-Mormons, but to systematically and carefully examine it for truth. Real truth can stand investigation and examination. It is not necessary to look at anti-Mormon sources to find out about the real Joseph Smith. Historical Mormon sources reveal an entirely different Joseph Smith than most Mormons have been shown. Mormons should insist that such publications, which are often withheld in sacred archives even from the Mormon public, should be opened at least to all Mormons.

At times some of this material has been made available and then withdrawn. We have done our best to be fair and honest with the truths we have discovered. We have ignored or passed over much extremely damaging information, *mostly from Mormon sources,* concerning Joseph Smith's morals, business ethics, truthfulness, treasure-hunting background, etc. We ask Mormons to investigate this honestly and thoroughly for themselves.

Truly, our Mormon friends need to heed Galatians 1:8 and indeed, we all do! "But though we, or an angel from heaven, preach any other gospel unto you than that which we have preached unto you, let him be accursed!"

Notes

1. Ora Pate Stewart, *We Believe.* Taken from Keith L. Brooks, comp., *The Spirit of Truth and the Spirit of Error* (Chicago, Moody Press, 1963), p.7.
2. Orson Pratt, *The Seer,* a publication founded by Orson Pratt in memory of the Prophet Joseph Smith, Jr. 1852, p. 255.
3. Bruce R. McConkie, *Mormon Doctrine* (Salt Lake City: Bookcraft, Inc., 1966), p. 138, see also pp. 81, 136.
4. McConkie, *Mormon Doctrine,* p. 47.
5. Brigham Young, *Journal of Discourses,* vol. 7, p. 289.

Special Comment

Many of these pre-Reformation groups of Christians, existing centuries before Martin Luther's time, as well as during and after his time, were called "ana-Baptists" in addition to whatever other name they were known by. Some of these groups held only a little of the truth, others were solidly Christian. See *"Trail of Blood"* by J.M. Carroll. Ross L. Range, 163 N. Ashland Avenue, Lexington, KY 40502.

CHAPTER THIRTEEN

The Final Authority

When God's people were enticed to consult the mediums and wizards who could perform wonders in the name of God, they were told, "To the law and to the testimony: if they speak not according to *this word*, it is because there is no light in them" (Isa. 8:20, italics added).

The law and the testimony obviously referred to the Word of God. The Bible is God's unchanging plumb line. Nothing else is!

Consider this: "All scripture is given by inspiration of God, and is profitable for doctrine, for reproof, for correction, for instruction in righteousness" (2 Tim. 3:16). "For the prophecy came not in old time by the will of man: but holy men of God spake as they were moved by the Holy Ghost" (2 Pet. 1:21).

These and many other Scriptures tell us that the Bible is the very Word of God. Fulfilled prophecy, historical and archaeological accuracy, unity and harmony beyond compare in a book with some 40 authors and written over a period of some 1500 years, lack of scientific errors common in other ancient books, the life and resurrection of Jesus, and its life-transforming power all combine to reinforce this claim.

This same God who gave the Word is well able to preserve it. He has promised to do just that; He has done it and He will continue to do it. God does not lie. "Heaven and earth shall pass away, but my words shall not pass away" (Matt. 24:35). To cast doubt on the Word of God is to take the side of atheists, unbelievers, skeptics and cultists down through the ages. It is to take sides against Christ and true Christians.

Jesus told us to search the Scriptures, in John 5:39, even to proving His claims: "Search the scriptures; . . . and they are they which testify of me." When Paul and Silas went to Berea with the claims of Christ and of the gospel, the Bereans were praised because they "searched the scriptures daily, whether those things [that Paul and Silas were teaching] were so" (Acts 17:11). The Bereans were using the Old Testament which had been given hundreds of years before and had been translated from the Hebrew into the Greek in a translation called the Septuagint. They did not quibble about the Bible being "the Word of God as far as it is translated correctly."[1]

How different from the Mormon way of finding truth!

The Mormon Test for Authority

Whereas the Bible teaches that we are to test the authority of preaching and Scriptures by other Scriptures, Mormons are taught to test the truth of the *Book of Mormon* by their *minds*, their *feelings* and by *prayer*.

McConkie says, "The spirit of revelation consists in having thoughts placed in one's mind by the power of the Holy Ghost" (*Mormon Doctrine*, p. 502). But the Bible has something else to say about one's mind. The Word of God says that we cannot trust our own thoughts because we have "reprobate" minds (Rom. 1:28), "carnal" minds (Rom. 8:7), "vain" minds (Eph. 4:17), "defiled" minds (Titus 1:15) and our thoughts continually lean toward evil (see Gen. 6:5; Matt. 9:4; 15:19).

In trying to verify the authority of Mormon teachings, Mormons sometimes declare that they had a "burning bosom," such as is mentioned in *Doctrine and Covenants:* "But, behold, I say unto you, that you must study it out in your mind, then you must ask me if it be right, and if it is right I will cause that your bosom shall burn within you; therefore, you shall feel that it is right" (*Doctrine and Covenants* 9:8). This *feeling*, this burning bosom "proved" the Holy Spirit was testifying to them of the truth of the *Book of Mormon* and Mormonism.

In addition to their minds and their feelings, Mormons are told to test the *Book of Mormon* by *prayer*:

"And when ye shall receive these things, I would exhort you that ye would ask God, the Eternal Father, in the name of Christ, if these things are not true; and if ye shall ask with a sincere heart, with real intent, having faith in Christ, he will manifest the truth of it unto you, by the power of the Holy Ghost" (Moroni 10:4, *Book of Mormon*).

Partly on the basis of this passage in Moroni, Mormons declare that if you ask God with a "sincere heart" He will manifest the truth of the *Book of Mormon* to you! The psychology of this, as well as the satanic trap, is obvious: You must be convinced that the *Book of Mormon* is true, otherwise you are insincere!

No one, especially if he has fallen for this false and unbiblical way of finding out the truth is going to want to admit to himself or others—or especially to God—that he was insincere when he prayed to Him about the truth of the *Book of Mormon*. If one is honest and sincere, he must test the *Book of Mormon* by the only test Moroni 10:4 offers; and if no "feeling" or "burning" or "inner conviction" occurs to assure him of the truth of the *Book of Mormon*, then he must be insincere. So, many people keep trying and eventually convince themselves, since they know very well they are sincere, that the *Book of Mormon* is true. Some work up feelings, some do not, but are convinced by their own sincerity, by others, by the delusion and trauma of the "test," and by the fact that if sincerity will prove the truth of the *Book of Mormon*, and they are desperately sincere, then the *Book of Mormon* must be true!

The relief Mormons feel after giving up the struggle and believing the *Book of Mormon*, further convinces them that they have had the witness of the Holy Spirit that the *Book of Mormon* is true.

Now if someone were to say to me, "Pray about it, prayer is the test of truth. When you pray, God will show you what is right," I would answer that for some sincere souls prayer sounds like the ideal solution. The problem? I *have* prayed about it and I got a different answer than others did. Others pray about the same things and get still an entirely different answer. If prayer were the solution, then Moslems, who pray five times a day, should get the same answer I do; however, their answers are all different than mine.

I know that my prayer is sincere, and I do not doubt that many other prayers are sincere too. Yet each thinks he is right. Prayer, sincere prayer, does not solve the problem. Moslems are certain they are right. I am certain I am right. You are certain you are right. Then how can we have different answers? Obviously, we must have a better test of truth, better proof than prayer, than "testimony," than feelings.

The Bereans did not depend on these things—they searched the Scriptures (see Acts 17:11). Peter said, "We have also a more sure word of prophecy; whereunto ye do well that ye take heed" (2 Pet. 1:19).

Reading the *Book of Mormon* and letting the Holy Spirit testify of its truthfulness to oneself is not God's approved way. *First*, this substitutes another test, another way, for God's way of determining truth or error.

Second, for the most part, Mormon doctrine is not even in the *Book of Mormon*. Though Mormons claim the *Book of Mormon* is the fullness of the everlasting gospel, it does not contain any of the following doctrines which form the heart of Mormonism: (1) Pre-existence, (2) Genealogies, (3) Baptism for the dead, (4) Celestial marriage, (5) Three degrees of glory, (6) Godhood promised to man, (7) Temporary hell, (8) Eternal progression. How can prayer and feeling or experience determine the truth of something that isn't even included in the book you are reading? The Holy Spirit does not lend Himself to such nonsensical "tests"!

Third, and most dangerous, the Holy Spirit is not the

only powerful spirit in this world. You might be deceived by trusting only in prayer and feeling or experience. The mighty evil spirit the Bible calls Satan is posing as an "angel of light," and deceiving all he can to an eternal hell. When we set aside God's prescribed way of finding truth, we are totally without protection and open to Satan's delusions.

Someone well asked, "Could a false church appear righteous?" The one who asked this question, a converted Mormon lady, added; "What would be the purpose of a wrong church if not to deceive? If someone were going to make counterfeit money, would they use red ink?"[2]

Notice Satan's program: "For such are false apostles, deceitful workers, transforming themselves into the apostles of Christ. And no marvel: for Satan himself is transformed into an angel of light. Therefore it is no great thing if his ministers also be transformed as the ministers of righteousness; whose end shall be according to their works" (2 Cor. 11:13-15).

Allen Beechick and Bruce Walters, two fine Christian men in our church, recently had a confrontation with several Mormon missionaries. The conversation went something like this:

Allen: "How do you know that the *Book of Mormon* is the Word of God?"

Mormon: "I have prayed about it and I have a *testimony* that I know that it is true and that Joseph Smith, to whom it was given, is a prophet of God."

Allen: "What is your *evidence* that the *Book of Mormon* is true and that Joseph Smith is a prophet of God? How do you 'know' it to be true, in either case?"

Mormon: "I know it is true because I have prayed about it and *feel* that it is true. I also know that it is true because the Mormon church has a living prophet to guide us into all truth."

Allen: "How do you know that this living prophet is a prophet of God?"

Mormon: "I have a *testimony* that our living prophet is a prophet of God."

Allen: "Can Satan give good feelings to deceive? What happens when your feelings say one thing and the Word of God says another? Which is more reliable and which do you believe? I have good feelings about receiving Jesus Christ by faith alone and being saved instantly and being sure of heaven, and this good feeling has already lasted 20 years. Why should your 'good feelings' be any more conclusive than mine? Don't you think the Bible is a much more reliable standard than my 'feelings' or 'testimony' or your 'feelings' or 'testimony'?"

We ask again, can a testimony make a false prophet true or make sense out of obvious nonsense? What can a testimony do to make this prophecy come true: Mormon president Heber C. Kimball prophesied that Brigham Young would become president of the United States.[3] What can a testimony do to nullify this statement: Polygamy will *never* be done away with.[4]

What can a testimony do to verify these revelations given in sermons by Brigham Young that he declared were Scripture: "Gold and silver grow, and so does every other kind of metal, the same as the hair upon my head, or the wheat in the field."[5] Young also taught that the sun as well as the moon were inhabited. Read it for yourself in *Journal of Discourses*, volume 13, page 271.

No amount of "testimony" can ever cover up the fact that these are false prophecies by Mormon prophets. We cannot help but believe that hundreds of thousands of honest Mormons want and deserve better than this. We believe that they can see that the "testimony" has been developed and used as a weapon to keep them in unquestioning ignorance and darkness. Brilliant doctors, lawyers and professors among the Mormons, who would never accept shoddy, unproven and dangerous theories but demand impeccable evidence in their professions, are locked into this system which forces them to accept "facts" like these by their "testimony." In this way they have confused faith with believing what they know is not true.

Biblical faith permits and demands objective, evidential reality, as well as subjective experience. Anything less fosters delusion and dishonesty.

Millions of Christians can testify to a tremendous "testimony" of certainty that the Bible is the *only Word of God*, that they have been saved instantly when they trusted Jesus, and that they are now sure of heaven forever with Jesus Christ. They have peace, joy and transformed lives since their conversion. However, any such testimony must be in full accord with the Bible and its truth or it is false. Feelings can be and have been manipulated. God would not leave our eternal destiny to be decided ultimately by "feelings" or "testimony" of fallible human beings. This is why He furnished so much tremendous evidence in the Bible that it is indeed the Word of God. This is why all claims of truth must be measured by the Bible. God will not bypass this, His final authority.

Authority of the Prophets

Prophets, in the sense of foretelling the future and getting their message directly from God, have fulfilled their role and been set aside in favor of the Son and His completed Word, the Bible: "God, who at sundry times and in divers manners spake in times past unto the fathers by the prophets, hath in these last days spoken unto us by his Son" (Heb. 1:1,2).

This is obvious for at least two reasons. *First,* any "gospel" given directly from God would have to be the same as the gospel of the Word of God *already fully given*; therefore, it would be unnecessary.

Paul declared, "I have fully preached the gospel of Christ" (Rom. 15:19). Not one thing needed to be added to the gospel. (See also Gal. 1:8,9.)

Second, the book of Revelation reveals the church age, the rapture, the tribulation, millennium and the consummation of all things into the eternal state. All time is covered. God has not forgotten anything so that He would have to add a divine PS by further revelation to a prophet.

Remember, the Old Testament foretold the coming of the Messiah, the Christ. The New Testament tells of the fulfillment of the Old—Christ has come. Hebrews chapters 7 and 8 speak of replacing the Old Covenant with the New Covenant. In Hebrews 13:20 this New Covenant is referred to as an "everlasting covenant." There is no mention in Scripture of a third, or "newer," covenant that might involve further revelation.

Jude 1:3 speaks of the "faith *once for all* delivered to the saints" (literal translation). There is no gospel left to give. There is no revelation left to give. It has already been fully given!

Since no other revelation is needed, prophets, in the sense of getting revelations directly from God and foretelling future events and recording them as God-given Scripture, are no longer in the church today. *All* such so-called prophets today are false.

The Mormons claim that Joseph Smith was a prophet. Read what the Scriptures say about those who preach any other gospel than what God has already given to us: "Many will say to me in that day, Lord, Lord, have we not prophesied in thy name? and in thy name have cast out devils? and in thy name done many wonderful works? And then will I profess unto them, I never knew you: depart from me, ye that work iniquity" (Matt. 7:22,23). "But though we, or an angel from heaven, preach any other gospel unto you than that which we have preached unto you, let him be accursed. As we said before, so say I now again, If any man preach any other gospel unto you than that ye have received, let him be accursed" (Gal. 1:8,9).

What then, is the final authority? The Bible, the Word of God! God has given it. God has preserved it. Any other work that does not square with the gospel already given, is not of God.

The Authority of the "Inspired Bible"

If Joseph Smith truly were a prophet of God, one of the first things God would have him do would be to correct any errors in His Word, the Bible! Surely this makes sense.

As a matter of fact, when Joseph Smith began to have some problems in coinciding what the *Book of Mormon* taught and what the Bible said, he received a "revelation" to translate the Bible and free it from all "error." God, he said, commissioned him to do this and gave him divine revelation in doing it. This Bible is called the *Inspired Version of the Bible*.[6]

Now immediately the question comes to mind, "If Joseph Smith translated the Bible into an accurate translation, why does the Mormon Article of Faith say, 'We believe the Bible to be the Word of God as far as it is translated correctly?'" The *Inspired Version of the Bible* can be purchased in the Deseret Book Store in Salt Lake City, a Mormon-owned business. Yet few Mormons (and exceedingly few non-Mormons!) even know the book exists.

Why don't the Mormons joyously bring out this perfect, without error, inspired Bible? Could it be that they cannot trust the *Inspired Version of the Bible* of Joseph Smith? If so, they condemn their prophet as a false prophet, even though he said he got the Bible directly from God, just as he did the *Book of Mormon*.

Perhaps the answer is that they know what the reaction would be if it were shown that Joseph Smith's *Inspired Version of the Bible* still contains virtually word-for-word, about 85 to 90 percent of the King James Bible. This might be embarrassing to the Mormons.

Even more embarrassing perhaps, would be the 17 verses Joseph Smith added to Genesis 50, in which he prophesied and says that he will bring salvation to his people: "And that seer will I bless. . . and his name shall be called Joseph, and it shall be after the name of his father. . . for the thing which the Lord shall bring forth by his hand shall bring my people unto salvation" (Gen. 50:33, *Inspired Version of the Bible*).

Jesus often referred to the Scriptures. It seems odd that He would have overlooked something as tremendously important as this passage. Odd too, that Revelation, which deals explicitly with latter days, never mentions Joseph Smith and the prophecy in Genesis!

In Summary

In the love of Christ, I counsel you, Mormon or

non-Mormon, to recognize that the Bible is reliable and the only final authority; that departure from it as the standard of truth brings chaos and confusion.

Suppose Satan inspired a book to either supplant or deny the Bible. If the book were judged by the Bible, Satan would be easily found out and thwarted. But if he declared the book he had written to be the Word of God, used some of the real Word of God in it, and used similar wording, the plot would thicken. Then suppose he suggested as proof, that we pray, and ask the Holy Spirit to show us if it was the Word of God or not, and if we were really *sincere* we would know the truth. And, in some cases at least, it might even be confirmed by a "burning in the bosom."

Obviously, Satan could cause us to do a flip-flop. We are no longer judging the book by the known Word of God, the Bible, as we are commanded to do. We are judging the book by feeling, and experience, and asking God to give us proof that something He has already clearly declared false is true! If our burning desire to know the truth and the psychology and emotion of calling on God and desperately seeking an answer doesn't produce some kind of feeling it would be strange indeed!

Could not Satan cause a "feeling" or a "burning in the bosom" to *prove* that the book he inspired was the Word of God? Of course he could. And he does!

Once Satan removes the Bible as a test or final authority, the foundation God gave for judging prophets, religious movements, etc., is lost! Then the person or cult claiming to have a vision, a revelation, a "burning in their bosom that God gave them," has an open field! In this way scores of religious movements and cults have been started.

As soon as we begin to put feelings, experiences, our own intellect, scientific speculations, new prophets or other Scriptures on a par with, and even above the Bible, we lose our foundation and completely reverse the situation. We then begin to judge the Bible by false criteria rather than testing the criteria by the Bible. Immediately, we become disobedient to God and doubt His truth. He can no longer answer our prayers for light and truth because He will not bless disobedience and sin! Even if God were to answer our prayer for discernment under these conditions, "the natural man receiveth not the things of the Spirit of God: for they are foolishness unto him" (1 Cor. 2:14).

I believe that the only reason I was delivered from becoming a Mormon is because I finally searched the Bible. The Holy Spirit opened my eyes to Jesus. My prayers were answered and I had sweet and precious feelings, *but the Bible was the catalyst*. The Bible made it happen! The Bible, not my feelings, was my authority!

When we trust in anything other than the Bible as the authority, we open the door to Satan's delusion that he is an angel of light and minister of righteousness. Satan not only deceives people into hell by making them "bad" people who lust for the things of the world, he also lures many into hell by making them "good" people. Just look at Romans 10:2,3: "For I bear them record that they have a zeal of God, but not according to knowledge. For they being ignorant of God's righteousness, and going about to establish their own righteousness, have not submitted themselves unto the righteousness of God."

This seems to be as perfect a description of the Mormons as it was of the religious but lost Jews of Paul's day.

In Luke 16:31, when the rich man in hell pleaded for someone to go from the dead and convince his brothers and save them from hell fire, God's Word declares, "If they hear not Moses and the prophets [the written Word of God], neither will they be persuaded, though one rose from the dead."

It is so difficult to be kind and yet speak the truth. We do not want to sacrifice truth on the altar of kindness, nor sacrifice kindness on the altar of truth. We have earnestly endeavored, by the grace of God, to keep the proper balance and "speak the truth in love." We know the cutting away of malignant tissue involves pain, however good the intentions of the surgeon, even with the use of the best anesthetic. But the results can be life, joy, and health.

Spiritual surgery is often painful also. The intentions may be good but the keen edge of the knife of truth may still cause some pain. The results, however can be eternal life, spiritual health, and great joy! God grant that it may be so to many of our readers!

Several weeks ago, I was presenting Christ and His free and instant salvation to two Mormon ladies. They were leaders in the library and visual aids department of their LDS church. Both ladies asked Jesus to save them.

One lady, who has four Mormon sons who served as missionaries, raised her head and exclaimed, "Vivian, Vivian, you know that burning feeling our leaders talk about and you never get, and you wonder what it is? I've got it, I've got it!" Needless to say, she based her instant salvation on Jesus and His word, but felt that this was a bonus. Christians do not ordinarily get or depend on such. God gave this dear lady a special bonus. True Christians do get a deep and abiding peace beyond anything else they have ever known.

Notes

1. Articles of Faith #8.
2. Janet Webster, in an open letter to Mormon friends. Used by permission.
3. Young, *Journal of Discourses*, vol. 5, p. 219.
4. Young, *Journal of Discourses*, vol. 3, p. 125.
5. Young, *Journal of Discourses*, vol. 1, p. 219.
6. Both Joseph Smith and Andrew Jensen in his LDS *Church Chronology* claim the *Inspired Version of the Bible* was completed July 2, 1833. So also claims *Documentary History of the Church*, vol. 1, pp. 324, 369; *Times and Seasons*, vol. 6, p. 802.

CHAPTER FOURTEEN

Mormon Salvation

When we speak of obtaining salvation most people recognize one of two ways whereby we think we might be saved: God's way, by free unmerited grace; man's way, by works. The Mormons teach that the way of salvation is by works.

Mormons divide salvation into two parts: (1) unconditional or general salvation, (2) conditional or individual salvation; McConkie adds a third, exaltation or eternal life, by dividing "individual" salvation.

General Salvation

Mormon theology claims that the death of Christ on the cross ransomed men from the effects of the Fall (see McConkie, *Mormon Doctrine*, p. 62; also 669,670) except for the incorrigible "sons of perdition" (those who fell with Lucifer). All mankind will eventually receive "general salvation," which will get everyone at least into the lowest of the three heavens or degrees of glory.

Stephen L. Richards, in his pamphlet, *Contributions of Joseph Smith*, claims that this salvation is equated with resurrection, for all men will be resurrected—atheists, pagans, unbelievers, etc.[1] It is difficult to fit this belief into John 3:18: "He that believeth on him is not condemned: but he that believeth not is condemned already, because he hath not believed in the name of the only begotten Son of God."

John 3:36 tells us that there is no salvation of any kind for those who do not believe, only condemnation: "He that believeth on the Son hath everlasting life: and he that believeth not the Son shall not see life; but the wrath of God abideth on him."

Resurrection cannot be equated with salvation as the Bible teaches it. All men will be resurrected: "And they [the dead] shall come forth; they that have done good, unto the resurrection of life; and they that have done evil, unto the resurrection of damnation" (John 5:29). To say that all men are saved because all are resurrected is to directly contradict the Word of God.

All men are resurrected, but those who believe in Christ and have been saved are resurrected 1000 years before the wicked dead. *None* in this first resurrection is lost. All these were saved through personally receiving Jesus as their Lord and Saviour. The wicked dead will be resurrected 1000 years later. None of the saved will be in the second resurrection. *All* those in the second resurrection will have rejected Christ and His salvation and they all will be lost (see Rev. 20:5,6). Two resurrections are clearly taught in the Bible. In the first resurrection *all* are saved! In the second resurrection, 1000 years later, *all* are lost!

Personal Salvation

The second part of the Mormon salvation is personal salvation, sometimes called individual or conditional salvation or exaltation. This salvation comes by grace plus baptism plus works.

Talmage says in *Articles of Faith*, "Redemption from personal sins can only be obtained through obedience to the requirement of the Gospel, and a life of good works."[2]

Can you imagine quoting that to the thief on the cross as he was dying? Thank God, Christ was there and not Mr. Talmage, or the thief would have been forever lost.

We have asked Mormons and other devotees of works for salvation, how many good works we had to do to be sure of our salvation. No one knows. Surely, if works in any degree were necessary, God would have prominently and repeatedly listed how many, what they are, and guaranteed us the certainty of our salvation when we had done them all. This isn't God's way. When the religious Jews thought they could be saved, or help themselves be saved by good works, they asked Jesus, "What shall we do, that we might work the works of God? Jesus answered and said unto them, This is the work of God, that ye believe on him whom he hath sent" (John 6:28,29). No single work or large amount of works will ever bring salvation.

A man may keep 1000 good laws during his lifetime and never break one of them. He may also do 1000 good works in addition to this. However, if he breaks one law, no matter how insignificant it may be, he must pay for it. A lifeguard may save 20 lives over a period of time. But if he deliberately and maliciously murders a man, he must face the penalty for his crime. The lives he saved in no way pay for the life he took.

Imagine someone running a red light, and being pulled over to the side by a policeman. And he says, "Hey, officer, you can't do a thing to me for going through that red light!"

The officer pushes his cap back on his head, sighs, and wonders if this is going to be one of those days. "O yeah," he answers noncommittally, "Why not?"

"Because I've driven through here at least a thousand times before and always stopped for the red light. I've kept the law 1000 times and broken it once. My good works outnumber my bad works 1000 to 1. Actually, you should reward me! You can't do a thing to me!"

Oh no? Try that approach some time and see how far you get. Would the law buy that facetious argument? Neither will God!

God's Salvation

In the first place, God cannot accept good works from a bad source, and He declares that all men are sinners, and therefore *lost*: "For all have sinned, and come short of the glory of God" (Rom. 3:23). It is not a matter of how far short each individual has come, but that *all* men have sinned and come short of the glory of God.

If every person were attempting to leap a 100-foot chasm, with a 10,000 foot drop to jagged rocks below, it would be purely academic as to how far some leaped, and how pitiful the efforts of others were. *All* would fail and be doomed because they were short of the mark, and that is God's point.

Not only that, but good works from an unrepentant

heart are contaminated, and are not considered good by God at all. In fact, Isaiah said, "All our righteousnesses are as filthy rags!" (64:6). If all our righteousnesses are as filthy rags to God, what an insult it must be to Him for us to try to buy our salvation with them. Many filthy rags would be even more insulting than a few.

God sent Jesus to die in bloody agony on the cross to totally pay for all our sins. How it must hurt Him when we insist on hanging the dirty rags of our good works on the cross to "help Jesus save us" rather than accepting this great gift of salvation.

The problem is deeper than just the sins we commit, however. The real problem is the *sin nature* every human being inherited from Adam. The sin nature is the sin factory that keeps producing sin. Not all factories produce the same kind of sin, and not all factories produce the same amount of sin. Some sins are gross, some are socially acceptable, even highly regarded in some circles. However, all are abominable to God. If we allow bottles to represent the sin produced by these sin factories, we might spend a lifetime destroying the bottles in a losing effort. The factory is still there, and though on occasion it may change the form or the brand of the product or slow down or speed up production, it is the same old sin factory.

God says in John 1:12, that the problem is that we are not children of God. Men by nature are *not* children of God! "But as many as received him, to them gave he power to become the sons of God, even to them that believe on his name." Now God would not ask us to *become* children of God if we already *were* children of God. He plainly says we have to receive Jesus in order to become children of God. He told religious but lost Nicodemus, "Ye must be born again" (John 3:7).

We are born again into the family of God by receiving Jesus Christ as our personal Lord and Saviour. We call believingly on Him to forgive us our sins, and come into our heart and life and make us children of God. This is the personal invitation He is waiting for. He immediately enters our life, washing away our sins through His shed blood, and gives us His free gift of everlasting life.

At the same time, He gives us a new nature as a child of God, and He begins to live His life through us, insuring a changed life. Then and only then, *after* we are saved, are our good works of any value to God whatsoever. Then and only then, *after* we are saved, for the first time God truly becomes our Father. He is not the Father of all men. He is the Father only of the saved, those born again into the family of God through receiving Christ. Of the unsaved, God says: "Ye are of your father the devil" (John 8:44). (See 1 John 3:8.)

Can you imagine a pig trying desperately to become a sheep by imitating a sheep? Suppose the pig became fed up with being a pig and noticed the sheep rambling about in the nice green pasture eating dry, clean, sheep food instead of slop. The pig manages to break out of the pig pen, find a dead sheep and clothe itself in the sheep wool. The pig learns to eat sheep feed, and slowly, agonizingly learns to bleat or talk sheep talk: "Oink, Bloink, Blah-h, Baa-a!"

Would the pig now be a sheep? Would it even be any closer to being a sheep? Would its change in outer appearance be enough? Would any of this change its basic pig nature? Would it matter in the slightest whether or not it was a "good" pig or a "bad" pig, by pig standards? Surely, we can all understand that a pig cannot become a sheep by acting like a sheep.

By the same token, no one can become a Christian by acting like a Christian. It does not matter how many "good" works or imitation Christian works we do, we can only become children of God by personally receiving Christ and being born again into God's family. Acting like a Christian, performing religious and other good works, is futile for salvation. We must be born again, and receive a new nature from God as children of God. Then, we will do good works for God, not in order to become Christians, but *because* we already are! (See Eph. 2:10.)

Faith Versus Works

Another rather obvious problem in working for our salvation in any degree is that God says of all men (unless they accept Christ and receive life through Him) that they are "dead in trespasses and sins" (Eph. 2:1). Just how much work can a dead man do, anyway?

It is true that in Christ, but only in *Christ*, are men made alive. Those in Christ have been made new creatures, with a new nature, new life, new desires, new power: "Therefore, if any man be in Christ, he is a new creature: old things are passed away; behold, all things are become new" (2 Cor. 5:17).

Mormons claim that in order to be able to claim personal salvation one must have faith in the Lord Jesus Christ, testify that Joseph Smith was a prophet of God, repent, be baptized into the Mormon church (the one true church) undergo the laying on of hands and keep the commandments. However, even after obeying all these requirements and believing there are three heavens and almost no hell, many Mormons are still fearful and uncertain. They admit they really don't know for sure where they will go when they die!

There is only one salvation taught in Scripture, and God says it is never gained by works. The first step anyone makes toward salvation is repentance of sin: "All we like sheep have gone astray; we have turned every one to his own way; and the Lord hath laid on him the iniquity of us all" (Isa. 53:6). Repentance in the Greek is *metanoia*, and simply means a change of mind about sin, self and Saviour; turning from going one's own way to going God's way. Repentance occurs simultaneously with salvation when one turns from sin to the Saviour.

Sin is basically following our old sin-nature, going our own way, being self-centered instead of Christ-centered. It is being the God, the Lord, the boss of our own life. It is managing our own affairs rather than submitting control to God. God cannot permit rival gods, however benevolent they may at first seem, anywhere in His universe. Rebellion and chaos would be the ultimate result. Salvation consists in receiving Jesus by faith and going God's way rather than our own.

Ephesians 2:8,9 makes it crystal clear: "For by grace are ye *saved* through *faith;* and that not of yourselves: it is the gift of God: *not of works, lest any man should boast*" (italics added).

We are saved, *not by works, not by works, not by works!*

The Mormon answer is to try to nullify this clear and unmistakable statement. They turn rapidly to James 2:20: "But wilt thou know, O vain man, that faith without works is dead." How true! The devils have a head belief and they are in hell forever (see Jas. 2:19). It takes a heart belief (the ruling, governing, choosing center of man's being; see Rom. 10:9,10) to save a man. Saving faith, if it is real, always produces good works, not in order to be saved, but as proof that one *has been* saved. Faith without works never lived!

In James 2:18 we are told to show our faith by our works. We cannot show something we don't already have, and if we have faith we have already been saved. James is pointing out that all the talk about faith in the world is useless if one does not have a changed life proving he has truly been saved. James is telling us to demonstrate our salvation.

James goes on and tells about Abraham and how he was justified by *works* (v. 21), but he *believed* God and it was accounted to him for righteousness (v. 23; see also Gen. 15:6). What is the answer? Abraham was justified in the sight of God by his faith. He was justified in the sight of men by his works. Men can't see faith, they can only see the works that saving faith produces.

Fourteen years after Abraham believed God he was circumcised as an outward sign of the covenant he already had with God. He had been saved 14 years *before* he was circumcised (see Gen. 17:9-11).

Then, around 40 years or so *after* he had believed God and been saved (many years before the birth of Isaac) Abraham *proved* his faith before men. He demonstrated his salvation, as James points out, by faithfully offering his son Isaac upon the altar (see Gen. 22). Here we see how faith that does not produce a changed life is dead. Faith that does not produce works that justify our claims of salvation is not saving faith at all.

Incidentally, dramatic transformation of character and life is the norm in evangelical Christianity. Mel Trotter was an alcoholic. All his desperate promises and efforts to quit proved in vain.

One sad and dreary day, his precious little baby died. In his grief the insatiable craving for whiskey filled his being, but Mel was abysmally broke. Finally in self-loathing but in abject desperation, he slipped up to the casket where the cold body of his little baby lay. His fingers trembled as he tore the shoes from the tiny little feet. Then he shuffled out to sell the shoes for money to buy a drink.

Some time later, Mel met Jesus Christ as his personal Lord and Saviour and was *instantly* and *forever* changed. He became a devout Christian, his thirst quenched by the Saviour. In the following years he founded over 60 missions to preach Christ to needy men and women.

Where, by the way, are the *Mormon missions on skid row?* Where are the alcoholics, prostitutes, murderers, drug addicts, who can testify to being instantly saved and changed by Mormonism? Of course, every program, whether religious or secular, educational or rehabilitational, can claim favorable results in rehabilitating these needy people, but we are talking about the change that takes place in a few minutes and lasts forever that only Christ can make. I have seen this transformation again and again, in a few moments, as people receive Christ. Changes in lifetime habits, in disposition, attitudes, temper, a sudden and imperishable certainly about salvation, death and heaven. A sudden influx of love and concern for others, whether in psychologists, lawyers, businessmen, prostitutes, alcoholics, farmers, drug addicts, fishermen, miners, Alaskan guides, school teachers, housewives or whoever.

To work for our salvation, then, insults God and puts us further in *debt*. He wants us to *work out*, demonstrate our salvation, *after* we have been saved. (See Phil. 2:12.)

It is difficult to see how words concerning works for salvation could be clearer than these God gave in Romans 11:5,6: "Even so then at this present time also there is a remnant according to the election of grace. And if by grace, then is it no more of works: otherwise grace is no more grace. But if it be of works, then is it no more grace: otherwise work is no more work."

Biblical grace is God's unmerited love and salvation extended to the *totally undeserving*, without works. Look at the thief on the cross again—no church, no baptism, no good works, just sin, sin, sin. Then this hopeless wretch calls on Jesus Christ, "Lord, remember me when thou comest into thy kingdom. And Jesus said unto him, Verily I say unto thee, To day shalt thou be with me in paradise" (Luke 23:42,43). Instant salvation! Full and free! No works, no church, no baptism, nothing but faith, asking and believing Jesus! Without doubt, the thief would have had a changed life had he come down from the cross, but as a result of, not the means to, his salvation.

Contrast this with the Mormon teaching on grace. Mormon grace consists in part of doing religious, church and temple good works and so *making oneself worthy* of the grace of God. Read again the statement quoted previously in this chapter from Talmage's *Articles of Faith*: "Redemption from personal sins can only be obtained through obedience to the requirements of the Gospel and a life of good works."

Here is why Mormon grace is false and why works can *never* get one to heaven: "For if Abraham were justified by works, he hath whereof to glory; but not before God. For what saith the scripture? Abraham believed God, and it was counted unto him for righteousness. Now to him that worketh [for salvation] is the reward not reckoned of *grace*, but of *debt*. But to him that worketh not, but *believeth* on him that justifieth the ungodly, his faith is counted for righteousness'' (Rom. 4:2-5).

We feel we must repeat with total conviction, *the Mormon religion is an elaborate doctrine of works, which denies the sufficiency of Christ alone to save*.

Christ, plus *nothing*, keeps us saved (once we fully commit ourselves by faith for salvation to Him). Anything else, the Bible declares to be heresy. Works follow salvation as proof of real salvation and to glorify Christ.

Dealing with the Mormon Illusion

Mormons react in several ways when confronted with irrefutable evidence that Mormonism is false. Some turn from the Mormon Jesus to the biblical Jesus and get saved and come out of Mormonism. Some are mentally convinced but emotionally cling to Mormonism because of family ties, fear, etc. Some denounce all evidence as lies, material taken out of context, anti-Mormon persecution, etc. Many just ignore the facts, and cling to the "testimony" the "Holy Ghost" has given them.

It is interesting but heartbreaking to note that even after Jim Jones and the People's Church had been thoroughly exposed, even after the Jonestown massacre, after Jones had been unmasked as morally depraved, after his departure from the biblical Jesus had been revealed, some people *still* believed in him, and were still loyal to the People's Temple. Some were still willing to die for him and his cult.

Some hard-core Mormons apparently have made their choice irrevocably and, unfortunately, eternally and may be completely impervious to facts. Their "testimony" from the "Holy Ghost" that Mormonism is true, that

Joseph Smith is a prophet of God, that their Mormon Jesus is real, and all other churches but theirs are apostate, is good enough for them.

Whatever or whoever Mormons receive their "testimony" from is certainly not the Holy Spirit of the Bible. Mormons claim that the Holy Ghost, with the Father and Son, is one of the personages of the Godhead. In Mormon theology this makes three separate and individual gods, one only in purpose, contradicting the Bible and revealing Mormons to be polytheistic. Yet Mormons admit that the Holy Ghost is a "personage of spirit" and does not have a body of flesh and bone, one of the Mormon requirements for being God. The Morman Holy Ghost can only be in one place at a time. When the Bible says the Holy Ghost fills many different people at the same time, and that He indwells all true Christians everywhere, Mormons interpret this as "the powers and influences that emanate from God." (Thank God for our *personal comforter*, the Holy Ghost of the Bible, a living Person dwelling in each of us who has been truly saved.)

Holy Ghost is just the old English translation of Holy Spirit, the same word is used and refers to the same person. Believe it or not, Mormons sometimes distinguish between these words as if the Holy Ghost differed from the Holy Spirit! Clearly, whatever is giving the Mormons witness to the "truth" of Mormonism, it is not the Holy Spirit of God!

Notes

1. Stephen L. Richards, *Contributions of Joseph Smith* (Salt Lake City: The Church of Jesus Christ of Latter-day Saints).
2. Talmage, *Articles of Faith*, pp. 85,87,478,479.

CHAPTER FIFTEEN

Biblical Salvation

A few years ago, in the predominantly Mormon field where we were sharing our Saviour, we gave a young Mormon lady and her Mormon husband much of the material contained in this book. He was not interested enough to read it thoroughly, but she was.

At two o'clock in the morning, she could stand it no longer. She shook her husband awake and told him she wanted to be saved. He shrugged her off and told her to shut up and go back to sleep. She called me as soon as she could.

As we knelt together she poured out her heart, confessed her lostness, her sin, and took Jesus as her Saviour and Lord. She reveled in coming from the darkness of Mormonism to the light of Christ. Within two months she virtually committed the Gospel of Matthew to memory, learning and understanding more Scripture in a few weeks as a Christian, than in all her life before as a Mormon.

We have discovered that there is no division of salvation into "general" and "personal" salvation. There is only one salvation, and that comes by receiving the Lord Jesus Christ.

Mormons and Biblical Salvation

Following are true experiences (although some of the names are fictitious) of Mormons who received this one salvation.

Tim O'Flannigan grew up in the Mormon church. His parents, now grown old, are still in the church. Youth activities were fun, and he readily absorbed the Mormon teaching both before and after his baptism into the Mormon church.

In spite of his Mormon testimony Tim began to drink and let other sins slip into his life. Marriage to breathtakingly lovely Jean, and the subsequent arrival of two precious children, should have quelled his restlessness, but they did not.

Jean was led to Jesus Christ by the sweet, consistent witness of a girl friend. Tim could not help but notice the change in her life but thought the last thing in the world he needed was "religion." He had plenty of that. Jean soon started coming to our church where she blossomed like a spring rose for Jesus Christ. Tim and I talked about his relationship with Christ. At first, he saw little difference in Mormon teaching and what the Bible said about salvation. Sometimes, he felt sure that he would go to heaven—well, one of the Mormon's three heavens anyway.

For awhile he avoided me, but he could not avoid the

impact of the Word of God and the sweet testimony of his wife's changed life. Secretly, Tim had to admit that there was something different, alive, far more real and vibrant about Jean's life and testimony than there was about the life and testimony of the many Mormons he knew so well. Turmoil filled Tim's heart. Undeniably, the Bible taught that salvation was a *gift*; Mormonism taught that you had to work for your salvation. Which was right? Verses like Romans 4:5, "But to him that worketh not, but believeth on him that justifieth the ungodly, his faith is counted for righteousness," smote him like a sledgehammer.

Tim surrendered. He called on Jesus Christ to save him from his sins and fill the empty spot in his heart that Mormonism never was able to fill. Jesus came into his heart, and Tim knew the testimony of joy and peace only the living Saviour can give, so different from his former Mormon testimony. Immediately after his salvation, Tim turned from Mormonism to follow Christ in baptism in our church. Christ forever filled that empty spot.

I recently received a letter a young LDS mother wrote after reading some of the material in this book and after I visited her. In the letter she said: "I have seen things happen that I never thought could or would. *It is beautiful*. I'm real glad you came, and God is part of my life now. I pray that God will help you reach more LDS people to know and understand the love of God. It really distresses me to think some of the most beautiful people I know may not be in heaven because of this false and hypocritical way the LDS teaches. . . I am now a true born-again child of God the Lord. What a beautiful feeling is with me each new day. I know thru the love and faith of God I'll be able to overcome my old teachings. Thanks again for helping me see the light."

Later, I had the joy of returning to her town, and leading her husband to Jesus Christ.

Brett Somers was a rather well-to-do Mormon, with a beautiful home, in Washington state. Both he and his wife were very active in the Mormon church. After years of faithful, even brilliant service in the Mormon church, Mrs. Somers became increasingly troubled about the lack of vital interest in talking about Jesus Christ she found among church leaders, officials, and her Mormon women friends. What she heard the leaders say and what she read in the Bible did not seem to agree. She dug deeply into the *Book of Mormon*, and other Mormon books, seeking to bolster her once flaming faith. She read carefully through the *Articles of Faith*, by Talmage, marking many passages. (I know! She gave me the book!)

I was holding evangelistic meetings in the vicinity and Mrs. Somers made an appointment with me. She asked me very careful, intelligent questions about Mormonism, the Bible and salvation. She took home some of the material I have included in this book. She asked the Christ of the *Bible*, not of *Mormonism*, into her heart. Now she has clearly, definitely, recommitted her life to Christ and made up her mind to leave the Mormon church.

Brett was in a quandary. Some of his wife's searchings had begun to trouble him. He went with her for a little while to an evangelical church. But he was a Mormon! Where was the answer?

God graciously opened the way for me to have an appointment with Brett. Slowly, carefully, prayerfully, I presented the gospel to Brett and answered questions from the Word of God, the Bible. Finally, I said, "Brett, Jesus loves you so much. He died for you and promises that if you call on Him to save you from your sins, He will do it.

Brett, will you call on Jesus Christ to save you, right now?"

Brett bowed his head, and simply, quietly invited the risen Christ to come into his life and save him from his sins. Oh, the unspeakable joy and radiance that shone from his tear-filled eyes as he lifted them to mine! I showed several Bible verses, such as Romans 10:13 and John 3:36, to him again and he quickly memorized and claimed John 3:36.

Then I asked Brett if he *knew* beyond the shadow of a doubt that Jesus had saved him and given him the wonderful gift of everlasting life. Brett gave a resounding Yes. We prayed together and Brett thanked the Lord Jesus Christ for saving him from his sins, from Mormonism, and from hell.

Brett and his wife were, by their request, excommunicated from the Mormon church and are very active in a Baptist church and vitally concerned about leading others to Christ. Now both Brett and his wife know what a real testimony for Jesus Christ is. They can't keep quiet about *Him*!

Some of the names in these testimonies are fictitious to protect the individuals involved. No one, who has not experienced it, can believe the intense pressure the Mormon church, Mormon leaders, relatives, loved ones, family and friends, can put on those who get saved and leave the Mormon church.

However the names in the following experience are true. Janet Webster printed and widely circulated her 12-page testimony.

Janet is a very lively lady and was an enthusiastic Mormon. She was in the process of acting as a missionary to two very good Christian friends, teaching them the six missionary lessons. Janet was sure her friends would soon see the "truth of the Mormon church," especially if they knew "of all its wonderful, beautiful, and glorious principles and doctrines." However, when she looked in the Bible for one of the Scriptures Mormons use to try to prove a doctrine, she found, to her chagrin and astonishment, that she had to read what the Bible said before and after the Scripture to understand its complete meaning!

This one experience led Janet to read more and more of the Bible and she became convinced it was God's perfect Word, and she saw her need for Jesus Christ. She accepted Him as her Lord and Saviour and turned from Mormonism forever.

She said in her letter, "How can I tell you of the blessed miracle which has happened to our family? By the marvelous, wonderful grace of God, we have been called out from darkness and redeemed by our precious Lord and Saviour, Jesus Christ."

Janet's daughter, Brenda, a student at Brigham Young University, came home to her "apostate," newly-Christian family. In time, the love of Christ and Christians won, and Brenda met Christ also.

Janet wrote cogently, "Suddenly it came into sharp focus. . . there are two camps (or sides) on this earth. On the first side, we have those who unreservedly uphold the Word of God (Bible), trusting it completely. And on the second side are those who would (and do) undermine (sometimes subtly) the Bible and proclaim that the Bible is not a supernatural book. Instead they believe their own intellectual ideas or scientific knowledge (Atheists), or new prophets and Scriptures (Spiritualists, Jehovah's Witnesses, Mormons, Bahai, Science and Mind, etc.) are to be trusted over the Bible.

Well, why not, you say? I can only tell you why not for me. First, please notice that there are many groups in the second camp, but there is only one group in the first: *born again Christians*, who feel there is no salvation in any particular denomination, or in following a prophet, or Pope, etc., but only in and through Jesus Christ. And Jesus Christ and Him crucified *only* do they preach. These Christians all belong to the same church—the church of Jesus Christ, even though they fellowship in many different denominations."

Janet went on to say that it was a glaring revelation to her as a Mormon, before she was converted to Christ, that she was in the same camp with atheists and all the other cults, who did not believe in the sufficiency or accuracy of the Bible. She realized the fallacy of the Mormon teaching, "We believe the Bible to be the Word of God as far as it is translated correctly."

Janet declared that she once thought Christians who believed they were saved by grace were given a free license to sin all they wanted to. Now, she knows how untrue this is. "How glorious it is to obey the Lord, not to gain salvation or exaltation, but just because you love the Lord, and knowing that because He died for you, your greatest desire in life is to live for Him! That can't compare with the idea of offering our puny works in exchange for exaltation."

Then Janet adds, "This is what *believing on Jesus* really means! It means that you believe Him when He tells us that the wages of sin is death, and so if we are going to be punished for our own sins (even one little unrepented sin), that means death—*spiritual death! Believing on Jesus* means we believe Him when He tells us He has died and paid in full the penalty for our sins and therefore, we will not be punished for our sins! And *believing on Jesus* means that you believe Him when He tells you that you must *accept Him as your* (personal) *Saviour.*"

Three days after Janet accepted Jesus Christ as her Saviour she knew for sure that the Mormon church was wrong, and she left it. She now has the wonderful joy of having seen God bring her family to Jesus Christ.

The Biblical God

God loves you and wants you to know that there is only *one God*. This *one God* created and is Lord over all the universe, stars, planets and all.

In the beginning *God* created the heaven and the earth''—Genesis 1:1. (See also John 1:3.)

"Before me there was *no God formed*, neither shall there be after me"—Isaiah 43:10. God was never a man, and man will never be God!

"From everlasting [that's eternity past] to everlasting [that's eternity future], *thou art God*!"—Psalm 90:2. God never progressed, earned or attained His way to being God; *He always was God.* (The Bible mentions *false* gods, but to believe that other gods really exist is pagan polytheism, not Christianity.)

Clearly, there is not now, and *never* will be, any other God on this planet or any other "world" or planet. There is forever only *one* God.

The Biblical Christ

There is one Saviour, Jesus Christ, who is the eternal God.

"For unto us a child is born, unto us a son is given: and the government shall be upon his shoulder: and his name shall be called Wonderful, Counsellor, *The mighty God*,

The everlasting Father, The Prince of Peace''—Isaiah 9:6.

Within the nature of God there are three eternal distinctions: God the Father, God the Son, and God the Holy Spirit, and there is only *one* God. Since Jesus is repeatedly called God, we must accept Him as God, or we accept another Jesus. In the Bible, ''the Word'' means Jesus: ''In the beginning was the *Word*, and the *Word* was with God, and *the Word was God!*''—John 1:1. ''Beginning'' here simply means ''from all time.'' As God was God *from all time*, so was Jesus Christ God—from the beginning, from all time! Jesus never progressed, worked, or attained His way into being God. *He always was God*.

God forbade forever the worship of any other God (Exod. 34:14), yet Jesus accepted worship as God on many occasions. ''And as they went to tell his disciples, behold, Jesus met them, saying, All hail. And they came and held him by the feet, and *worshipped him!*''—Matthew 28:9.

Good Works Cannot Save You

God loves you and wants you to know that ALL men are lost sinners and *must* be born again.

All men have a sin nature and there is NO general salvation. The Bible says in Romans 3:23: ''For all have sinned, and come short of the glory of God.'' This means we are all lost sinners. Romans 3:10: ''There is none righteous, no, not one.''

Sin is going our own way (Isa. 53:6). It is being the God, manager, boss, Lord of our own life. It is being self-centered instead of Christ-centred.

''All our righteousnesses are as filthy rags''—Isaiah 64:6; ''Now to him that worketh [for salvation] is the reward not reckoned of grace, but of debt. But to him that worketh not, but believeth on him that justifieth the ungodly, his faith is counted for righteousness"—Romans 4:4,5.

An apple tree is an apple tree; it bears apples. So, we sin *because* we have a sin-nature. Beating the apples off the tree does not change the nature of the tree! So, getting rid of some sins does not change our nature!

Besides, how much *good works* can a *dead* man do? As natural (unsaved) men we are all "*dead* in trespasses and sins"—Ephesians 2:1.

John 5:24: "Verily, verily, I say unto you, He that heareth my word, and *believeth* on him that sent me, *hath* everlasting life, and shall not come into condemnation [judgment], but *is passed* from death unto life."

What Is Real, Biblical Salvation?

Salvation Is a Free Gift

God loves you and wants you to know salvation is not by works, it is a *gift*. Personally receiving Christ, trusting Him alone to save us, is God's way of salvation.

Romans 6:23: "For the wages of sin is death; but the *gift* of God is eternal life through Jesus Christ our Lord." We cannot make ourselves "worthy" of the grace of God. Salvation is a free gift for the unworthy, the undeserving, which we all are. "Christ died for the ungodly"—Romans 5:6.

Ephesians 2:8,9: "For by grace are ye saved through *faith*; and that not of yourselves: it is the gift of God: not of works, lest any man should boast."

We Need a New Nature!

God loves you and wants you to know that there is

only *one* way of salvation, that is through rebirth.

John 3:7: "Ye must be born again." John 1:12 tells us how. "As many as received him, to them gave he power to become the sons of God, even to them that believe on his name." Accepting Jesus is the *only* way to be *born again*.

We are not by nature children of God. We must receive Christ in order to become the children of God.

Jesus alone can cleanse us from sin and change our nature; 1 Peter 2:24: "Who his own self bare our sins in his own body on the tree." Jesus took our place and shed His blood to cleanse us from sin. No amount of "good works" can wash away one sin or change our nature.

Salvation occurs when we call believingly on Jesus to save us. He then comes into our life and we become children of God with a new nature.

Although salvation is not by works, true salvation always produces a changed life. Christ comes in by personal invitation as Lord and Saviour to change our life and live His life through us.

Salvation Is Instant

God loves you and wants you to know *salvation is instant*. The moment we repent, turn from our sins to Jesus, He saves us. As the hymn says, "Just as I am without one plea, but that thy blood was shed for me." Christ said to the unbaptized, unsaved thief on the cross (an instant salvation response to the thief's believing call), "Today shalt thou be with me in paradise"—Luke 23:43. (*Paradise* being the same place Paul saw as the heaven of God, 2 Cor. 12:2-4.) Jesus granted salvation for a harlot: "Go thy way, thy faith hath saved thee!"—see Luke 7:50. Instant salvation!

Salvation includes accepting Jesus Christ as both Lord (God, Lord, new manager of our life) and Saviour. It involves heart (the ruling, governing, choosing, center of our being) belief. Romans 10:9: "That if thou shalt confess with thy mouth the Lord Jesus [Jesus as Lord], and shalt believe in thine heart that God hath raised him from the dead, thou shalt be saved."

Salvation Is Simple

God loves you and wants you to know that *salvation is simple*. Romans 10:13: "For whosoever shall call upon the name of the Lord, shall be saved." "The blood of Jesus Christ his [God's] Son, cleanses us from all sin"—1 John 1:7.

We must personally call believingly on Jesus to save us. This is how we receive Him. If we do so call, He *must* save us or God would be lying, and God *cannot* lie. If Jesus loved us enough to die to save us, would He then turn us down when we call on Him? *Of course not!*

God loves you and wants you to be saved. Would you like to receive Jesus as your Lord and Saviour right now? Here is a prayer you can pray right now, meaning it with all your heart:

"Lord Jesus Christ, come into my heart and life. Cleanse me from all sin by your shed blood. Make me a child of God. Give me your free gift of everlasting life, and let me know that I am saved, now and forever. I *now* receive you as my very own personal Lord and Saviour. In Jesus' name, amen."

Did Jesus save you or did He lie? He *had* to do one or the other. According to Romans 10:13, if you called believingly on Him, He has saved you and you are cleansed from your sin.

Salvation Is Certain

You can *know* you are saved, not just by *feeling*, but because God's Word says so! Memorize John 3:36: "He that believeth on the Son *hath* everlasting life." What do you have right now, according to God's Word? Where would you go if you were to die right now, according to God's Word? "(We walk by faith, not by sight:) we are confident, I say, and willing rather to be absent from the body, and to be present with the Lord" (2 Cor. 5:7,8).

If you now know that Jesus has saved you, according to His word, please take time right now and thank Him out loud for saving you as we pray.

First John 5:13: "These things have I written unto you that believe on the name of the Son of God; that ye may *know* that ye *have* eternal life."

Salvation Is Believing!

Choose to believe Christ, feelings or no feelings, and He will prove His reality to you as you step out on faith that He has kept His word and saved you.

Three men step aboard the same elevator bound for the seventh floor where they all want to go. One is laughing, one is crying, one is poker-faced, unemotional. All three of them get to the seventh floor, regardless of their feelings, because they *believed* and committed themselves to the elevator. So it is with trusting Christ—feelings or no feelings. He will save you instantly and see you through to heaven.

The reality of your salvation will be shown in your love-response in obeying and following Jesus Christ. John 14:23: "If a man love me, he *will* [not if, maybe, and or but] keep my words." If you are truly saved, you *will* obey!

Among other things, this means you will come *out* of Mormonism and follow the biblical Christ!

True Salvation Produces Good Works,
Obedience to Christ

To *work for* salvation shows unbelief in the sufficiency of Jesus Christ alone to save us. However, true salvation, true faith, *always produces* good works!

James 2:20: "But wilt thou know, O vain man, that faith without works is dead?"

Apple trees produce apples. True Christians produce good works. Apples are products of the tree and prove that it is an apple tree. But it was an apple tree before it produced apples. In the same way, good works *never produce* a Christian; they merely prove he is one. Second Corinthians 5:17: "Therefore if any man be in Christ, he is a new creature [creation]: old things are passed away; behold, all things are become new."

We must *have* salvation in order to *demonstrate* it, just as we must have a car before we can demonstrate it!

More than Head Belief

Does salvation actually work? For nominal Christians who may be religious but have only a head belief in Christ, the answer is definitely no! Unfortunately, many churches have members who are nominal Christians. I was a nominal Christian. On such the cultists feed.

For those who turn believingly to Jesus Christ with all their heart, the answer is a thrilling, resounding yes!

I owe a debt to the Mormons and to John, my Mormon friend, mentioned in the first chapter. Because of John, I discovered that my head religion was not enough. I truly came to know Christ as my personal Lord and Saviour.

Now, I want to share Him with you.

God loves all of us so very much, so much that He sent Christ to shed His blood on the cross for us. Even more to the point God loves you. Will you turn away from sin and self to the Saviour? God says we are all sinners, and that means we are *all lost*. You will never be truly saved, till you admit that you are lost! Until you can admit that, you insult God, and accuse Him of letting His Son die for you when there was no need! Let us go over the way of salvation one more time. Your decision about Christ will determine your destiny. We pray God in His love will enable us to make the way crystal clear.

Exactly how do I turn to Christ? "As many as received him, to them gave he power to become the sons of God, even to them that believe on his name" (John 1:12). You must confess to God that you are a lost sinner, and receive Jesus Christ as your Saviour. Instantly, He will save you and you will be born again, a child of God with a new nature.

How do I receive Him? Accept Jesus as the eternal God who is bodily resurrected from the dead. You must "confess with thy mouth the Lord [God, Boss, new Manager of your life] Jesus [Saviour from sin and hell], and shalt believe in thine heart that God hath raised him from the dead, [then] thou shalt [absolutely, not maybe] be saved" (Rom. 10:9).

What do I do to receive Him? Call with all your heart, believingly on Him! "For whosoever shall call upon the name of the Lord shall be saved" (Rom. 10:13). If you call believingly, Jesus will *have* to save you or He would be lying, because He promised. He cannot lie! Besides, if He loved you enough to die in your place in broken, bloody, lonely agony on a cruel cross, would He turn you down when you call on Him to save you? Of course not!

Simply pray: "Lord Jesus Christ, please save me from all my sins. Cleanse me by your shed blood. Give me your free gift of everlasting life. Come into my heart and life right now. Make me a child of God, and let me know that I am saved, now and forever. I now receive you as my very own personal Lord and Saviour."

The Christ you are receiving is the eternal biblical Christ, who always has been and always will be God, from everlasting to everlasting.

Did Christ save you—not according to your feelings but according to the Word of God? Then simply thank Him out loud for saving your soul and giving you eternal life.

Memorize, right now, the first part of John 3:36, "He that believeth on the Son hath [right now] everlasting life." So, the moment you believed, God said He gave you everlasting life!

Find a church that teaches the blood of Christ and makes salvation clear, and believes the Bible and the Bible alone. Join it, and attend regularly as God commands true Christians in Hebrews 10:25.

Follow Christ in baptism to show the world that your sins were washed away when you were saved (see Acts 10:47,48), and to show that you are dead to the old life and resurrected with Him to the new life.

Read slowly through the Gospel of John. Confess to others that Christ has saved you. Share Christ constantly with others (see Acts 1:8). The greatest responsibility and joy in all the world, other than being saved, is leading others to know Christ!

Pray often, and tell Jesus every day that you love Him and thank Him for dying on the cross for you and for saving you! If you sin, confess it instantly, whether in thought, word or deed and thank God for His instant forgiveness (see 1 John 1:9). A Christian can sin, but a true Christian cannot continue to live habitually in sin. Let Christ live this new life through you. Tell Him you love Him and daily give Him permission to live His life each day through you.

Come out of Mormonism if you care about your soul, and the souls of others you will influence either for heaven or hell. "For what shall it profit a man, if he shall gain the whole world, and lose his own soul" (Mark 8:36).

If you are truly saved, God says you will obey Him: "Jesus answered and said unto him, If a man love me, he will keep my words: and my Father will. . . come unto him, and make our abode with him" (John 14:23).

Do not be overly concerned about feelings. God wants you to walk by faith, not by feelings and sometimes He will completely remove all feelings to see if you are going to walk by faith in Him and in His Word. At other times there may be inexpressible joy and peace, but feelings or not, His Word is true.

Here is that valuable illustration again. Three men waiting on the first floor, want to go to the seventh floor of a building. One is laughing, one is crying, and one is stoical. Their feelings do not matter at all. What matters is that they all trust the elevator to get them to the seventh floor. So they step into it and commit themselves to it, and the elevator takes all of them to the seventh floor.

So it is with coming to Christ. It does not matter greatly whether you cry or laugh or have little or no feeling. If you trust Christ to save you and commit yourself to Him, He will get you to heaven as He promised, feelings or no feelings. But the very realization that one has been truly saved from sin and from eternal hell, sooner or later, will bring a sense of relief and peace, but not always at the very moment of salvation.

Just as you must take medicine before it can take effect, so must you trust Christ and His Word, after calling on Him, before He can give you more feelings of joy, peace and His love than you ever dreamed possible.

Here are some verses you may want to learn. In any event they will be very helpful to you in your Christian life.

Acts 1:8: "But ye shall receive power, after that the Holy Ghost is come upon you: and ye shall be witnesses unto me both in Jerusalem, and in all Judea, and in Samaria, and unto the uttermost part of the earth."

First John 1:9: "If we confess our sins, he is faithful and just to forgive us our sins, and to cleanse us from all unrighteousness."

First John 3:14: "We know that we have passed from death unto life, because we love the brethren. He that loveth not his brother abideth in death."

How God loves us! It is my prayer that I have not hindered His love from flowing through me, even though God led me to point out the errors in Mormonism. God loves the Mormon people, and, as far as I know my heart, so do I. God does not love Mormonism, which teaches people about another God, another Jesus, to their eternal loss.

If this book has been a blessing to you, please share it with as many people as you can in this desperate day of darkness and incredible urgency. Pray much for its use for Jesus, and for souls for Him.

Appendix: The Way to Salvation

Dr. Norman Lewis of Western Conservative Baptist Seminary, Portland, Oregon, states that every true Christian is confronted with the "inescapable command" to witness to all men who are without Christ.

"Go ye therefore, and teach all nations, baptizing them in the name of the Father, and of the Son, and of the Holy Ghost: Teaching them to observe all things whatsoever I have commanded you: and, lo, I am with you alway, even unto the end of the world" (Matt. 28:19,20).

"But ye shall receive power, after that the Holy Ghost is come upon you: and ye shall be witnesses unto me both in Jerusalem, and in all Judea, and in Samaria, and unto the uttermost part of the earth" (Acts 1:8).

When you combine this great admonition with John 14:23, "Jesus answered and said unto him, If a man love me, he will keep my words," truly the responsibility to share Christ with all men, including Mormons, is inescapable. If we love Jesus, if we believe men are lost, if we believe in heaven and hell, we *must* share with Mormon friends as well as with others who need Jesus.

Following are questions that will show you, dear Mormon friends, the way to salvation.

(Italicized words in quoted passages are added by the author.)

1. The Bible says there is only one God who created all universes, planets and worlds. Joseph Smith and other Mormon leaders teach that there are many Gods. Which do you believe?

The Bible

"*Before* me there was no God formed, neither shall there be *after* me" (Isa. 43:10).

"Is there a God beside me? Yea, there is no God; I know not any" (Isa. 44:8).

Mormon Writers

"And the *Gods* ordered, saying: let the waters under the heaven be gathered together unto one place, and let the earth come up dry; and it was so as they ordered; and the gathering together of the waters pronounced they, great waters; and the *Gods* saw that they were obeyed" (Joseph Smith, *Pearl of Great Price*, Abraham 4:9,10; published by The Church of Jesus Christ of Latter-day Saints, Salt Lake City, Utah, 1967).

"If we should take a million of worlds like this and number their particles, we should find that there are more Gods than there are particles of matter in those worlds"

(Orson Pratt, *Journal of Discourses*, vol. 2; published by F.D. & S.W. Richards, Liverpool, 1854; reprint ed. Salt Lake City, Utah, 1966, p. 345).

Comment

Obviously, God declares there never has been, is not now, and never will be any other God in this or any other world, on this or any other planet.

For additional information see chapter 7, "The Fatal Flaw," in this book.

2. The Bible teaches that God never originated as a man, that He was God from all eternity past. The Bible also teaches that there will never be any other God. Mormonism teaches that God was once a man before He became God. Mormonism also teaches that men may someday become Gods. Which do you believe?

The Bible

"From everlasting to everlasting, *thou art God*" (Ps. 90:2).

"For I am God, and not man" (Hos. 11:9).

"I am the first, and I am the last; and *beside me there is no God*" (Isa. 44:6).

"Before me there was no God formed, neither shall there be after me" (Isa. 43:10).

Mormon Writers

"God himself was once as we are now and is an exalted *man,* and sits enthroned in yonder heavens!" (Joseph Smith, *Teachings of Prophet Joseph Smith;* published by Deseret Book Co., Salt Lake City, 1969, p. 345).

"Remember that God our Heavenly Father was perhaps once a child, and *mortal* like we are and rose step by step in the scale of progress, in the school of advancement" (Orson Hyde, *Journal of Discourses*, vol. 1, p. 123; published by F.D. and S.W. Richards, Liverpool, 1854; reprint ed. Salt Lake City, Utah, 1966).

"The Lord created you and me for the purpose of becoming *Gods like Himself*" (Brigham Young, *Journal of Discourses*, vol. 3, p. 93).

"As man is, God once was; as God is, man may be" (Lorenzo Snow, former president of the Mormon church, *Millenial Star*, vol. 54; also Milton R. Hunter, *The Gospel Through the Ages*, pp. 105, 106).

Comment

According to the Bible, God never progressed His way into being God, He always was God. Clearly man did not exist prior to God. Clearly too, since God declares there will *never* be any other God, men will *never* become gods.

For additional information see chapter 8, "The Truth About Adam-God," and chapter 9, "Contradictions Concerning the Person of God," in this book.

3. The Bible teaches that Jesus Christ always was God. Mormonism teaches that there was a time when Jesus Christ was not God. Which do you believe?

The Bible

"But thou, Bethlehem Ephratah, though thou be little among the thousands of Judah, yet out of thee shall he come forth unto me that is to be ruler in Israel: whose goings forth have been from old, *from everlasting*" (Mic. 5:2).

"In the beginning *was* the Word [Jesus], and the Word was with God, and the Word *was God*" (John 1:1).

"Before Abraham was, *I am*" (John 8:58).

Mormon Writers

"Christ the Word, the First born, had of course *attained* unto the status of Godhood while yet in pre-existence" (booklet, *What the Mormons Think of Christ;* published by The Church of Jesus Christ of Latter-day Saints, p. 36).

"Jesus *became* a God and reached His great state of understanding through consistent effort and continuous obedience to all the Gospel truths and universal laws" (Milton R. Hunter, *The Gospel Through the Ages;* Deseret Book Co., Salt Lake City, 1945, p. 51).

Comment

God was God from the beginning and so was Jesus Christ God from the beginning, *from all time*. Jesus Christ *always was and is God*. Jesus told Phillip, in John 14:9, "He that hath seen me hath seen the Father."

For additional information see chapter 7, "The Fatal Flaw," under the subhead, *The Christ,* in this book.

4. Deuteronomy 18:20-22 says that God's test for a prophet includes 100 percent accuracy in fulfillment of his prophecies, or the prophet is a false prophet. Many of Joseph Smith's prophecies were never fulfilled. According to the biblical test, was Joseph Smith a true prophet or a false prophet?

The Bible

"But the prophet, which shall presume to speak a

word in my name, which I have not commanded him to speak, or that shall speak in the name of other gods, even that prophet shall die. And if thou say in thine heart, How shall we know the word which the Lord hath not spoken? When a prophet speaketh in the name of the Lord, *if the thing follow not, nor come to pass*, that is the thing which the Lord hath not spoken, but the prophet hath spoken it presumptuously: thou shalt not be afraid of him'' (Deut. 18:20-22).

Mormon Writers

Prophecy given by Joseph Smith, September 1832: New Jerusalem and its Temple are to be built in Missouri *in this generation* (Joseph Smith, *Doctrine and Covenants* 84:1-5; published by The Church of Jesus Christ of Latter-day Saints, 1968).

"The Latter-day Saints just as much expect to see a fulfillment of that promise during the *generation that was then in existence in 1832* as they expect that the sun will rise and set tomorrow. Why? Because God cannot lie. *He will fulfill all His promises*" (Apostle Orson Pratt, *Journal of Discourses*, vol. 9; published by F.D. and S.W. Richards, Liverpool, 1854; reprint ed. Salt Lake City, 1966, p. 71).

This prophecy was not fulfilled, therefore it is *false*.

Prophecy given by Joseph Smith sometime between 1831 and 1844: Nauvoo House to be built and to belong to the Smith family forever (Joseph Smith, *Doctrine and Covenants* 124:56-60; published by The Church of Jesus Christ of Latter-day Saints, 1968). Smith was killed in 1844 and the Mormons were driven from Nauvoo. The house no longer belongs to the Smith family. The prophecy was *false*.

Prophecy by Joseph Smith: "The coming of the Lord which was nigh . . . *even 56 years should wind up the scene*" (Joseph Smith, *History of the Church*, vol. 2, p. 182; published by Deseret News Publishers, Salt Lake City, 1902-1912). This prophecy was *false*.

Comment

Joseph Smith fails God's test for a true prophet. He was *not* a prophet of God.

For additional information see chapter 3, "Joseph Smith—Prophet of God?" in this book.

5. The Bible says that Christ was begotten by the Holy Spirit. Mormon prophet, Brigham Young, said Christ was not begotten by the Holy Ghost. Which do you believe?

The Bible

"For that which is conceived in her is of the Holy Ghost" (Matt. 1:20).

"The Holy Ghost shall come upon thee . . . therefore also that holy thing which shall be born of thee shall be called the Son of God" (Luke 1:35).

Mormon Writers

"The child Jesus . . . was not begotten by the Holy Ghost" (Brigham Young *Journal of Discourses*, vol. 1; published by F.D. and S.W. Richards, Liverpool, 1854; reprint ed., Salt Lake City, Utah, 1966, pp. 50, 51).

Comment

Would a true prophet of God contradict the Word of God?

For additional information see chapter 7, "The Fatal Flaw," in this book.

6. *The Bible teaches that God made Adam and gave him life. Brigham Young taught that Adam "is our father and our God and the only God with whom we have to do." Which do you believe?*

The Bible

"And the Lord God *formed* man of the dust of the ground, and breathed into his nostrils the breath of life; and man became a living soul" (Gen. 2:7). "For Adam was first *formed*, then Eve" (1 Tim. 2:13).

Mormon Writers

"When our father Adam came into the Garden of Eden, He came into it with a celestial body and brought Eve, *one* of his *wives*, with him. He helped to make and organize this world. He is Michael, the Arch-angel, the Ancient of Days! about whom holy men have written and spoken. He [Adam] is our Father and our God and the only God with whom we have to do" (Brigham Young, *Journal of Discourses;* vol. 1; published by F.D. and S.W. Richards, Liverpool, 1854; reprint ed. Salt Lake City, Utah, 1966, p. 50).

Comment

To deny the Adam-God doctrine is to admit that Brigham Young is a false prophet. To accept it denies God's Word, the Bible.

For further information see chapter 8, "The Truth About Adam-God" and chapter 9, "Contradictions Concerning the Person of God."

7. The Bible calls the study of genealogies foolish. Mormons make extensive use of genealogies in their system of works, baptizing for the dead, etc. Which do you believe is right?

The Bible

"But *avoid* foolish questions, and *genealogies*, and contentions, and strivings about the law; for they are *unprofitable* and *vain*" (Titus 3:9).

"Neither give *heed* to fables and endless *genealogies* which minister questions, rather than godly edifying which is in faith: so do" (1 Tim. 1:4).

Mormon Writers

"Before vicarious ordinances of salvation and exaltation may be performed for those who have died . . . they must be accurately and properly identified. Hence, *genealogical research* is required . . . The Church maintains in Salt Lake City one of the world's greatest *genealogical societies*. Much of the genealogical source material of various nations of the earth has been or is being microfilmed by this society; *millions of dollars* are being spent; and a reservoir of *hundreds of millions* of *names* and other data about people who lived in past generations is available for study (McConkie, *Mormon Doctrine*, pp. 308, 309).

Comment

Genealogical records were destroyed in Jerusalem in A.D. 70 by the Romans under Titus, underlining God's closing the door on genealogies, since Jesus had come and fulfilled their purpose.

For additional information on genealogies, see chapter 10, "Priesthood and Genealogies" in this book.

8. The Bible, the Church and history cast strong doubt on the Mormon claim that they have "new" or "further" revelation. Which do you believe?

The Bible

"For I testify unto every man that heareth the words of the prophecy of this book, If any man shall add unto these things, God shall add unto him the plagues that are written in this book: And if any man shall take away from the words of the book of this prophecy, God shall take away his part out of the book of life, and out of the holy city, and from the things which are written in this book" (Rev. 22:18, 19).

"I will build my church; and the gates of hell shall not prevail against it" (Matt. 16:18).

"Beware of false prophets, who come to you in sheep's clothing, but inwardly they are ravening wolves" (Matt. 7:15).

Mormon Writers

"On the morning of a beautiful spring day in 1820 there occurred one of the most important and momentous events in this world's history. God, the Eternal Father and His Son, Jesus Christ, appeared to Joseph Smith and gave instructions concerning the establishment of the kingdom of God upon the earth in these latter days" (LeGrand Richards, *A Marvelous Work and a Wonder;* Salt Lake City, Deseret Book Co., 1971, p. 7).

"Containing *Revelations* Given to Joseph Smith, Jr. The Prophet" (*Doctrine and Covenants;* published by The Church of Jesus Christ of Latter-day Saints, 1968).

Comment

The book of Revelation gives us the picture of the church age, the tribulation, the millennium, and the consummation of all things on into the eternal state. God did not "forget" anything that would make it necessary to add a divine PS by further revelation.

"This book" in Revelation 22:18,19, certainly seems to apply primarily to the book of Revelation. However, the all-knowing God who knows the future *certainly* knew which book would be placed at the end of the Bible, and that the Bible is and was referred to as a unit, or book. It seems more than a coincidence that the most powerful warning in the Bible concerning its words or adding to its prophecies should be on the *last* page, in the *last* chapter, of the *last* book of the Bible, by the *last* prophet, with the *last* true and certain prophecies.

No prophet has arisen since biblical days who can foretell the future with the 100 percent accuracy required of a true prophet. *None*, since New Testament days, has met the test, proving conclusively that the prophetical gift of foretelling the future has been withdrawn, and that there is no "new" or further revelation from God.

For additional information see chapter 13, "The Final Authority," in this book.

9. Do you, as a Mormon, understand that opening the door to "new" or further "revelation," the truth of which is determined in part by "feeling," "testimony," or a "burning in the bosom," makes it possible for you or anyone else to claim revelations from God and construct any kind of teaching you want? Could you have confidence in a religion that is constructed from such "revelations"? Do you believe the word of a discredited "prophet" (one whose prophecies failed) who said he had "new" revelation, or do you believe the Bible?

The Bible

"But though we, or an *angel* from *heaven*, preach *any other gospel* unto you than *that which we have preached unto you*, let him be accursed" (Gal. 1:8).

"And no marvel; for Satan himself is transformed into an *angel of light*. Therefore it is no great thing if *his ministers also* be transformed as the *ministers of righteousness;* whose end shall be according to their works" (2 Cor. 11:14,15).

"Thy *Word* is a lamp unto my feet, and a *light* unto my path" (Ps. 119:105).

Mormon Writers

"I received the *First Visitation of Angels*, which was when I was about fourteen years old" (Joseph Smith, quoted in the *Deseret News*, May 29, 1852).

"By and by an obscure individual, a young man, rose up, and, in the midst of all Christendom, proclaimed the startling news that God had sent an *Angel* to him" (Orson Pratt, Apostle, *Journal of Discourses*, vol. 13; published by F.D. and S.W. Richards, Liverpool, 1854; reprint ed. Salt Lake City, Utah, 1966, pp. 65, 66).

"But behold, I say unto you, that you must study it out in your mind; then you must ask me if it be right, and if it is right I will cause that your bosom shall *burn* within you; therefore, you shall *feel* that it is right" (Joseph Smith, *Doctrine and Covenants* 9:8).

Comment

Here you see that the claims of Mormonism are similar to scores of others, such as Christian Science, that have added other "inspired" books and Rev. Moon of the Unification Church who claims he had a vision of Jesus in 1936. These teach that they have had further revelation, visits by angels, visions, etc., for the purpose of "understanding" or adding to Scripture. You also see that the proof they claim shifts your attention away from the Bible as full and final authority, so that anything goes.

Incidentally, no amount of "testimony," "burning in the bosom" or "feeling" can make Joseph Smith's prophecies come true, or turn a false prophet into a true prophet.

For additional information see chapter 13, "The Final Authority," in this book.

10. The Bible teaches that hell is eternal. Mormonism teaches that hell is not eternal punishment for all lost men. Which do you believe?

The Bible

"And these shall go away into everlasting punishment: but the righteous unto life eternal" (Matt. 25:46).

"He that believeth on the Son hath everlasting life: and he that believeth not the Son shall not see life; but the wrath of God *abideth* on him" (John 3:36).

"And whosoever was not found written in the book of life was cast into the lake of fire" (Rev. 20:15).

Mormon Writers

"Eternal punishment is God's punishment: everlasting punishment is God's punishment; or in other words it is the *name* of the punishment God inflicts. He being eternal in his nature. Whosoever, therefore, receives

God's punishment, receives eternal punishment whether it is endured one hour, one day, one week, one year, or an age" (Elder John Morgan, pamphlet, *The Plan of Salvation*, published by The Church of Jesus Christ of Latter-day Saints, 1970, p. 29).

"In The Church of Jesus Christ of Latter-day Saints, *there is no hell. All* will find a measure of salvation" (Apostle John Widtsoe, *Evidences and Reconciliations*, p. 216; same statement found in *Joseph Smith—Seeker After Truth*, Salt Lake City, 1951, pp. 177, 178).

Comment

The same Greek word from which everlasting and eternal are translated, *aionios,* is used to describe the eternal continuance of heaven, hell and God. If one is eternal all are. Revelation 14:11, picturing some of the lost already in hell, declares that they have "no rest night nor day," and that "the smoke of their torment ascendeth up forever and ever." The choice is clear, either the Bible or Mormon teaching.

For additional information, see chapter 11, "Some Distinctive but Dubious Doctrines of Mormonism."

11. The Bible teaches that David and Paul, both murderers, were forgiven and that "the blood of Jesus Christ, his Son, cleanses us from all sin." Joseph Smith's teachings say that murder is an unforgivable sin. Which do you believe?

The Bible

(After David confessed to murdering Uriah, and taking his wife, Bathsheba), "The Lord also hath put away thy sin; thou shalt not die" (2 Sam. 12:13).

"And Saul, yet breathing out threatenings and *slaughter* against the disciples of the Lord, went unto the high priest" (Acts 9:1). "And I persecuted this way unto the *death*, binding and delivering into prisons both men and women" (Acts 22:4).

"The blood of Jesus Christ, his Son, cleanseth us from all sin" (1 John 1:7).

Mormon Writers

"And, now, behold, I speak unto the church. Thou shalt not kill; and he that kills shall not have forgiveness in this world, nor in the world to come" (Joseph Smith, *Doctrine and Covenants* 42:18; also 132:26, 27; published by The Church of Jesus Christ of Latter-day Saints, 1968).

"Hopes of reward through so-called Deathbed repentance are vain" (Bruce McConkie, *Mormon Doctrine*, p. 631).

Comment

Saul was responsible for the death of Stephen and others. Yet Saul, the murderer, became Paul, the missionary, from one vital encounter with the risen Christ on the Damascus road. His sins were forgiven. He was cleansed by the blood of the Lord Jesus Christ.

For additional information see chapter 15, "Biblical Salvation," in this book.

12. The Bible teaches that all men are lost sinners needing salvation, and that only those who personally trust Christ are saved. Mormonism teaches that resurrection is salvation, and since all men will be resurrected, all men are therefore saved. They call this "general salvation." Which do you believe?

The Bible

"For all have sinned, and come short of the glory of God" (Rom. 3:23).

"And this is the will of him that sent me, that every one which seeth the Son, and believeth on him, may have everlasting life: and I will raise him up at the last day" (John 6:40).

"Jesus said unto her, I am the resurrection, and the life: he that believeth in me, though he were dead, yet shall he live: and whosoever liveth and believeth in me shall never die" (John 11:25).

"Believe on the Lord Jesus Christ, and thou shalt be saved" (Acts 16:31).

Mormon Writers

"There will be a General Salvation for *all* in the sense in which the term is generally used, but salvation, *meaning resurrection*, is not exaltation" (Stephen L. Richards, pamphlet, *Contributions of Joseph Smith*, published by The Church of Jesus Christ of Latter-day Saints, p. 5).

"*All* men are *saved* by grace alone without any act on their part, meaning they are *resurrected*" (Apostle Bruce McConkie, *What the Mormons Think of Christ*, p. 28, pamphet currently published by The Church of Jesus Christ of Latter-day Saints).

Comment

Mormons equate salvation with resurrection. Everybody is *not* automatically saved whether he believes or not. Resurrection is not salvation. There will be a resurrection to damnation for those who do not believe as well as a resurrection to salvation (John 5:28,29; Acts 24:15).

For additional information see chapter 14, "Mormon Salvation," in this book.

13. The Bible says that all salvation is by faith alone in Jesus Christ alone. Mormonism teaches that by doing good works man must make himself "worthy" of individual or personal salvation. Which do you believe?

The Bible

"As it is written, There is *none righteous, no, not one*" (Rom. 3:10).

"For I bear them [unsaved, religious Jews] record that they have a zeal of God, but not according to knowledge. For they being ignorant of God's righteousness, and going about to establish their own righteousness, have not submitted themselves unto the righteousness of God" (Rom. 10:2,3).

"He that believeth on me hath everlasting life" (John 6:47).

"Wherefore he is able also to save them to the uttermost that come unto God by him, seeing he ever liveth to make intercession for them" (Heb. 7:25).

Mormon Writers

"For we know that it is by grace that we are saved, *after all we can do*" (Joseph Smith, *Book of Mormon*, 2 Nephi 25:23).

"Redemption from personal sins can only be obtained through obedience to the requirements of the gospel, and a *life of good works*" (James Talmage, *Articles of Faith*, published by The Church of Jesus Christ of Latter-day Saints, 1952, pp. 478, 479).

Comment

As stated and proven scripturally, Christ's blood cleanses from all sin, and He saves to the *uttermost*, and there is no salvation that is fuller, higher or greater.

Good works including baptism, come *after* a person has been saved. They demonstrate salvation and prove its reality. Never does God accept our good works as a means to salvation (see Eph. 2:8,9). Baptism is also a symbol that we have been saved, not a way by which we must be saved. Acts 10:44-48 says: "While Peter yet spake these words, the Holy Ghost fell on all them which heard the word . . . Then answered Peter, Can any man forbid water, that these should not be baptized, which have received the Holy Ghost as well as we? And he commanded them to be baptized in the name of the Lord." The thief on the cross and the publican in the temple, Luke 18:9-14, were all saved without baptism.

For additional information see chapters 14 and 15.

14. The Bible teaches that we are sinners and must be born again to become children of God by receiving Christ. Mormonism teaches that we are all children of God. Which do you believe?

The Bible

"Except a man be born again, he cannot see the kingdom of God" (John 3:3).

But as many as *received him*, to *them* gave he power *to become* the *sons* of God, even to them that believe on his name" (John 1:12).

Mormon Writers

"Man is in reality a child of God . . . In the Mormon

concept the phrase, the fatherhood of God and the brotherhood of man, takes on a new and powerful meaning" (Elder Gordon B. Hinckley, pamphlet, *What of the Mormons?*; published by The Church of Jesus Christ of Latter-day Saints, 1975, p. 6).

"All men and women are in the similitude of the universal Father and Mother, and are literally the sons and daughters of Deity" (Joseph Smith, *Man: His Origin and Destiny*, pp. 351, 355).

Comment

God would not tell us to *become* children of God by receiving Christ and being born again, if we *already were* by nature children of God.

See chapter 14, "Mormon Salvation."

15. The Bible says true Christians can and do know they are saved, here and now, and they are sure of going to be with Jesus forever. Can you, as a Mormon, say that you are absolutely sure you have personal salvation right now? That you will go to the "highest" heaven to be with Jesus Christ forever?

The Bible

"These things have I written unto you that believe on the name of the Son of God; that ye may *know* that ye *have* eternal life, and that ye may believe on the name of the Son of God" (1 John 5:13).

"He that *hath* the Son *hath* life; and he that hath not the Son of God hath *not* life" (1 John 5:12).

Mormon Writers (Author's comment)

I have quoted many Mormon writers on the subject of

good works for salvation. Since we can never know when we have done enough good works, or whether we are accepted of God, if salvation in whole or in part comes by good works, it is obvious that Mormons are very uncertain about true personal salvation. I have talked with scores of Mormons, high and low in the church, and almost none of them could claim they knew for sure that they would go to the "highest" (really the only) heaven to be with Jesus Christ forever. If such a claim is made, it is usually qualified on the basis of continued good works, faithfulness to the Mormon church and ordinances, or just the general idea that since there are three heavens they surely should reach one of them. Really, Mormons do not know where they are going when they die. Their main hope is in the invention of a discredited Mormon prophet and his myth of three heavens or degrees of glory. They at least feel pretty sure they won't go to hell. However, all men will go either to heaven or hell, according to the Bible, and any other hope is a false hope.

16. The Bible tells us to beware of false Christs, and false prophets. According to Mormon prophets and writers, you as a Mormon are trusting in a different God, a different Christ, and a different way of salvation from the biblical God, Christ and the way of salvation. All of your beliefs are based on the writings of Joseph Smith, who is proven to be a discredited prophet, not a prophet of God. Do you want to face the judgment and eternity trusting the Mormon gods, or the God of the Bible?

The Bible

"And Thomas answered and said unto him, [Jesus] My Lord and my God" (John 20:28).

"If thou shalt confess with thy mouth the Lord Jesus, and shalt believe in thine heart that God hath raised him from the dead, thou shalt be saved. For with the heart man believeth unto righteousness; and with the mouth confession is made unto salvation" (Rom. 10:9,10).

Mormon Writers

"As man is, God once was: as God is, man may be" (James E. Talmage, A Study of the *Articles of Faith*, published by The Church of Jesus Christ of Latter-day Saints, 1957, p. 430).

"Christ the Word, the Firstborn, had of course attained unto the status of Godhood while yet in pre-existence" (B.R. McConkie, *What the Mormons Think of Christ*, published by The Church of Jesus Christ of Latter-day Saints, p. 36).

"He [Adam] is our Father and our God and the only God with whom we have to do" (Brigham Young, *Journal of Discourses*, vol. 1, 1966, p. 50).

"The child Jesus . . . was not begotten of the Holy Ghost" (Brigham Young, *Journal of Discourses*, vol. 1, pp. 50, 51).

"For we know that it is by grace that we are saved, after all we can do" (Joseph Smith, *Book of Mormon* 2 Nephi 25:23).

Comment

The choice is clear, Mormonism or Christianity, *Joseph Smith or Jesus Christ*.

For additional information see chapters 7 and 14 in this book.

17. The Bible teaches instant and complete personal

salvation through Jesus Christ. Mormons do not believe in instant and complete personal salvation. Which do you believe?

The Bible

"For whosoever shall *call* upon the name of the Lord shall be saved" (Rom. 10:13).

Mormon Writers

"Redemption from personal sins can only be obtained through obedience to the requirements of the Gospel, and a life of good works" (James E. Talmage, *Articles of Faith*, published by The Church of Jesus Christ of Latter-day Saints, 1952, pp. 85, 87).

Comment

How long does it take to *call*, to ask Christ to save you?

18. Would you like to ask the biblical Lord Jesus Christ to save you right now? God loves you and wants you to be saved.

Here is *exactly* how you can be saved: Just pray if you mean it, the best you know how, with all your heart, "Lord Jesus Christ, come into my heart and life. Cleanse me from all sin by your shed blood. Make me a child of God. Give me your free gift of everlasting life, and let me *know* that I am saved now and forever. I now receive you as my very own personal Lord and Saviour. In Jesus' name, Amen."

Did you mean this prayer? Then did Jesus save you? He promised that "Whosoever shall call upon the name of the Lord shall be saved" (Rom. 10:13). If you called believingly on Him, He had to save you or He lied. According to His Word He *cannot* lie! So, did He save you? You can *know* you are saved right now, not just according to your feeling, but because *God's Word says so*. To wait for feeling is to deny faith!

Now let's read John 3:36 out loud three times: "He that believeth on the Son hath everlasting life." What do you have right now according to God's Word? If you were to die right now where would you go, according to God's Word? If you *know* that Jesus has saved you according to His Word, thank Him out loud for saving you!

The reality of your salvation will be shown in your love-response in obeying and following Jesus Christ. "If a man love me, he will keep my words" (John 14:23). If you are truly saved, you will obey Christ's command. Naturally, this includes coming out of Mormonism.

You will grow in assurance and in His love as you:
(1) Attend faithfully a church that believes in the Bible and the Bible *alone,* and that believes the blood of Jesus Christ *alone* can cleanse from sin!
(2) Confess Christ in public and be baptized.
(3) Pray daily.
(4) Read the Bible daily. Start with the Gospel of John.
(5) Share Christ with others.
(6) Confess your sin instantly.
(7) Let Jesus live His life through you.
(8) Turn away from anything that would hinder you from following Christ.

Comment

Real love cares enough to tell the truth. Jesus loves

you, my Mormon friend, and so do I love you, enough to want you to be saved and be in heaven with me forever, loving and serving the Lord Jesus Christ together.

Floyd C. McElveen
Box 1717
Port Orchard
Washington 98366-0179

Bibliography

Bjornstad, James. *Counterfeits at Your Door*. Glendale, CA: Regal Books, 1979.

Budvarson, Arthur. *Book of Mormon—True or False?* Concord, Calif.: Pacific Pub. Co., 1959.

Cowan, Marvin W. *Mormon Claims Answered*. Published by Marvin W. Cowan, 1975.

Hunter, Milton R. *The Gospel Through the Ages*. Salt Lake City: Deseret Book Co., 1945.

McConkie, Bruce R. *Doctrines of Salvation*. Salt Lake City: Bookcraft, Inc., 1954.

_____*Mormon Doctrine*. Salt Lake City: Bookcraft, Inc., 1966.

_____*What the Mormons Think of Christ* (tract). Salt Lake City: Deseret News Press, no date.

McElveen, Floyd C. *The Mormon Revelations of Convenience*. Minneapolis: Bethany Fellowship, Inc., 1978.

McKay, David O. *Gospel Ideals*. Salt Lake City: The Church of Jesus Christ of Latter-day Saints, 1953.

Nelson, Dee Jay. *The Joseph Smith Papyri, Part 2*. Salt Lake City, 1978.

Richards, LeGrand. *A Marvelous Work and a Wonder*. Salt Lake City: Deseret Book Co., 1950.

Richards, Stephen L. *Contributions of Joseph Smith*. Salt Lake City: The Church of Jesus Christ of Latter-day Saints.

Roberts, B.H. *A Comprehensive History of The Church of Jesus Christ of Latter-day Saints*. Salt Lake City: Deseret News Press, 1930.

Smith, Joseph, Jr. *The Book of Mormon*. Salt Lake City: The Church of Jesus Christ of Latter-day Saints.

_____*Doctrine and Covenants*. Salt Lake City: The Church of Jesus Christ of Latter-day Saints.

_____*Inspired Version of the Holy Scriptures*. Independence: Herald Pub. House, 1955.

_____*The History of the Church of Jesus Christ of Latter-day Saints*. 6 vols. Salt Lake City: Deseret News, 1902-12.

_____*The Pearl of Great Price*. Salt Lake City: The Church of Jesus Christ of Latter-day Saints, 1958.

Smith, Joseph Fielding, comp. *Teachings of Prophet Joseph Smith*. Salt Lake City: Deseret News Press, 1958.

Talmage, James E. A Study of the *Articles of Faith*. 36th ed. Salt Lake City: The Church of Jesus Christ of Latter-day Saints, 1957.

Tanner, Jerald. *Mormonism:* A Study of Mormon History

and Doctrine. Clearfield, Utah: Utah Evangel Press, 1962.

Tanner, Jerald and Sandra. *The First Vision Examined.* Salt Lake City: Modern Microfilm Co., 1969.

———*The Changing World of Mormonism.* Chicago: Moody Press, 1979.

———*Joseph Smith's 1826 Trial.* Salt Lake City: Modern Microfilm Co., 1971.

———*Mormonism—Shadow or Reality.* Salt Lake City: Modern Microfilm Co., 1975.

Turner, Wallace. *The Mormon Establishment.* Boston: Houghton Mifflin Co., 1966.

Widtsoe, John A. *Evidences and Reconciliations.* Salt Lake City: Bookcraft, Inc., 1969.

———*Joseph Smith—Seeker After Truth.* Salt Lake City: Bookcraft, Inc., 1951.

Whitmer, David. *An Address to All Believers in Christ.* Reprint; Searcy, Ark.: Bales Bookstore, 1960.

Wilson, Robert Dick. *A Scientific Investigation of the Old Testament.* Chicago: Moody Press.

In addition to the books named above I have been in contact with the following students in Mormonism who have assisted and encouraged me: Jim Bjornstad, Jerry Urban, Wesley P. Walters, Einar Anderson, and Wally Tope.

From MORMON ILLUSION To GOD'S LOVE

Floyd C. McElveen

Table of Contents

Introduction		Pg. 3
Chapter 1	This Is The Way	Pg. 5
Chapter 2	The Christ Changed Life	Pg. 25
Chapter 3	God's Word . . . Still Infallible	Pg. 48
Chapter 4	Some Vital Differences Examined	Pg. 62
Chapter 5	Brigham Young, Adam-God, and Mormon Revelation	Pg. 71
Chapter 6	God, Gold Plates, and Joseph Smith the Prophet	Pg. 86
Chapter 7	Facing Further Facts and Fruits of Mormonism	Pg. 97

Introduction

Truly, our heart cries out with Paul, "Brethren, my heart's desire and prayer to God for Israel is, THAT THEY MIGHT BE SAVED." This is our motive, our cry to God, our appeal to Mormons. That is why this book was written, to share the love of Jesus with Mormons and bring them to a saving knowledge of Jesus Christ.

After much prayer and counsel, we have rearranged and remodeled FROM MORMON ILLUSION TO GOD'S LOVE. Even though we received many favorable comments, we believe God has led us in this move for the following reasons:

ONE. The Mormon Illusion has already dealt with Mormonism enough to reveal its unbiblical basis and show Mormons their need of the biblical Christ. Since some of the materials in this next book were a duplication, we felt it better to move right to the heart of our concern. Our purpose is to present Jesus Christ and His salvation and love as clearly and powerfully as possible.

Some of the material formerly included in this book will now be found in Chapters 3 through 7. Mormon's responses to the first edition of this entire volume, to other LDS problems, and our answers to those responses will also be found there. Please read THIS IS THE WAY first, and then by all means read the Chapters 3 through 7.

TWO. We believe the new format makes for a smoother transition into the very heart of why this book was written. We want to inform the unwary about Mormonism. We want to equip Christians to reach Mormons. Hopefully, the book will help do this. Most of all, we love Mormons and want to reach them for the Lord Jesus Christ before it is forever too late. Please, beloved Mormon friends and others, open your heart and let Jesus guide you as you read the following chapter, THIS IS THE WAY.

CHAPTER 1
This Is The Way

Step 1. ONE GOD. God loves you and wants you to know that there is only ONE GOD.

This ONE GOD created and is LORD over all the universe, stars, planets and all. Gen. 1:1. "In the beginning GOD created the heaven and earth."

Isaiah 43:10B . . . "Before Me there was NO GOD FORMED, neither SHALL there be after Me."

God was NEVER a man, and man will NEVER be GOD! As the eternal God He became the *God-man* Jesus, to die for us, but for all eternity He was God, not man.

Ps. 90:2B . . . "From everlasting (that's eternity past) to everlasting (that's eternity future) THOU ART GOD!

God never progressed, earned or attained His way to being God, HE WAS ALWAYS GOD. (The Bible mentions false gods, but to believe that other gods really exist is pagan polytheism, not Christianity.)

Clearly, there is not now, and NEVER will be, any other God on this planet or any other "world" or planet. There is forever only ONE god. Men *cannot* become Gods—none ever has, none ever will!

Isaiah 46:9B, . . . "For I am God, and there is none else; I am God, and there is none like Me." Again—43:10B . . . "Before Me there was no God formed, neither shall there be after Me!!!"

Step 2. ONE SAVIOUR, JESUS CHRIST, WHO IS ETERNALLY GOD.

Isaiah 9:6 . . . "For unto us a child is born, unto us a Son is given, and the government shall be upon His shoulders, and His name shall be called wonderful, counselor, THE MIGHTY GOD, THE EVERLASTING FATHER, the Prince of Peace." Within the nature of God there are three eternal distinctions, God the Father, God the Son, and God the Holy Spirit, and there is only ONE God. Since Jesus is repeatedly called God, we MUST accept Him as God, or we accept another Jesus. In the Bible, the Word means Jesus (John 1:14) . . . "In the beginning was the *Word,* and the Word was with God, and THE WORD WAS GOD!" Beginning here simply means, "from all time." As God was God *from all time,* so was Jesus Christ, God, FROM THE BEGINNING, FROM ALL TIME! Jesus never progressed, worked, or attained His way into being God, HE ALWAYS WAS GOD.

God forbade forever the worship of any other God, Ex. 34:14; yet Jesus accepted worship as God on many occasions. Matt. 28:9 . . . "And as they went to tell His disciples, behold Jesus met them, saying All Hail. And they came and held Him by the feet and WORSHIPPED HIM!" No wonder Thomas cried out to Jesus "My Lord and my God."

Unfortunately, Man has a sin-nature that separates him from true worship of God.

Step 3. ONE SIN-NATURE

An apple tree is an apple tree BEFORE it bears apples. It bears apples BECAUSE it is an apple tree.

So, we sin BECAUSE we have a sin-nature. An apple

tree is just as much an apple tree by nature, whether it bears one apple or a thousand! So it is with a sinner.

One sin or a thousand is *not* the point! The point is, we *all* have a sin nature that *must be changed*.

Beating the apples off the tree does NOT change the nature of the tree! So, getting rid of some sins does not change our nature!

John 3:7 . . . "Ye MUST be born again." John 1:12 tells us how . . . "To as many as received Him to THEM gave He the power to BECOME the sons of God, even to them that BELIEVE on His name."

We are NOT by nature children of God. We must receive Christ in order to BECOME the children of God.

We are sinners by Nature and Choice. Sin is the fruit of our sin-nature, of each of us as sinners. Sin is "going our own way," Isaiah 53:6. It is being the God, Manager, Boss, Lord of our own life. It is being self-centered instead of Christ-centered.   Eph. 2:8 & 9 . . . "For by grace are ye saved through faith; and that not of yourselves: it is the gift of God: Not of works, lest any man should boast." Rom. 3:10B . . . "there is NONE righteous, no not ONE."

Rom. 4:4-6 . . . "Now to Him that WORKETH (for salvation) is the reward not reckoned of grace, but of DEBT. But to Him that WORKETH NOT but BELIEVETH on Him that justifieth the UNGODLY, His FAITH is counted for righteousness.

Salvation is not by works, it is a GIFT. Personally receiving Christ, trusting Him alone to save us, is God's way of salvation.

Rom. 6:23 . . . 'For the wages of sin is death, but the GIFT of God is eternal life through Jesus Christ, our Lord."

We cannot make ourselves "worthy" of the grace of God. Salvation is a free gift for the unworthy, the undeserving, which we all are. Christ died for the "ungodly" . . . Rom. 5:6.

A dog does not bark in order to become a dog. He barks because he already is a dog. His barking helps demonstrate the fact! Just so, we do not do good works in order to become Christians (be saved). We do good works *after* we are saved (become Christians) to demonstrate the fact that we have been saved!

"All our righteousnesses are as filthy rags." . . . Isaiah 64:6B.

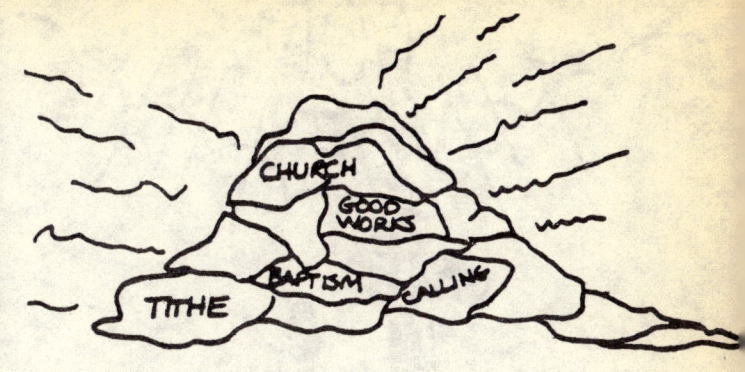

BEFORE SALVATION

Step 3. ONE SIN-NATURE (CONT'D). We are sinners by nature and choice.

Rom. 3:23 . . . "For ALL have sinned and come short of the glory of God." This means we are all LOST sinners.

BESIDES

How much *Good Works*
can a *Dead* man do?

As natural men we are ALL,
"DEAD in trespasses and sins." Eph. 2:1B.

Although salvation is not by works, true salvation always produces a changed life. Christ comes in by personal invitation as Lord and Saviour to change our life, and live His life through us.

THE BLOOD OF JESUS CHRIST, GOD'S SON, CLEANSES US FROM ALL SIN. I John 1:9

Too Late After Death!

Now Is The Time To Be Saved!

Step 4. ONE CHANCE.

II Cor. 6:2B . . . "Now is the accepted time, NOW is the day of salvation." There is NO chance after death. Heb. 9:27 . . . "And as it is appointed unto men once to die, but AFTER THIS THE JUDGMENT!" There is NO general salvation for all men because of Christ's death, but ONLY individual salvation for those who believe. John 3:36 . . . "He that *believeth* on the Son hath everlasting life; and he that BELIEVETH NOT THE SON SHALL NOT SEE LIFE: BUT THE WRATH OF GOD ABIDETH ON HIM!" All men are resurrected, but the unsaved dead are resurrected to DAMNATION, not salvation (John 5:29; Rev. 20:3-6).

Rev. 20:15 . . . "And whosoever was not found written in the book of life was cast into the lake of fire." Nowhere in the Bible is anyone EVER said to have been saved after they died. Today is the day of salvation.

Matt. 7:13 . . . "Enter in at the narrow gate; for wide is the gate, and broad is the way, that leadeth to destruction, and many there be who go in that way;"

Vs. 14 . . . "Because straight is the gate and narrow is the way, which leadeth unto life, and few there be that find it."

According to God's Word, the vast multitude of men are on the road to Hell, and to the resurrection unto damnation, John 5:29, unless they personally invite Christ into their life as Lord and Savior.

Death ends all hope for the lost.

SIN NATURE—SINNER

John 3:7 . . . "Ye MUST be born again."

Suppose a pig tried to become a sheep by ACTING like a sheep. Suppose the pig were clothed in sheep wool, ate sheep feed and even learned to bleat like a sheep. Would that *change* its pig nature and make it a sheep?

Would it matter whether or not the pig was "good" or "bad" by pig standards? So it is with trying to *act* like a Christian in order to become a Christian! It takes a miracle—the new birth, to make one a child of God, a Christian.

Step 5. ONE WAY OF SALVATION.

Jesus alone can cleanse us from sin and change our nature. I Peter 2:24 . . . "Who His own self bore our sins

NEW NATURE—CHRISTIAN

in His own body on the tree." *Not* just Adam's sin, but our own personal sins. Jesus took our place and shed His blood to cleanse us from sin. No amount of "good works" could wash away one sin or change our nature.

Salvation is instant. The moment we repent and turn to Jesus from our sins He saves us. "Just as I am without one plea, but that thy blood was shed for me."

Christ said to the unbaptized, unsaved, no good works, thief on the cross, in INSTANT salvation response to the thief's believing call; Luke 23:43B . . . "Today shalt thou be with Me in paradise." (The place Paul saw as the Heaven of God, I Cor. 12:2-4.) INSTANT salvation for a harlot. Luke 7:50B . . . "Go thy way, thy faith HATH SAVED THEE!" INSTANT salvation in response to the publicans believing call. Luke 18:14A . . . "This man went down to his house justified."

Saul the murderer was changed to Paul the Apostle from one vital encounter with the living Christ.

Salvation includes accepting Jesus Christ as both Lord (*our* God, Lord, new manager) and Saviour. It involves heart (the ruling, governing, choosing, center of our being) belief. Rom. 10:9 . . . "That if thou shalt confess with thy mouth the Lord Jesus (Jesus as Lord) and shalt believe in thine HEART that God hath raised Him from the dead, thou SHALT be saved.

We thus turn from our sins, our self, and our way to God's way. When we believingly call on the Lord Jesus Christ, He enters our life, cleanses us from sin, makes us children of God by the new birth, and gives us the free gift of salvation, with new, abundant, everlasting life. Heaven becomes our certain home, and His peace our possession.

There is no magic in the few puffs of air emitted from our vocal cords as we call on Christ. Yet He said, "Out of the abundance of the *heart* a man speaketh." If our call is from the heart, using our God-given power of choice to believe in Christ, *God Always Responds* and *Saves! He Promised!*

Salvation is simple. Rom 10:13 . . . "For WHOSOEVER shall CALL upon the name of the Lord, SHALL BE SAVED!"

We must personally CALL *believingly* on Jesus to save us. This is *how* we RECEIVE HIM. If we do so call, He MUST save us or God would be lying, and God CANNOT lie. If Jesus loved us enough to die in bloody agony to save us, would He then turn us down when we called on Him? OF COURSE NOT!

"THE BLOOD OF JESUS CHRIST, GOD'S SON, CLEANSES US FROM ALL SIN." I John 1:9

God loves you and wants you to be saved. Would you like to receive Jesus as your Lord and Saviour right now?

Just pray, if you mean it the best you know how, with all your heart, this prayer, or a similar one.

"Lord Jesus Christ, come into my heart and life. Cleanse me from all sin by your shed blood. Make me a child of God. Give me your free gift of everlasting life, and let me know that I am saved, now and forever. I NOW receive you as my very own personal Lord and Saviour. In Jesus' name, amen."

Did Jesus save you or did He lie? He HAD to do one or the other according to Rom. 10:13, if you called believingly on Him. Which did He do?

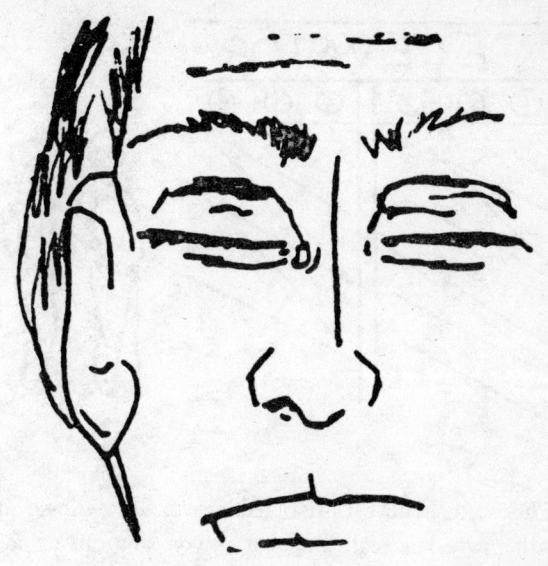

SALVATION IS CERTAIN.

You can *know* you are saved, not just by *feeling*, but because God's Word says so! Memorize John 3:36A . . . *read it three times* . . . "He that believeth on the Son HATH everlasting life." What do you have right NOW according to God's Word? Where would you go if you were to die right now, according to God's Word?

If you KNOW that Jesus has saved you, according to His Word, please thank Him out loud for saving you as you pray.

I John 5:13A . . . "These things have I written unto you that believe on the name of the Son of God, that ye may KNOW that ye HAVE ETERNAL LIFE.

Choose to believe Christ, feelings or no feelings, and He will prove His reality to you as you step out on faith that He has kept His word and saved you. Three men step aboard an elevator bound for the third floor where they all want to go. One is laughing, one is crying, one is poker-faced and unemotional. All three of them get to the third floor, regardless of their feelings, because they BELIEVED the elevator would get them to the third floor, acted on their belief and committed themselves to the elevator. So it is with trusting Christ, feelings or no feelings.

The reality of your salvation will be shown in your love-response in obeying and following Jesus Christ. John 14:23A . . . "If a man love Me, he WILL (not if, maybe and/or but) keep My words." If you are truly saved, you *will* obey!

To work FOR salvation shows UNBELIEF in the sufficiency of Jesus Christ alone to save us.

However, true salvation, true faith, ALWAYS PRODUCES good works! James 2:20 . . . "But wilt thou know, O vain man, that *faith without works is DEAD.*"

Apple trees do *not* have to produce apples in order to become an apple tree! Apples are products of the tree and prove that it is an apple tree. So, good works *never* produce a Christian, they merely *prove he is one*.

II Cor. 5:17 . . . "Therefore if any man is IN CHRIST, he is a NEW CREATION, old things are passed away; behold, all things are become new."

We must have salvation in order to *demonstrate* it, just as we must HAVE a car BEFORE we can demonstrate it!

True Christians Produce Good Works.

Find a church that makes salvation clear, that believes the Bible, and the Bible *alone,* that believes the blood of Christ alone can cleanse from sin. Attend church *faithfully*. Heb. 10:25 and I John 3:14. Follow Christ in baptism to picture your sins being washed away, AFTER you have been saved, Acts 10:47, 48 and to picture your death with Christ to the old life, and your resurrection with Him to new life. Pray daily, I Thess. 5:13, John 15:7. Confess sin instantly, I John 1:9. (A Christian can sin, but a true Christian cannot continue habitually in sin. I John 3:9.) Read the Bible daily, Acts 17:11, I Peter 2:2.

Confess Christ publically. Luke 12:8-9.

Share Christ with others constantly. Acts 1:8.

Begin memorizing at least a verse a week. Thank God every day that Jesus has saved you and thank Him for all things, good and bad. I Thess. 5:18.

Obey Him, believe Him, feelings or no feelings, by faith.

Believe Him for His victory, thank Him and step out on faith and He will prove His victory in your experience.

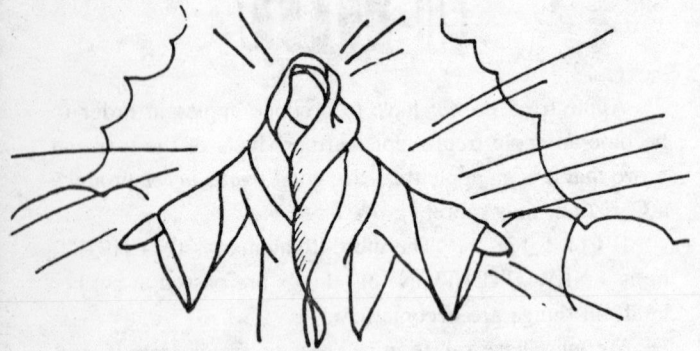

Step 6. ONE HEAVEN.

John 14:3 . . . "And if I go and prepare a place (one ONLY, not THREE), I will come again and receive you unto myself . . . that where I (JESUS) am, THERE ye may be also!" Matt. 13:24 . . . "And then shall He send His angels and shall GATHER TOGETHER His elect, from the four winds, from the uttermost part of the earth to the uttermost part of heaven." I Thess. 4:16-17 . . . "For the Lord Himself shall descend from heaven with a shout, with the voice of the archangel, and with the trump of God; and the dead in Christ shall rise first; then we which are alive and remain shall be caught up together with them in the clouds, to meet the Lord in the air, and so shall we ever be with the Lord."

Jesus will be in the HIGHEST HEAVEN, the ONLY Heaven of God, and all His people will be with Him forever.

The Heaven of God is sometimes called the third heaven, to distinguish it from the other two heavens, one of the stars and planets, and one of the clouds and atmosphere.

This third heaven is the ONLY Heaven of God, and all the church-age saints will be with Him forever in heaven. It is where both Paul and the thief on the cross went, as paradise is also called the third heaven. Compare Luke 23:43 with II Cor. 12:2-4.

Jesus will reign as Lord of Lords in this HIGHEST HEAVEN, the ONE Heaven of God, and all true Christians will be with Him forever.

Christian families will be together forever, *not* separated on different planets as "Gods."

ONE HEAVEN OF CLOUDS & ATMOSPHERE
Ps. 147:7, Deut. 28:12.

ONE HEAVEN OF SUN, MOON, STARS & PLANETS
Gen. 1:17

Since in heaven we will be one family in Christ, and since He is called our heavenly bridegroom desiring and deserving our fullest love and adoration, marriage and reproduction there have forever ceased. Matt. 22:30 . . . "For in the resurrection they neither *marry,* nor are given in marriage, but are as ANGELS OF GOD in heaven." God is clearly saying here that there is NO MARRIAGE, and NO STATE OF BEING MARRIED in heaven, as we will be like the angels there. The angels of God are always mentioned in the masculine gender. They are NOT married, there are no "angel babies," being born in heaven. Sex in the human sense is not mentioned of them.

ONE HEAVEN OF GOD Isa. 66:1

TO THOSE WHO HAVE JUST ACCEPTED CHRIST!

To wait for feeling to believe Christ is to deny faith. Feeling will come in God's time, however, AFTER you have chosen by your *will* to believe God's Word and fully trust, commit yourself to, Christ. Salvation includes joy, but only AFTER the will has chosen Him by faith.

Let Jesus live His life through you, that's true Christianity. Share Christ by life and lip. God's purpose is now yours. Reach the lost at any cost. Acts 1:8, Luke 19:10, John 20:21.

Lay aside anything in your life that would hinder you, shame Christ, or cause others to stumble. *He* is your victory, I Cor. 15:57, Gal. 5:16. Surrender daily to the Holy Spirit's control of your life.

Finally, begin THIS SUNDAY a life of faithfulness to Christ by attending a gospel preaching church. We do not decide Monday morning whether we are going to work or not, that is a settled conclusion. Neither, if we are really serious Christians (neither deceiving ourselves or being deceived), do we decide on Sunday morning whether or not we are going to church? If we truly love Jesus that was settled forever when we committed our lives to Him. Now we *Follow Him!*

REMEMBER:

To work FOR salvation shows UNBELIEF in the sufficiency of Jesus Christ alone to save us.

However, true salvation, true faith, ALWAYS PRODUCES good works! James 2:10 . . . "But wilt thou know, O vain man, that faith without works is DEAD."

Please share with us your decision for Christ or desire for more information by mailing the response card in this book. It would help us if you indicated the topic for which you are seeking additional information.

HIGHLY RECOMMENDED READING:
"MORMONISM, SHADOW OR REALITY,"
"THE CHANGING WORLD OF MORMONISM," Jerald & Sandra Tanner
"MORMON CLAIMS ANSWERED," Marvin Cowan
"TO MORONI WITH LOVE," Ed Decker
"BEYOND MORMONISM: AN ELDER'S STORY," James Spencer
"MORMONISM, MAMA AND ME," Thelma Geer

If you have difficulty finding any of these books, please contact Gospel Truths for help.

ADDRESS OF THE AUTHOR:
Floyd C. McElveen
Box 1717
Port Orchard, WA 98366-0179
(Sketches by Ginger Lake—some based on originals by Karen Davis)

Beloved Mormon friends, a great exodus is beginning to take place from the Mormon church. At the very time when Mormons have recently doubled in number, God is beginning to work in His great love and power. The "You took it out of context," "Why do you teach such lies about Mormonism?", "Why are you persecuting us?" excuses have worn thin for many heart-hungry Mormons. The references from Mormon sources are given and many intelligent Mormons are checking them out and finding what we say is not "out of context," but exactly what their leaders taught, said, and did. Only dishonest people would claim something is out of context unless they have fully checked out the context the statement comes from; otherwise, it is only a shallow excuse which honest Mormons will not use. In just the last several years, thousands of Mormons have turned to Christ. Some, of course, and we say this with real tears, will never believe, having their minds blinded by Satan. Others have hardened their hearts until God has sent them "strong delusion that they should believe a lie, that they all might be damned who believe not the truth . . ." II Thess. 2:11-12. However, Mormonism shows definite signs of crumbling, and we plead with you, Mormon friends, if you value your soul, if you really care about your loved ones, if you really want true salvation, turn to the Biblical Christ and away from Mormonism while there is yet time.

The hour is late, the need is urgent. In the name of Jesus, I beseech you, please act now! If you need help or desire further documentation please write Gospel Truths immediately.

Floyd C. McElveen

CHAPTER 2
The Christ Changed Life
John 14:23
New Life Discipleship Follow-up

This chapter will introduce you to God's way of growth in your new Christian life. The eight headings below are discussed in some detail. As Jesus clearly said in John 14:23, ". . . If a man love me he WILL keep my words . . ." True salvation results in love for and obedience to Jesus Christ.

1. Be baptized. Acts 2:41, 16:31-33, Acts 10:47-48.
2. Confess Christ before men. Luke 12:8-9, Rom. 10:9-10.
3. Attend church faithfully. Heb. 10:25, I John 3:14.
4. Read the Bible daily . . . Study it . . . Memorize special verses. I Peter 2:2, II Tim. 2:15, Ps. 1:2, 119:1, Joshua 1:8, Col. 3:16-17.
5. Pray daily, I Thess. 5:17, Jeremiah 33:3, Rom. 8:32, Matt. 18:19, 21:22, I John 5:14-15.
6. Confess sin instantly. Proverbs 28:13, I John 1:9.
7. Share Christ . . . Witness . . . Win the lost. Acts 1:8, Proverbs, 11:30, Luke 5:10, 19:10, John 20:21, Psalms 126:6.
8. Let Jesus live His life through you. I Cor 15:57, Col. 3:1-4, Gal. 2:20, 5:16. Live not by feeling, but by faith. Faith-root, feeling-fruit.

DECISION, PLEASE

The definite decision for Christ is necesary and important. Life or death, Heaven or Hell, hinge upon this decision. That is why we stress the need of crystallizing belief into a concrete act of accepting Christ. We are told in the Bible to call, to receive, to be born again, to open the door.

Agrippa believed the prophets, Paul said, but was not a Christian; he did not personally receive the risen Christ. The devils believe and tremble, God says, but they are doomed to Hell forever. Obviously then, there is a belief which falls short of saving faith in Christ, short of the act of receiving Him as Saviour and Lord, unconditionally.

A young man can love a young woman and she can return that love; yet they can remain apart in deepest frustration and sorrow until death. They do not belong to each other until in the simple act of marriage each consents to receive the other and forsake all others. So it is with Christ. One may profess to believe in Him, to love Him, and yet never receive Him, call on Him, open the door to Him for salvation. Saving faith then requires the act of calling on and receiving Christ and being born into the family of God. Then we are new creatures with new desires, new power, and new life (II Cor. 5:17).

Regardless then of how much we convince ourselves we love Him and believe in Him, we must call on Him, receive Him, open the door to Him, invite Him in by a definite decision or act of faith as the Bible says. Rom. 10:13 . . . "For whosoever shall call upon the name of the Lord shall be saved."

HOW TO DO IT

If you are willing to make this definite decision for Christ right now, you may pray after this manner:

"Dear God, I confess that I am a sinner. I believe that you sent your Son to die on the cross for my sins. I want to receive Jesus into my heart, and I do open my heart and life to Him right now. Dear Jesus, come into my life and be my Lord and Saviour."

To further nail down this definite decision, you may wish to sign your name to the following statement:

I have today received Jesus Christ as my Lord and Saviour. I am claiming by faith His promise of sins forgiven and His gift of eternal life.

Signed: _____

Date: _____

WELCOME TO GOD'S FAMILY

Congratulations! You have just become a child of God! You have just been born-again, born from above, born of the Spirit of God into the forever family of God! You are a new creation in Christ. Your sins are washed away by His shed blood. You have a new future, a new family, and a new Father! We have just shown you from God's Word how you can be saved and know it for sure from Rom. 10:13, John 3:36, and I John 5:13 (We suggest you memorize these verses). You can rejoice with all your heart that Jesus is yours and you are His forever, that Heaven and not Hell is your eternal home, and that He will be with you in a new and vital way now and forever. Salvation is instant but, the results last forever!

Choose to believe Christ, feelings or no feelings, and He will prove His reality to you as you step out on faith that He has kept His word and saved you, when you called believingly on Him. Rom. 10:13 . . . "For whosoever shall call upon the name of the Lord shall be saved." Since God cannot lie, you can now KNOW that Jesus has saved you, according to God's Word.

NOTE: This important illustration one more time!

Three men step aboard an elevator bound for the third floor where they all want to go. One is laughing, one is crying, one is pokerfaced, unemotional. All three of them get to the third floor, regardless of their feelings, because they BELIEVED the elevator would get them to the third floor, acted on their belief, and COMMITTED THEMSELVES to the elevator. So it is with trusting Christ, feelings or no feelings.

The reality of your salvation will be shown in your love-response in obeying and following Christ. John 14:23 . . . ". . . if a man love me, he WILL (not if, maybe, and/or but!) keep my words." If you are truly saved, you *will* obey! Clearly, obedience does not save you, or help you get saved, or help you stay saved. Eph. 2:8, 9 . . . "For by grace are ye saved through faith; and that *not of yourselves; it is the gift* of God; *not of works,* lest any man should boast."

Just as clearly, the love-response to Christ of good works, because of gratitude and love, because of His new life in you, will flow from you when truly saved. James says emphatically, James 2:20 . . . "But wilt thou know O vain man, that faith without works is dead?" Titus warns also, Titus 1:16 . . . "They profess that they know God; but in works they deny Him, being abominable, and disobedient, and unto every good work reprobate." Jesus gave a parable in Luke 8:5-18 which speaks powerfully to these shallow head, but not heart believers, also. Read it!!!

Finally, Heb. 6:9 unequivocally states, "But, beloved,

we are persuaded better things of you, and things that accompany salvation though we thus speak."

To sum up: To work FOR salvation shows unbelief in the sufficiency of Jesus Christ alone to save you. However, true salvation, true faith always produces good works. An apple tree is an apple tree before it ever produces an apple. It produces apples because it *already is* an apple tree, *never* in order *to become* an apple tree. So it is with the Christian, good works demonstrate the salvation we already have. Obedience is the proof that we have been saved, our love-response to our Saviour, the evidence of the new life now dwelling in us, and enables us to grow in Him.

As II Cor. 5:17 declares . . . "Therefore if any man be in Christ, he is a new creature; old things are passed away; behold all things are become new." How delightful! How exciting!

Now let me share with you how to begin and continue with your new life of love-response, obedience and growth in Christ. As a real child of God, I know you will be ready to obey the Lord Jesus Christ, just as God's Word says you will in John 14:23.

1. BE BAPTIZED

The waters of baptism cannot wash away one sin. That was done the moment you were saved by the shed blood of the Lord Jesus Christ. But God commanded that we be baptized as soon as we have been saved. Just as the approximately 3,000 converts in Acts 2:41 were baptized the day they were saved, and the jailer in Philippi was baptized the very night he believed and was saved, Acts 16:31-33, so we should be baptized as soon as possible after we are saved. Baptism is an outward picture of an inward cleansing by the blood of Christ. It comes after salvation; before salvation it has no value or meaning. It pictures on the outside what Christ has already done on the inside. Even more important, Biblically, it pictures our death to the old life with Jesus, identifies us with His death for us, identifies us with His burial for us as we go down under the water of Baptism, and identifies us with His risen life as we rise from the water of Baptism as He bodily arose from the grave. We are thus publically forever declaring our identification with the Lord Jesus Christ, our death to the old life, and declaring our new life in Him. Acts 10:47, 48, clearly shows the order, salvation, then baptism. See also Rom. 6:1-4.

Baptism is by immersion since that is exactly what the original word meant, and since that alone fulfills the picture of death, burial, and resurrection which the Bible presents as a picture of our identification with Christ.

Stated another way, when we have been saved, God counts it that we died with Christ in His death, were buried with Him, and rose with Him to new life. Baptism pictures this! Beautiful! *Do it,* not in order to be saved, but because you have *already* been saved, and now want to fully love and obey Him!!

2. CONFESS CHRIST BEFORE MEN

Luke 12:8, 9 . . . "Also I say unto you, whosoever shall confess me before men, him shall the Son of man also confess before the angels of God: But he that denieth Me before men shall be denied before the angels of God."

Open, public confession of Jesus Christ is Biblical evidence and confirmation of salvation. That is why many of our churches give public invitations so that before a friendly, loving crowd praying for just such miracles, you may acknowledge Christ. *God* commanded confession before men. If those early disciples in Jerusalem had declared that salvation was a private thing between them and God only, and had refused to confess God before men, often hostile, murderous men, the gospel would have never spread beyond Jerusalem, and we would be on our way to Hell without a Saviour! So *confess Christ before men,* in church as a good beginning, and wherever God leads. It is tremendously strengthening!

3. ATTEND CHURCH FAITHFULLY

Heb. 10:25 . . . "Not forsaking the assembling of ourselves together, as the manner of some is, but exhorting one another; and so much the more, as ye see the day approaching." "Assembly" and "church" have virtually the same meaning in this context, so God is saying not to forsake the "churching" of ourselves together. The New Testament knows nothing of a true Christian living in isolation from the local church. We immediately become part of the body of Christ upon our salvation. Each of us have gifts to share with one another; we form different but essential parts of the body of Christ. We attend church both to give and receive. God gave godly men with special gifts to serve the church, officers called pastors to oversee and feed us, and deacons also. He carefully created the church, and gave special ordinances to the church, Baptism and the Lord's Supper. He is not about to ignore His beloved church, and meet with some disobedient Christian gone A.W.O.L. in the woods or in some "spiritual" fellowship that bypasses His church. Frankly, to despise the local church is to despise the Lord of the local church, whether one is aware of it or not. The Bible says that Christ is the head of the church, and the church is His body. Just as it would be nonsense to marry a person's head and have nothing to do with their body, so it would be nonsense to "marry" Christ, (be joined to Him eternally through conversion) and have nothing to do with His body, the church. It is true there are sometimes hypocrites in the church, but that only proves the Bible true, for Christ predicted such in His parable of the tares and wheat. He will tend to that in due time.

The thrilling thing is that you are now a part of the family of God, filled with brothers and sisters with whom you will spend eternity! Sharing their joys and burdens, being discipled to be more and more like Jesus Christ, to His glory!

So, ATTEND CHURCH FAITHFULLY! This is one of the surest evidences that you have truly been saved. I John 3:14 . . . "We know that we have passed from death unto life, because we LOVE the brethren . . ." If we love Jesus and the brethren we will be delighted to be with them in church.

Be sure to find a church that clearly believes the Bible, and the Bible only, to be the inspired, infallible Word of God. Find a church that believes that Jesus Christ's blood cleanses from sin and that depends on Him alone for salvation.

4. READ THE BIBLE DAILY

I Peter 2:2 . . . "As newborn babes, desire the sincere milk of the Word, that ye may grow thereby." As food is to you physically, so the Word of God is to you now spiritually. Ask God to help you understand each time you read it, and He will. Start with the gospel of John, then read I John, then the New Testament, and then the Old Testament. God's Word gives growth, strength, helps you to avoid sin, (Psalms 119:11), illuminates your daily walk with God, brings peace, knowledge and wisdom, heightens joy, and lessens danger. Joshua 1:8, Psalms 1:2, Col. 3:16-17. If possible, it is best to read your Bible and pray early in the morning before facing the day, just as it is best to tune your instruments before playing in the orchestra; but any time is acceptable. It has been well said, "This book will keep you from sin, or sin will keep you from this book." *Memorize special verses!* (See also II Tim. 2:15).

5. PRAY DAILY . . . AND MORE OFTEN!

I Thess. 5:17 . . . "Pray without ceasing." You now have a hot-line to heaven through the Lord Jesus Christ. God *promises* to answer prayer. (Jeremiah 33:3, Matt. 18:19, Matt. 21:22, I John 5:14-15) Reading the Bible is God talking to you, prayer is you talking to God (tho' He speaks to your heart as you pray, also) and witnessing is your talking for God. Praise God, worship Him, thank Him, and ask Him for your needs believingly every day. *Very important:* tell the Lord Jesus Christ, preferably out loud, every day, that you love Him and thank Him for dying on the cross for you and giving you eternal life. It is amazing what this will do for you, in warmth, love, and abiding fellowship. *(It turns your mountains into molehills!)*

Together, prayer and Bible-study form the essence of our communication with Jesus. Love in its practical application is spelled T-I-M-E. The quintessence of our love for

God is expressed and enhanced by the time we spend with Him in prayer and Bible-study. Those who profess to have no time for prayer and Bible-study may call into questions the reality of their relationship with Jesus Christ. A person claiming that he has no time for Bible-study, for prayer, to live for God, is like a bird declaring that it has no time to fly, or a fish claiming it has no time to swim. For this, they were created. To love God, spend time with Him, get to really know Him and serve Him, for this, we were created. At the very least, neglect insures leanness of soul, defeat and heartbreak instead of triumph and joy. Through prayer and Bible-study we tap God's love and power, and grow into mature Christians established in doctrine and practice, and most of all Christlikeness. The fruit of the Spirit, love, joy, peace, longsuffering, gentleness, goodness, faith, meekness, temperance, will flow from us to His glory and attract others to Him! Besides, what a thrill it is to see the God of the universe answering your prayers.

It is probably true that no Christian is any stronger, or better, or greater, than his prayer life! It is doubtful if anything worthwhile has ever been accomplished except by prayer . . . often much prayer. Even as a new babe in Christ, like the first call of a baby to its mother, your prayers are very precious to God. Begin the habit of prayer and Bible-study right now. Perhaps the greatest reward of all is that, as you daily focus in on Christ through prayer and Bible-study, you become like Him! II Cor. 3:18. As a plant looks to the sun and is transformed by photosynthesis, so let us look to Jesus in prayer and Bible-study, and we will be transformed into His likeness by Christosynthesis! Christ now actually dwells in you and intercedes for you! Pray in confidence and boldness in His name.

6. CONFESS SIN INSTANTLY . . . HONESTLY . . . AND AVOID IT!

Prov. 28:13 . . . "he that covereth his sins shall not prosper, but whosoever confesseth and forsaketh them shall have mercy." Christians can still sin, because although we have a new nature, we still have the old nature, but God has made provision in Christ. I John 1:9 . . . "If we confess our sins, He is faithful and just to forgive us our sins, and to cleanse us from all unrighteousness." Instant confession, of the thought before the deed is done, avoids much sorrow and heartbreak, but thought or deed should be confessed to God, for instant forgiveness and virtually unbroken fellowship, turning by His strength from that which caused us to stumble. Remember, a Christian can sin, but a true Christian cannot live in sin.

First, because when we came to Christ, we repented of our sins (changed our minds about sin, self and the Saviour) turning from self and sin as the Lord of our life (Rom. 10:9 . . . "That is thou shalt confess with thy mouth the Lord Jesus [literally, *Jesus as Lord*], and shalt believe in thine heart that God hath raised Him from the dead, thou shalt be saved.") *Secondly,* because, though we are sometimes surprised by sin, I John 3:9 tells us, "Whosoever is born of God doth not commit (habitually practice or continue in, literally) sin." To illustrate, a pig and a sheep could be taken, washed, perfumed, beribboned, petted and kept in one's home. But if someone left the door open, the pig would head for the first mudhole and wallow happily in it; that is the pig nature. The sheep might fall into the same mudhole, ('I've seen some very dirty sheep'), but would get out as quickly as possible. It is not a sheep's nature to wallow happily in a mudhole, even though it might fall into it, and so it is with the true Christian. He can never again wallow happily in sin, and will seek to flee from temptation, to avoid sin, but he can still sin. *Thirdly,* we are told, I John 2:15 . . . "Love not the world (not speaking of trees, birds, etc. but the wicked world system presided over by Satan) neither the things that are in the world. If any man love the world, the love of the Father is not in him." Sin and the world are what Jesus saved us from. There is no point in going back into them any more than there would be for Lazarus to crawl back into the tomb, after Jesus raised him from the dead, to have fellowship with rotting corpses. The Bible says we have passed "from death to life," and these are the things of death. Nevertheless, when we do sin, instant confession and instant forgiveness are the answer. Sonship can never be broken; fellowship can, and sin breaks fellowship between us and God. Agreeing with God about our sin honestly in confession instantly restores that sweet fellowship. (See God's promise in I Cor. 10:13!)

7. WITNESS . . . SHARE CHRIST WITH OTHERS . . . WIN THE LOST!

Acts 1:8 . . . "But ye shall receive power, after that the Holy Ghost is come upon you; and ye shall be witnesses unto me both in Jerusalem, and in all Judea, and in Samaria, and unto the uttermost part of the earth." Also, Matt. 4:19 . . . "And He saith unto them, 'Follow me, and I will make you fishers of men.' " (Those not fishing, call into question the reality of their following, obviously.) We are saved to be conformed to the image of Christ, to bring glory to Him. However, the very heart of this is sharing Christ and winning others to Him. *Purpose* . . . Luke 5:10B . . . ". . . from henceforth thou shalt CATCH men. (Actually, WIN them, NOT just fish for them.) *Promise* . . . "He that goeth forth and weepeth, bearing precious seed shall doubtless come again rejoicing, bringing his sheaves (the *harvest, souls*) with him." Prov. 11:30 . . . "The fruit of the righteous is a tree of life; and he that winneth souls is wise." See Dan. 12:3, and Ezek. 33:8. *Priority* . . . Luke 19:10 . . . "For the Son of Man is come to seek and save that which was lost." His Priority and Purpose . . . John 20:21 . . . "Then said Jesus to them again, 'Peace be unto you; AS THE FATHER HAS SENT ME, EVEN SO I SEND I YOU.' " . . . now becomes our Priority and Purpose! May we also, by His loving grace, be consumed as was Paul, with his passion for the Lost . . . for His great heaviness and continual heart sorrow, caused Him to cry out, Rom. 9:3 . . . "For I could wish that myself were accursed from Christ for my brethren, my kinsmen according to the flesh."

Winning souls!! . . . THIS is the one thing we can do to make Jesus and the angels of HEAVEN rejoice! (Luke 15:9-10) There is also rejoicing in the hearts of those reached for Christ, and rejoicing in our own hearts, and in the church!

God's command and Christ's love within compel us to witness and win souls to our Savior. Also, more souls being saved, more people being conformed to His image, brings *more glory to Him.* Other motives: the joy of sharing good news, seeing messed-up lives transformed and made abundant here and how in this life, desire to share heaven with as many as possible, the growth and joy that occurs in oneself as we witness and share Him, the demonstration of the power and compassion of Christ, and last but not least, *saving precious lost souls from the awfulness of an eternity in the lake of fire!!* Truly, if salvation is the most important thing ever to happen to us, and it is, and if we "Love our neighbors as ourselves" as God commands, then love constrains us to share Christ with them to deliver them from sin and Hell. This is the most wonderful privilege and purpose known to man, sharing Christ, and winning the lost to glorify Him forever!

Begin by sharing what Christ has done for you and tell those to whom you witness how it can happen to them. Share the Bible verses that brought you salvation and assurance in Christ. You will become more and more effective as you revel in His love, learn His word, and share Him more and more with others.

8. LET JESUS LIVE HIS LIFE THROUGH YOU!

I Cor. 15:57 . . . "But thanks be to God which giveth us the victory through our Lord Jesus Christ." We cannot live the Christian life in our strength, He clearly said, "without Me ye can do nothing," but we can live it in HIS strength. Letting Jesus daily live His life through you, being filled and controlled by His Holy Spirit, Eph. 5:18, takes much of the strain out of Christian life. Thus we can, Rom. 6:11 . . . ". . . reckon ye also yourselves to be dead indeed unto sin, but alive unto God through Jesus Christ our Lord." And we can, Gal. 5:16 . . . ". . . Walk in the Spirit, and ye shall not fulfill the lust of the flesh." We are NOT to live by feelings, but by FAITH, and as we step out on God's Word, feelings or not, we will find His Word true, His presence real, and the feelings ultimately will follow, as the *fruit*, never the *root* of our Christian life. The surrender mentioned in Rom. 12:1-2 is the reasonable step for a serious Christian, and Rom. 8:28 will leap to life and make I Thess. 5:18 its expression! Now that you are His, bought by His blood, give Him cheerfully and willingly, *first,* yourself, *followed* by your time, talents and treasure (tithes and offerings), Mal. 3:10, I Cor. 16:1-2. Love is the compelling motive in the Christian life, not legalism, which can be a slavish, mechanical obedience to stated laws out of fear or force, bringing constraint and unhappiness.

Thus a young wife could obey a list of rules posted daily by her husband. Yet love, a higher motive, an inner response to share and/or surrender to someone else for their good, would cause the young wife to seek ways to please her husband, rules or no rules, and something he expressed that she knew would please him would bring joyous response. This response would be done in complete freedom and bring happiness and peace. So it is with the Christian and Christ. Obeying is not legalism, it is the *attitude,* the motive, toward rules, toward obedience, which determines that. We cannot merit growth, but we can cease to hinder His love working in us by obeying rather than disobeying. Some have stretched the grace of God to cover living in disobedience to Him. It is true that God loves us as much when we fail as He did before we failed, and that is wonderful! It is also true that when I picked up my babies because I loved them, if they had a dirty diaper, I did not love them less, nevertheless, I hastened to change the diaper, and so does God. He does not, He cannot leave us in the state in which He found us. Those who turn back— never real—are covered in I John 2:19 and Luke 8:5-18. READ!!

This is what the true grace of God, the unmerited favor, the free flow of His marvelous love on undeserving sinners REALLY does ... Titus 2:11-14 ... "For the grace of

God that bringeth salvation hath appeared to all men, teaching us that, DENYING UNGODLINESS AND WORLDLY LUSTS, WE SHOULD LIVE SOBERLY, RIGHTEOUSLY, AND GODLY, IN THIS PRESENT WORLD, looking for that blessed hope, and the glorious appearing of the great God and our Saviour Jesus Christ; who gave Himself for us, that He might redeem us from all iniquity, and purify unto Himself a peculiar people zealous of good works."

Beloved, when you met Jesus, you met the Living God, for He *is* God. He is risen bodily. He is alive, and He is God. John 20:28, I Tim. 3:16. He is now your life. Col. 3:1-4. He can meet all your needs. Phil. 4:13, 19; I Peter 5:7; John 14:1-3, 27.

The shimmering splendor of His life, new life, eternal life, is yours forever! Love His people, love the Word, and love the lost for Him! God bless you! I John 5:13.

LAST WORDS IN HIS LOVE

Many Christians have found their lives gloriously transformed by Christ. He has fulfilled their deepest needs, calmed their fears, curbed their restlessness, taken away their guilt, lifted their burdens, given them His sweet and abiding peace. Their life is full and abundant, they revel in His love, they enjoy the Christian life, and love other Christians. Jesus is all in all to them, His life is now their life, and they love it.

Many others, unfortunately, though they say the same things about Jesus, claim they know Him, and love Him, are still wallowing most of the time, or much of the time, in the slough of despond. They are still restless, unfulfilled, often swallowed up in troubles, bad habits, sin, self-pity, barely able to keep their heads above water in the Christian life, much less bring any glory to Christ, grow, mature and be faithful as Christians, lead others to Christ, or be real pillars (pillows, maybe!) . . . in the church.

Some, of course, have never been truly saved, profession or not. However, many others are like a person who goes to the doctor, gets a prescription, with eight ingredients in it, and scratches out one or several of the ingredients before he gives it to the druggist to be filled. Then, after less than desirable, or even disasterous results, he blames the doctor or the druggist for the medicine not working. He may even lose faith in the doctor, or claim he is a fraud. Tragically, some do this in the Christian life. We must do what the great physician prescribes to enjoy and grow successfully in the Christian life. Love, loving Jesus, is the bottom line, but we must not take lightly II John 6a . . . "And this is love, that we walk after his commandments."

1. Victory is a gift basically, as salvation was. II Cor. 15:57.
2. Know that you are dead to sin. Rom. 6:11. (Sin is NOT dead to you!)
3. Yield yourself to Jesus as one alive from the dead. Rom. 12:1-2.
4. Believe, accept, reckon, rely on, claim, and live these facts by FAITH not FEELING.
5. This is all true because of your identification with Christ in His death, burial and resurrection.
6. Claim His control, the filling of His Holy Spirit, by faith. Gal. 5:16, 2:20.

We must exercise the power of the Holy Spirit in our lives by faith. While He provides the power, WE do it by faith that He is working in and through us. As Ryrie well said, "God's working is not suspended because I work; neither is God's working always apart from my working." God bless you in your new life!

Perhaps the greatest secret of that new life is to really believe and claim Rom. 8:28 and to *show that* confidence in Christ constantly. How? Practice always the following verse by faith, not feeling—for all thing "good" and "bad":

I Thess. 5:18 . . . *"In everything give thanks, for this is the will of God in Christ Jesus concerning you."*

For information or help, see tear-out pages in the back of this book.

"From Mormon Illusion to God's Love" was written by Floyd C. McElveen. He is also the author of *"THE MORMON ILLUSION,"* a best-selling book God is using worldwide to reach Mormons and others for Christ.

However, as the national evangelist for the Conservative Baptist Home Mission Society, he is on the road a lot, and does not have the staff or Mormon material for further, indepth follow-up. So send the tear-out page off first! Then, if you want to share your decision for Christ with McElveen, this would be a total joy to him!

Floyd C. McElveen
Box 1717
Port Orchard, WA 98366-0179

"The Mormon Illusion" and *"From Mormon Illusion To God's Love"* can be obtained as separate books. *"The Mormon Illusion"* from Regal/Gospel Light, in Ventura, Calif. or purchased or ordered from any Christian book store. *"From Mormon Illusion to God's Love,"* can be ordered from *Saints Alive In Jesus,* P.O. Box 1076, Issaquah, Washington, 98027.

The church you attend is going to have a great deal to do with your growth, perception of God and His purpose for you, and your outreach. The following is a list of things you should look for in a true New Testament Church.

1. Find a church that believes the Bible, and the Bible only, to be the inspired, infallible (without error) Word of God.

2. Find a church that believes and teaches that the blood of Jesus Christ, God's Son, cleanses from all sin, a church that clearly tells you that depending on Jesus alone is the way of salvation. Any church that claims to be 'the one true church', flee from IMMEDIATELY!! Your soul is at stake. There are many fine Christians in many different churches and denominations. No church saves you or helps save you. Only Jesus can do that!

3. There are false churches, nevertheless . . . the Bible calls them "Synagogues of Satan." Be careful and prayerful and trust God to lead you and give you peace when you have prayerfully and scripturally searched for and found a Bible-believing and living church. He will!

4. Be sure the church talks much, freely and with joy, about the precious shed blood of the Lord Jesus Christ. I Peter 1:18-19. Read the constitution. Check with people and pastor.

5. Find out what the church teaches about being born-again. If it is anything other than receiving Jesus Christ, as Lord and Saviour, Leave!! Salvation is not by works, or baptism, or anything else. This comes after salvation, to demonstrate your salvation. Never before salvation in order to help Jesus save you. That would be heresy! (Check chapter, "This is the Way.")

6. Be sure the church believes in the virgin birth, sinless life, death on the cross for our sins, and bodily resurrection of the Lord Jesus Christ. Ask! Accept no hedging!

7. Be sure the church believes in instant salvation, Luke 7:50, Romans 10:13, and that they believe John 3:36a, "He that believeth on the Son hath everlasting life . . ."

8. Be sure the church believes that there is now, always was, and always will be one God, existing as three eternal distinctions in what the Bible calls the Godhead, God the Father, God the Son, and God the Holy Spirit. One God.

9. Be sure the church believes in an eternal heaven and an eternal hell.

10. On the practical level, see if the church is bearing the fruit of the Holy Spirit, love, joy, peace, long-suffering, gentleness, goodness, faith, meekness, self-control. See if there is a genuine friendliness, a concern, love for one another. No church is perfect, expect that! But there should be progress in this direction even when failures occur, as they surely will!

11. Be sure they are trying to reach the lost. Be sure also that they have a missionary program. See if the leaders in the church, and many of the people, give evidence that God has changed their lives through Jesus Christ.

Reading is so vital to your life as a Christian. I suggest you take several good Christian magazines such as *Moody Monthly* or other Christian magazines. Reading the Bible is more important than reading all the other books put together. However, support books are extremely vital, as God has gifted some in the body of Christ to write in specific areas to help you grow, win others, and glorify Him. Here is a partial list. Get them and read them if you can. Very helpful for every serious Christian is a concordance to locate every word or verse in the Bible, with clear definitions . . . Strong's, Young's or Cruden's concordance. A Bible dictionary such as *The New Bible Dictionary* by J. D. Douglas, published by Eerdman's, one of the best, or a smaller, less expensive one. A good commentary is needful, such as Matthew Henry's, or one by Jamieson, Fausset and Brown, or something like the Pulpit Commentaries, etc. for those who wish to dig deeper. W. E. Vine's *Expository Dictionary of New Testament Words* is a must! *Word Studies in the Greek New Testament* by Kenneth Wuest is tremendously helpful. I remember reading through Strong's *Systematic Theology* a few weeks after I was saved. Most of it was helpful and delightful. Get it at least to refer to. Get acquainted with your Christian bookstore.

FOR APOLOGETICS: (Evidence for the Bible)
- *Evidence That Demands a Verdict* and *More Evidence That Demands a Verdict* by Josh McDowell
- *Science Speaks* by Peter Stoner
- *Countdown* by G. B. Hardy
- *The Seal of God* by F. C. Payne
- *Know Why You Believe* by Paul E. Little
- *You Must be Joking* by Michael Green
- *Mere Christianity* by C. S. Lewis
- *Who Moved the Stone?* by Frank Morrison
- *Basic Christianity* by John Stott
- *Why I am a Christian* by Terry Winters
- *The Messiah in Both Testaments* by Fred John Meldau

A Lawyer Examines the Bible by Irwin W. Linton
The Genesis Flood by Morris and Whitcomb
Therefore Stand by Wilbur Smith
Alleged Discrepancies in the Bible by John Haley
The Reason Why by R. A. Laidlaw
The Twilight of Evolution by Henry Morris
The Harmony of Science and Scripture by Harry Rimmer
Also several books by Francis Schaeffer

PRAYER:
Power in Prayer by E. M. Bounds
Prayer, Asking and Receiving by John R. Rice
How I Know God Answers Prayer by Rosalind Goforth

BIBLE:
The Inspiration of the Scriptures, God-Breathed by L. Gaussen
The Inspiration and Authority of the Bible by Benjamin B. Warfield
Our God-Breathed Book—The Bible by John R. Rice

FOR BEGINNING BIBLE STUDY:
A General Introduction to the Bible by Norman L. Geisler and William Nix
Introduction to the New Testament by H. C. Thiessen

BOOKS FOR HELP AND OUTREACH:
The Christian's Secret of a Happy Life by Hannah Whitall Smith
Your Reactions are Showing by J. A. Petersen
The Trinity in the Universe by Nathan Wood
Things to Come by Dwight Pentecost

The Cult Explosion by Dave Hunt
Through Gates of Splendor by E. Elliott
Athlete and Pioneer by C. T. Studd
Evangelism Explosion by James Kennedy
Discipleship Evangelism by Ken Stephens
Loving God by Church Colson
Dare to Care Like Jesus by Leslie Flynn
Peace, Prosperity, and the Coming Holocaust by Dave Hunt
The Act of Marriage by Tim Lahaye
Know the Marks of Cults by Dave Breese
James Dobson's books on *Marriage and Family*

Some of the material in the last several chapters of *God's Word, Final, Infallible and Forever* was previously published by Scripture Press in books by McElveen, *Christianity, Sense or Nonsense* and *Straight Thinking About Crooked Ideas*.

CHAPTER 3
God's Word . . . Still Infallible

Tens of thousands of copies of my book, God's Word, Final, Infallible, and Forever, were distributed in Utah. Many thousands more were distributed elsewhere. Many Mormons and others, praise God, have come to Christ through the book, all glory to Him. However, a frequent response by our Mormon friends is, "The Bible is full of contradictions, mistakes, and missing parts. It was the Word of God as originally given, but transmissions and translations have riddled it. There are 150,000 variants in the various manuscripts and translations of the New Testament alone. This is why we say that we only believe the Bible insofar as it is translated correctly."

We maintain that the Word of God is still Final, Infallible and Forever. The question is, why do some people honestly believe that the Bible is not fully trustworthy? For instance, Orson Pratt, in his book, Divine Authenticity of The Book of Mormon, foolishly claimed, "Who knows that even one verse of the Bible has escaped pollution, so as to convey the same sense now that it did in the original?" This is unbelief, pure and simple, and a denial of what God said he would do in preserving His Word. Hundreds of words, and whole chapters, including even the italicized words, were taken word for word from the Bible and reproduced without change in the Book of Mormon. To then claim the 'purity' of the Book of Mormon, and the pollution of the Bible, as Mormon Apostle Pratt did, is to ravish reason.

Consider the following reasons God's Word is . . . Still Infallible.

One. God's clear declaration. God, who cannot lie, said in the Bible, His immutable Word, Mt. 24:35, "Heaven and earth shall pass away, but my words shall not pass away." He also said, Mt. 5:18, "For verily I say unto you, Till heaven and earth pass, one jot or one tittle shall in no wise pass from the law, till all be fulfilled."

2 Tim. 3:16 declares, "All scripture is given by INSPIRATION OF GOD, (Gk. Theopneustos . . . God-breathed) and is profitable for doctrine, for reproof, for correction, for instruction in righteousness." These and other Bible verses state that God gave His Word infallibly through sinful, imperfect men by His sovereign guidance, and that He will preserve it infallibly through sinful, imperfect men by His sovereign guidance.

Unbelievers in God's promised preservation of the Bible, whether Mormon or non-Mormon, need to come to grips honestly with one clear fact. One cannot logically believe in the Inspiration of the Word of God without of necessity believing in the Preservation of God's Word, the Bible. We cannot accept the one and deny the other if we claim to believe God. Both irrefutably stand or fall together. God said so. God's Word tells us He knows the end from the beginning. His foreknowledge is infallible. He knew all about the difficulties of transmission, translations, emendations of the text, variants, and man's frailties. In spite of this, God, who cannot lie, said He would give His perfect, infallible Word to man, and He did. He said He would preserve that infallible Word, and He has. If God had allowed His Word, the Bible to become hopelessly polluted after giving it, then the giving of it would have been an exercise in futility. This is very unlike a sovereign, all-knowing, all-powerful God.

Two. Prophecy. From 700 to 1000 years before the coming of Christ, God foretold of Him. He foretold that Jesus is God. (Isaiah 9:6) Over 300 meticulous prophecies were given concerning His birth, time and place of birth, life, death and resurrection. All of these prophecies were fulfilled literally and precisely, 33 of them on the day He died on the cross. As foretold, He died pierced, with transgressors, was offered vinegar to drink, had His garments gambled for, and was buried in a rich man's tomb. These prophecies and many others like them, were preserved perfectly down through the long centuries of transmission, copying and re-copying, and translation of the manuscripts. Not one single error polluted the exact fulfillment of God's Word! Neither the alleged deletions or additions of bad men, or the mistakes of good men were allowed to mar the text. Suppose, in the text, someone had substituted orange juice, or some other drink, for 'vinegar.' Suppose someone had emended the text to read that Jesus would die with rich men and be buried at sea. The possibilities are endless. Yet the Bible was preserved perfectly down through the centuries, and the prophecies concerning Jesus were fully, perfectly, precisely, literally fulfilled. This is a mathematical impossibility by chance. It is double proof that Jesus was God incarnate, as He claimed, and that the Bible is the sure and certain Word of God. Furthermore, it is a good test case to prove that God can and has preserved His Word, all objections and difficulties notwithstanding. Can God no longer do what He did then, and what He definitely promised to do?

For a good example of God's performing His Word, and seeing to it that it is perfectly, literally fulfilled, consider the promise of the coming of the Lord Jesus Christ given in Isaiah 9:6-7. After stating exactly what would occur, God said, "The zeal of the LORD of hosts will perform this." . . . not the faithfulness of man. It did not depend upon man, though men were used in its fulfillment.

The *Inspiration* and *Preservation* of God's Word is absolutely necessary to the fulfillment of prophecy. The fulfillment of prophecy also proves the inspiration and preservation of God's Word. Hundreds of prophecies concerning Jesus, the Jews, people, events, kings, cities, nations, etc. have been fulfilled perfectly. Many of these prophecies have been preserved for hundreds, even thousands of years. Some ancient prophecies concerning the end times, Russia, the Jews, current conditions, and the soon coming of Jesus Christ are being fulfilled even now. This effectively does away with the false charge sometimes made by unbelieving liberal 'christian' scholars, that the prophecies were given after the event occurred. If God allowed His Word, and His prophecies, to be marred or changed, He would be a liar, His purported Word untrustworthy or uncertain. His prophecies would be useless, or fail, and He Himself would be a false prophet! As shown by fulfilled prophecy, God has kept His promise and preserved His Word.

Three. Jesus Christ. The most devastating fact of all, is that to deny the preservation of the Bible, pits one squarely against the Lord Jesus Christ! When Jesus began His ministry on earth, the Bible had been through centuries upon centuries of transmissions, attacks, emendations, countless copies, and a translation apparently from the Hebrew into the Greek, the Septuagint. Yet Jesus quoted freely and without reservation from the Word of God. Some scholars claim He also quoted freely from the Greek translation of the Hebrew Bible, the Septuagint. He never once warned the people about something missing, or something added to the Bible. He never once had to correct an error in the text. More than a thousand years had gone by in the transmission of the Word of God. Jesus verified it as having been preserved with incredible and perfect accuracy. It is no wonder that He declared that the Word of God could not be broken, and that Heaven and Earth would pass away, but the Word of God would never pass away!

One powerful point needs to be emphasized. God's Word declares that He knows the end from the beginning. (Acts 15:18) God knew in advance before He even gave His Word to man, that there would be difficulties in translations or transmissions of His Word. We are aware of these difficulties. So are many honest evangelical scholars. However, Jesus quoted the Scripture texts with complete confidence. Some of the texts He quoted were a thousand and more years old. Jesus was God the Son in human flesh. (1 Tim. 3:16) He would never have quoted, as the Word of God, texts that were in error. He quoted from all sections of the Word of God. (Luke 24:27) It is therefore a simple but irresistible deduction that God had not allowed transmissions and translations to introduce error into His Word in the long centuries before Jesus came. In spite of the difficulties of translations and transmissions, God had kept His Word unpolluted then, as He promised. He has continued to preserve His Word unpolluted as He promised, overruling the fallibility of sinful, mistake-prone men. Like Teflon, God's Word sheds vital error from its eternal truth. Is this point clear? God, knowing everything in advance, including the difficulties of preserving His Word, nevertheless declared that He would so preserve it. If it has not been preserved, He lied. He cannot lie. He has preserved His Word, difficulties notwithstanding. If Jesus had such complete confidence in the Bible, and in God's preservation of it, WHY CAN'T WE?!!!

Four. Natural man vs. Spiritual man. As used in the Bible, natural man is unsaved, not born-again. A spiritual man is saved, born-again, having the Spirit of God dwelling within. God's Word says, 1 Cor. 2:14, "But the natural (unsaved) man receiveth not the things of the Spirit of God: for they are foolishness unto him: neither can he know them, because they are spiritually discerned." Regardless of a man's I.Q. he cannot fully understand the Word of God until he is saved. Then the Spirit of God, the Author of the Bible, dwells within him, and opens the Bible up to his renewed mind. Dr. B.H. Carroll before his conversion was a bitter and brilliant skeptic. He was writing a book entitled, 6,000 Contradictions in the Bible. One night at a simple brush arbor revival meeting, B.H. Carroll accepted Jesus Christ. He rushed home to his manuscript, and studied the rest of the night. He declared that neither then or later could he find one single contradition in the Word of God. Natural, unsaved men sometimes believe that they see contradictions in the Bible where none exist. Many of us experienced this when we were natural men, before we were saved. B.H. Carroll after his conversion became a great defender of the Bible, and an outstanding scholar and theologian.

Five. Differences vs. contradictions. A distinction here is absolutely necessary. Often differences corroborate a story, and may be strong proof for its reality and accuracy, as any lawyer knows. Contradictions on the contrary, prove a story or a supposed event to be false. As Josh McDowell says, a thing cannot be A and non-A at the same time. It cannot be raining and not raining at the same place at the same time. Differences can and have been harmonized by Bible scholars. Contradictions, which are irreconcilable, cannot be harmonized in any honest way. Differences exist in the Word of God. Irreconcilable contradictions exist in the Book of Mormon, D&C, Pearl of Great Price, and in Mormon Doctrines. Biblical scholars have easily harmonized the Biblical differences in the resurrection account, the account of Paul's conversion, and other alleged contradictions. Sometimes careless reading causes claims of a 'contradiction.' Other supposed contradictions disappear when checked in the original language. Example: Acts 9:7, "The men which journeyed with him (Paul) stood speechless, *hearing* a voice, but seeing no man." Acts 22:9, "And they that were with me saw indeed the light, and were afraid, but they *heard not* the voice of Him that spake to me." Scholars of the Greek language such as Arndt and Wuest, point out that 'to hear' (akouo) in Acts 9:7 is used with the genitive, but in Acts 22:9, with the accusative. In the first instance, noise reached the ear, but no indication is given that the person understands what he hears. In the second instance, the hearing includes mental comprehension of the message spoken. That makes the explanation simple and clear. Paul is saying that his associates were aware of noise, of sounds, but did not 'hear' in such a way as to understand what was being said.

(Differences in the resurrection account can and have been easily harmonized. Contradictions in the 9 or so accounts of Joseph Smith's First Vision *cannot* be. We ask Mormons to attempt to do so honestly.)

Please notice. When a possible explanation is given to a Bible difficulty, it is UNREASONABLE to state that the passage contains a demonstrable error. This is particularly true because God's integrity is at stake. It is also because in thousands of instances where the Bible has been falsely accused of error or contradictions, it has proven to be true and its critics false, when all the facts were in. Therefore, all men, particularly those who claim to be FRIENDS of the Bible and of its God, should at least give the benefit of the doubt to God and His Word, UNLESS ABSOLUTE AND IRREFUTABLE PROOF IS GIVEN TO THE CONTRARY.

I plead with honest Mormons to consider carefully what crowd they are in when they deny that God not only gave, but preserved, His Word. This is precisely what the ENEMIES of God and His Word say. This includes liberal 'Christian' scholars, such as the 125 who wrote the 'Interpreters Bible' and major on 'higher criticism'! They hide their attack on God's integrity and His Word behind such euphemisms as 'intellectual honesty.' It includes atheists, unbelievers, infidels, agnostics, cultist in general, and skeptics of every hue.

The FRIENDS of God, born-again Christians, conservative scholars, evangelicals, fundamentalist, (and this vast number includes tens of millions of Christians and thousands of conservative Christian scholars), trust the word of God completely. They love it, defend it and use it. The allegations of such books as 'The Interpreter's Bible,' Tom Paines 'Age of Reason' etc. have been easily met and routed by superb evangelical scholarship, such as Josh McDowell's Evidence that Demands A Verdict, and More Evidence That Demands A Verdict.

Satan has long been in the business of saying, "Yea, hath God said?" Mormons, or 'Christians' who say they are friends of God and His word, and then deny what He said and tear down His Word, position themselves on the side of the ENEMIES of God. Mormons do not seem to be able to distinguish between unbelieving liberal attacks on the Bible, and Christian scholarship. They often quote such liberal attacks on the Bible with glee, as 'Christian' scholarship!

I am not a great scholar. I do not profess to be one. I am an ordinary Christian Jesus Christ has saved, and allowed to do some modest research. I believe my book, 'God's Word, Final, Infallible, and Forever,' while deliberately refraining from dealing with all possible objections, gives compelling and unanswerable reasons to prove that the Bible is God's Word, and that He has preserved it.

Few Mormons and skeptics in general seem to have read the tremendous books of Biblical Apolegetics produced by gifted evangelical scholars. I refer to such books as Gaussen's classic, 'Theopneustia,' meaning God-breathed, The Inspiration of the Bible, or Warfield's, The Inspiration and Authority of the Bible, or McDowell's, Evidence That Demands A Verdict, or More Evidence That Demands A Verdict. Even such books as Geisler's and Nix's, A General Introduction To the Bible, or Peter Stoner's, Science Speaks, or John W. Haley's, Alleged Discrepancies of the Bible, seem to be read by very few Mormons. They know alleged discrepancies, as the skeptics and ENEMIES of God's Word do. They seldom seem to know the answers, as the FRIENDS of God and His Word do.

Sadly, I am forced by many encounters over many years to agree with the words of Irwin W. Linton, in his book, "A Lawyer Examines the Bible." "So invariable had been my observation that he who does not accept wholeheartedly the evangelical, conservative belief in Christ and the Scriptures has never read, has forgotten, or never been able to weigh—and certainly is unable to refute—the irresistible force of the cumulative evidence upon which such faith rests, that there seems ample ground for the conclusion that such ignorance is an invariable element in such disbelief. And this is so, even though the unbeliever be a preacher, who is supposed to know this subject if he know no other." (pg. 45). Linton claimed that in 25 years of interviewing skeptics of the inspiration and preservation of the Word of God, and often of its Christ, He had never found one that had read even ONE of the great books on Christian Evidences or Apologetics for the Bible.

Six. Accuracy. Peerless scholar Robert Dick Wilson declared that the fact that the Bible mentions 40 Kings from 2,000 B.C. to 400 B.C. with each appearing in chronological order with reference to kings of the same country, and with respect to kings of other countries, proves the Bible mathematically. He said that there was only one chance in 750,000,000,000,000,000,000,000,000 that this accuracy is mere circumstance. The point I wish to make, however, is that the Bible had to be preserved flawlessly for this accuracy to be possible!

Seven. . . . Jots, Tittles . . . and Variants. God not only declared that, ". . . holy men of God spake as they were moved by the Holy Ghost," to give us the Bible, (2 Peter 1:21b), but declared that Heaven and Earth would pass away, but, ". . . My words shall not pass away." Also, He claimed that not one jot or tittle would fail to persevere until it was fulfilled. The very words of Scripture are vitally important. Jesus used the Greek word Elias, for the translation from the Hebrew of the name of Elijah. He also quoted from the Old Testament, sometimes using the exact words listed there, sometimes using slightly different words to give the exact same meaning. Apparently then, this does no violence to the words of the Word of God, or to its meaning.

When Jesus and the Apostles quoted that which was

essential to the preservation of a doctrinal point, they rested their case on the exact words of the Old Testament text, and in Paul's case, even on one letter, seed, not seeds, to prove a vital point! Even the *letters* of God's Word were inviolate! (See Genesis 13:15, and Gal. 3:16, distinguishing between the singular and the plural.) This indicates that after nearly two thousand years of transmission, copying, etc. even the *letters* of the words of God's Word were perfectly preserved.

However, we have some elasticity here, as shown when Jesus quoted the Old Testament. Suppose there is some variation in the text, or translation. Suppose that God gave the same concept, doctrine, or teaching, five or ten different places or more in the Bible, as He often does. This is sometimes done in the same words, sometimes in different words. Suppose that through the centuries, one or some of the words in one of these places get changed or emended. Does that change God's Word one jot or tittle in reality . . . or affect the teaching or concept at all? Absolutely not.

Variants cannot simply be equated with error. There are some 200,000 variants in New Testament manuscripts. There are about 5,500 copies of the Greek manuscripts of the New Testament, and more than 18,000 copies of these manuscripts. Josh McDowell has identified 24,633 such manuscripts to date. The variants involve such things as scribal mistakes and intended corrections, in fact, the greatest number of textual problems come from additions . . . not deletions! These variants involve only about 10,000 places. (There are over 850,000 words in the Bible!) Ezra Abbot claims that 95% of the variants do not involve error at all, but are merely various readings rather than rival readings. Phillip Schaff wrote that only 400 of these variants affected the sense of the passages they were in, only 50 were of any real significance, and of these, not one affected "an article of faith or a precept of duty which is not abundantly sustained by other and undoubted passages, or by the whole tenor of scriptural teaching." Quoted from "A General Introduction To The Bible," Geisler and Nix, pg. 366. A.T. Robertson, world reknown authority in the Greek, and a Biblical Scholar, declared that there is concern for textual criticism in only about one thousandth part of the entire text!! That has been greatly reduced by new manuscripts and further study. It is important to note that one misspelled word in 3,000 different manuscripts IS COUNTED AS 3,000 VARIANTS! What real difference does it make if the word 'color' is spelled some times in some places in some cultures as 'colour?' What real difference does it make if one manuscript, or even translation, says that Jesus wept, another says Jesus cried, and another that Jesus shed tears? Does this in any way do violence to God's preservation of His Word, even the jot's and tittles, when nothing He said or meant has been compromised?

Faith is not just subjective. It is not believing what we know is not true. God furnishes objective evidence. Acts 1:3, "To whom also He shewed himself alive after His passion by many infallible proofs, being seen of them forty days, and speaking of the things pertaining to the kingdom of God: . . ." A 'burning in the bosom' is not enough. God asks us to believe because of evidence, MANY INFALLIBLE PROOFS, which confirms His Word, and the witness to us of His Holy Spirit, confirming our faith. This avoids delusion and deception.

This is why I could not in good conscience plead for the Bible, if it had been found to contain proven contradictions and errors, if its history had proven to be fallacious. I could not support it or believe in it; if none of the numerous cities it mentions could be found, if its geography was unsound, if archeology controverted its claims. I could not plead for it, or defend it as the Word of God, if its prophecies had failed. The very opposite is true of the Bible. We can look at a Bible map, and KNOW where things happened, check out its cities, read both Biblical and secular history of its Kings, and rely with complete confidence on its archeological digs, completely supporting Biblical claims. (Not so, the Book of Mormon, it has NO MAPS, of any reliability whatsoever, no archeological sites of evidence, no proof whatsoever that any of its massive cities and kingdoms ever existed)!

To say the Bible 'contains' the Word of God, or that it is the Word of God insofar as it has been translated correctly, is a "cop-out." The Bible has been translated correctly, notwithstanding some few difficulties remaining. Any book of such antiquity, with thousands of years of transmissions, translations, etc. with less than one thousandth part of its text in question, is unique among all books, an incredible miracle book obviously preserved by God! God has preserved His Word, as He promised. Thousands of manuscripts are available to compare and correct minor textual aberrations, which barely make a ripple in the mighty river of God's Word flowing down through the centuries. Biblical scholars abound who have harmonized every difference, and answered every claim of 'contradiction' adequately.

To believe in a God big enough to create and sustain the universe, but not big enough to create and sustain a book which reveals Himself, is illogical. To deny what He plainly said He would do in preserving His Word is unbelief. To deny that He has given and sustained His Word as He Promised, and call oneself a 'christian' is ignorance, dishonesty, or treachery. Either God is right, or His critics are. Which side are you really on, Mormon friends? My prayer is that Mormons and non-Mormons alike who have honest doubts, will examine the evidence and claim, believe and obey John 7:17. Then read through the gospel of John very carefully and prayerfully.

To all who read this, the shortest, safest way out of confusion is to lay all your doubts at the foot of the cross. Take Rev. 3:20 *seriously, literally, and believingly.* Invite the Biblical Lord Jesus Christ, God in the flesh, who shed His blood for you and bodily rose from the dead, to come into your heart and life right now. Ask Him and trust Him to forgive your sins, save you instantly, and be your Lord and Saviour forever. Believe Him, thank Him, that He did just what you asked and He promised, and live accordingly in obedience to Him and His Word. He will make Himself real to you. Your doubts will flee, and the Bible will be a new book to you.

(Notice please! Recently, a number of students at Brigham Young University were reading this book. They were told that the Bible contained errors, and that obviously the author of this book was not aware of them, (or perhaps unable to deal with them). Therefore, they were told, everything this author said was to be discredited.

The example was given of a man whose age was listed incorrectly according to another biblical reference. John Haley's book was written specifically to answer scores of these claims for honest truth-seekers. *(ALLEGED DISCREPENCIES IN THE BIBLE.)* However, that is not the purpose of this book, nor does space allow for it.

There is NO real answer to the powerful, irrefutable evidence from prophecy, mathematical probability, and God's own words as to the inspiration and preservation of the Bible this book presents. The few grains of sand, due to minor problems in translation, which are clung to by those who would deny the Word of God, are overwhelmed by the rushing mighty river of God's Word!)

CHAPTER 4
Some Vital Differences Examined

As we have already indicated in the INTRODUCTION to "From Mormon Illusion to God's Love," we care about Mormons. Inevitably, we will receive many letters accusing us of hate, of persecuting Mormons, etc. This is always true of whatever group is being exposed. My heart aches for those who realize they have been misled, and moreover, that their precious friends and loved ones have also been misled. If sincerity were enough to get one to heaven, thousands of dear Mormon people would be saved, but, unfortunately, it is not. Doctors have made sincere mistakes that cost patients lives, many have made sincere mistakes that proved fatal.

Please believe me when I say that I would rather suffer immense loss, perhaps even of life itself, than mislead one Mormon to Hell. Some may call it hate, to expose Mormonism and show them the true way of salvation, but they will have to answer to God for judging my motives, not to me. I always thought it was love to want to be with someone forever with Jesus in heaven, and to do everything possible to see that they know Jesus and go to heaven instead of Hell. I want Mormons to know the biblical Jesus. I want them to be saved, now and forever. I want to spend eternity with them in heaven with Jesus. This is my heart's motive, as God is my witness. If that isn't love, what is?

What, dear Mormon friends and other readers, would you think of a man asleep in a burning house, if someone ran in and woke him up, and he cried out, "Leave me alone, why are you persecuting me?"

Mormons do not seem to understand that saying they are the 'One True Church, and that all others are false, and have no authority, right to baptize, or to practice church ordinances' is one of the greatest attacks and insults imaginable to hundreds of millions of Christians, from the time of Christ to now. To say that God told Joseph Smith this only adds to the persecution. This is an attack on dear children of God serving Christ in hundreds of different denominations and millions of churches. (See PGP, Joseph Smith, 2:19). Of course, Mormons hasten to declare that others may worship when and how they please, and want themselves to be accorded the same right as Americans. We do gladly recognize that wonderful privilege for them and for us. What they are saying however, is that such worship is apostate, futile, false and without 'authority' unless it is Mormon.

Sixty-six million Christians are estimated to have died for their faith in Jesus Christ, many singing hymns to Jesus while they were burned or torn asunder. They were tortured, burned and beaten, (and some still are!) lived in caves, and willingly died for the Lord Jesus Christ during those thousand and more years Joseph Smith claimed the gospel, the church and true Christianity had disappeared from the earth! I am speaking of men like John Hus, and John Wycliffe, and millions like them, as recorded in history in books such as "Foxes' Book of Martyrs." God must weep, as our hearts do, for the injustice of so foul a claim against His dear saints! Certainly we have the right to defend them, and Christians now also, against such an attack.

It definitely is not 'persecution' of Mormons to do so. It's an act of cowardice, confirming honest but misled Mormons in their fatal error, if we do not.

It is certainly true that God told HYPOCRITES not to judge in Matthew 7:1, (tho' Mormons have judged Christians as false from the very beginning of the LDS church), but God told CHRISTIANS in John 7:23, to judge righteous judgement. By God's grace, that is what I am attempting to do.

Simply stated, however, I believe Mormons in general are lost and on their way to Hell, whether they believe it or not. I would be a monster, however much I talked about 'tolerance' and 'love' and not 'offending' if I did not warn them, whatever the price, whatever the cost.

Love must warn them. Love CANNOT do less. We love Mormons, not Mormonism, as Jesus loves the sinner, but not his sin.

We state again the four basic reasons why Mormons need the Biblical Lord Jesus Christ and His salvation.
1. The God, (or gods) of Mormonism is not the God of the Bible.
2. The Christ of Mormonism is not the Christ of the Bible.
3. The prophet of Mormonism is not a prophet of God.
4. The salvation of Mormonism is not the salvation of God as revealed in His Word, the Bible.

Please bear with me, Mormon friends, while we examine some of the teachings of Mormonism. I will try to be fair, and 'speak the truth in love,' as God admonishes us to do. God will certainly be the final judge of that, but most of all, I pray He will enable you to see His truth and His love, and be delivered to trust in Christ alone for your salvation.

Joseph Smith taught that there was a time when God was not God. ". . . I will tell you how God came to be God. We have imagined and supposed that God was God from all eternity. I will refute that idea and take away the veil, so that you may see." (Teachings of Prophet Joseph Smith, pg. 345). "As man is, God once was. As God is, man may be." (Lorenzo Snow, also James Talmage, Articles of Faith, pg. 430).

This is in total contradiction to Isaiah 43:10b, ". . . Before me there was no God formed, neither shall there be after me," as well as to Psalm 90:2b, ". . . From everlasting to everlasting thou art God." There have never been any other Gods anywhere, anytime, anyplace. There is ONE God, with three eternal distinctions, God the Father, God the Son, and God the Holy Spirit. No human being or any other being, Mormon or otherwise, will ever become a God. God *alone* always was God, always has been God, and always will be God, *alone*. Note Is. 44:6b, ". . . I am the first, and I am the last; and beside me there is no God. 44:8b, "Is there a God beside me? Yea, there is no God; I know not any." Is. 46:9, "Remember the former things of old: for I am God, and there is none else; I am God, and there is none like me."

Notice also that even though Joseph Smith said the "Gods" helped "organize and form the earth," and also that the "Gods" organized or created the heavens, light and darkness, and even man, in PGP, Abraham, Ch. 4, God said differently. In Genesis 1:1, His word says that God created the heaven and the earth. In Is. 44:24b, God said, "I am the Lord that maketh all things; that stretcheth forth the heavens *alone;* that spreadeth abroad the earth *by myself.*"!!

God also said, in Jeremiah 10:11, "Thus shall ye say

unto them, the gods, that have not made the heavens and the earth, even they shall perish from the earth, and from under these heavens." God went on to say that He made the earth by His power. If there *were* other 'Gods' they would perish, Mormon or otherwise, because God said He made the heavens and the earth *alone*, and all 'Gods' that did not make the heavens and earth shall perish! It is simply another way in which God affirms that there are no other Gods, never has been, never will be, and shows Joseph Smith to be a false prophet. To believe that there are other gods, whether one worships them or not, makes God a liar.

Mormons teach that God was once a man before He became God, and had to work, attain, earn, progress his way to Godhood. According to Mormon theology, there is a God who fathered the God of this sphere, and a God who fathered that God, and so on. There is also a Mother God. The Mormon God is not omnipresent, as is the Biblical God, but has a body that limits Him to being in one place at a time. The Mormon God is polygamous and has many wives, by which all of our spirits were produced in sexual unions. Check out this statement in Articles of Faith, by James Talmage, pg. 430. "We believe in a God who is Himself *progressive*, whose majesty is intelligence; whose perfection consists in eternal advancement—a being who has attained His exalted state by a path which now His children are permitted to follow, whose glory it is their heritage to share. In spite of the opposition of the sects, in face of direct charges of blasphemy, the Church proclaims the eternal truth, 'As man is, God once was; as God is, man may be." (For information from Mormon sources on these subjects, see Orson Pratt's 'The Seer' pg. 132, 172, Joseph Fielding Smith's 'Doctrine of Salvation', Hunter's 'Gospel Through the Ages'. Many other Mormon sources confirm the above teachings, including some of the teachings of Brigham Young.)

Mormons also teach that Jesus Christ was not always a God, but had to earn, attain, progress His way into being God. Bruce McConkie, in the tract, 'What The Mormons Think of Christ' states, "Christ the Word, the Firstborn, had of course *attained* unto the status of God while yet in pre-existence." We answered this false claim about Jesus Christ on pg. 73-74 of the *Mormon Illusion*. Other Mormon statements about Jesus state that He is not virgin-born, (Brigham Young, J.D. Vol. 1, pg. 50, 51) is a spirit brother of Satan, is not one in nature, essence and substance with God the Father and the Holy Spirit, is polygamous, and cannot indwell all believers as He promised and as the Bible repeatedly says He does. He can only be in one place at a time, according to Mormon theology. This is manifestly a very different Jesus than the real, biblical Jesus. (Check Orson Pratt's statements in The Seer, pg. 158, and Religious Truths Defined, pg. 44., Journal of Discourses Vol. 13, pg. 282.) We are warned of such false Christs in Matthew 24:24. Micah 5:2 speaks of Christ as being '. . .from everlasting," John 1:1-3, 14 tells us that Jesus always was with God, and that He always WAS God, There was never a time when He was not God. John 1:3, says that Jesus created ALL things, He was never Himself created, as Satan and the angels were. 1 Tim. 3:16 declares that He as "God was manifest in the flesh." Therefore He was called God, and accepted worship as God, John 20:28, Mt. 28:9. The Biblical Christ indwells all true believers everywhere simultaneously, thus making them children of God, and new creatures in Christ, with a new, changed life. READ Gal. 2:20, 2 Cor. 13:5, Col. 1:27, and Eph. 3:17 for biblical proof.

Considering the millions of planets, and other galaxies, with other gods, the Mormon God may amount to little more than a sort of planetary tribal deity in this vast universe. He has little in common with the Almighty God of the Bible and of Christians. His very Godhood may be at risk in this vast and dangerous Universe.

As for God 'fathering' all of our spirits, if God neglected all the multipled billions of chores and worlds He is responsible for, including hearing and answering prayer, and spent 30 minutes per wife, day and night, in sexual union, it would take Him approximately 1,800,000 years to father the present population of the earth! This population is expected to double in a few decades, not to mention the billions that have gone on before. This is not even counting on the 9 months pregnancy, the raising of the family, or in fact, doing ANYTHING else! How torturous to father spirits, and keep them waiting for bodies for what is now billions of years!

This seems very unlike a God of love, or at least, a very unlikely way of doing things.

While speaking here of God and of Jesus, it is important to point out that Mormons believe that God the Father is one God, and God the Son is another God. They teach that God the Father's name is Elohim, while Jesus is a completely separate God named Jehovah. These two Gods are one in purpose only, according to Mormonism. This undeniably gives them two Gods to worship and serve, contrary to Biblical doctrine, not to mention myriads of other Gods they believe exist. Not to mention also, Adam-God, "the only God with whom we have to do." according to Brigham Young. Or the exalted men who have become 'Gods'. The truth is, Jehovah and Elohim are names used interchangeably, over and over again, for the ONE TRUE

God. It is very important we understand the Old Testament translators' system for communicating which name for God is being used. 'LORD' (written with all capitals) is recorded when referring to Jehovah. 'God' (written with a capital G and small od) is recorded when referring to Elohim. 'Lord' (written with a capital L and small ord) is recorded for Adonai, still another name used for the same God. These different names were used to emphasize different attributes of God; such as the self existent one (Jehovah), the strong, faithful, covenant keeping God (Elohim), or our sovereign master (Adonai). There are many other names for the one God, which space prevents discussing. Some are listed below. Notice for example, Deut. 6:4b: 'The LORD (Jehovah) our God (Elohim) is one LORD: (Jehovah). (Also see Is. 43:10, Is. 44:6, Is. 48:16 and Is. 61:1) Jesus is called Elohim, he is also called Jehovah. God the Father is called Elohim, he is also called JEHOVAH. This is because God the Father, God the Son, and God the Holy Spirit, are— one God! ($1 \times 1 \times 1 = 1$) The Bible even calls this one God JEHOVAH ELOHIM. It makes as little sense to try to separate these two names for God, and claim they represent separate Gods, as it does to separate Jehovah-Jireh, Jehovah-rophe, Jehovah-M'Kaddsh, Jehovah-shalom, Jehovah-tsidkenu, or Jehovah-shamah. To say that each of these names—(all used of God as descriptive attributes)—stands for a separate God would be inaccurate! El and El-Shaddai are other names used of the one true God in some special relationship to His people. THEY DO NOT SIGNIFY DIFFERENT GODS! Often the Bible uses the expression, 'the LORD thy God." In Hebrew, this is JEHOVAH thy ELOHIM. It is used to identify *one* God, not *two*, much as saying 'Virginia, thy wife.' 'JEHOVAH your ELOHIM,' is also a common expression, as in Deut. 4:2. Deut. 4:35, is even more definite, ". . . JEHOVAH *he is* ELOHIM: . . ." Could words be plainer or clearer? The Mormon God simply is not the God of the Bible. JEHOVAH and ELOHIM are not two Gods, but two names identifying the one true God!

CHAPTER 5
Brigham Young, Adam-God and Mormon Revelation

Perhaps here would be a good place to deal with several revealing Mormon doctrines. Brigham Young stoutly declared, "No man or woman in this dispensation will ever enter the celestial kingdom of God without the consent of Joseph Smith!" (Journal of Discourses, Vol. 7, pg. 289). Regardless of whether Mormons claim he was speaking here as a prophet or not, (a clever Mormon evasion often invoked) several things are immediately evident. In the light of John 14:6, "Jesus saith unto him, I am the way, the truth, and the life: no man cometh to the Father, but by me," this is blasphemy. Consider also 1 Tim. 2:5, "For there is one God, and one mediator between God and men, the man Christ Jesus." Acts 4:12, speaking of Jesus, "Neither is there salvation IN ANY OTHER: for there is none other name under heaven given among men, whereby we must be saved."

Brigham Young was giving recorded, documented teaching, supposedly from God to his LDS church, definitely as a 'living prophet.' However, even if Mormons should claim that he was not here 'speaking as a prophet,' it makes no real difference. Brigham Young was defining his beliefs. No man could be a Christian, much less a prophet of God, who held such beliefs. Woe to those who follow such a man and his teachings as a prophet of God.

This, however, is just the tip of the iceberg. Brigham Young also taught, "The only men who become Gods, even the Sons of God, are those who enter into polygamy." (Journal of Discourses, Vol. 11, pg. 269; Vol. 3, pg. 266.) He taught, "Jesus Christ was not begotten by the Holy Ghost," thus denying the virgin birth, Journal of Discourses, Vol. 1, pg. 50-51. This is in direct contradiction of Mt. 1:20b, ". . . for that which is conceived in her IS OF THE HOLY GHOST." He taught that the sun was inhabited, (Journal of Discourses, Vol. 13, pg. 271.) He also declared quite clearly, "I have never yet preached a sermon and sent it out to the children of men that they may not call Scripture. Let me have the privilege of correcting a sermon, and it is as good Scripture as they deserve." (Journal of Discourses, Vol. 13, pg. 95, also pg. 264). Obviously, he was claiming divine inspiration for His sermons, on a par with the Scriptures of God's Word. Obviously also, he had many years to read and correct anything recorded in the Journal of Discourses. Such sermons could not even be published, and certainly not continue to be published, without his approbation as 'living prophet' and president of the church.

Brigham Young taught that God came to earth in the flesh and had physical relations with Mary to beget Jesus Christ. He said, "The birth of the Saviour was as natural as are the births of our children; it was the result of natural action. He partook of flesh and blood—was begotten of his Father, as we are of our fathers." (Journal of Discourses Vol. 8, pg. 115.)

This fits in with what Brigham Young taught about Adam being our God, in his famous Adam-God doctrine. Speaking of Adam, on April 9, 1852, in a major address heard, recorded, and believed by many Mormons, Brigham Young said, ". . . he is our father and our God, and the ONLY GOD WITH WHOM WE HAVE TO DO." (Journal of Discourses, Vol. 1, pg. 50-51.) Brigham Young clarified EXACTLY what he meant two years later on Feb. 19, 1854. He made it clear that Adam was the Father of Jesus Christ in physical union with the virgin Mary. Speaking of Jesus, he declared, "Who did beget Him? His father, and His father is our God, and the FATHER OF OUR SPIRITS, and he is the framer of the body, the God and Father of our Lord Jesus Christ. Who is He? He is FATHER ADAM." (Brigham Young Paper, Feb. 19, 1854, call number MSF 219 #81, Church Historians Office, Salt Lake City, Utah.) Though thousands of Mormons then came to believe this doctrine of Adam-God as taught by Brigham Young for over 20 years, Mormons today generally deny it. Former Mormon president Spencer Kimball called it *false doctrine* in Church News, Oct. 9, 1976.

The problem for our Mormon friends is severe. Thousands of Mormons had a testimony during Brigham Young's time that Adam was God, and the direct father of Jesus Christ. Now thousands of Mormons have a testimony that this doctrine is not true, and Spencer Kimball and many Mormons for years have denied that Brigham Young even taught it!! Just recently, however, after years of denial, Bruce McConkie confessed in a letter to Eugene England, Feb. 19, 1981, that Brigham Young did indeed teach that Adam was God. Now a tract, "What about the ADAM-GOD THEORY," has been published by Van Hale of Mormon Miscellaneous, clearly admitting that Brigham Young taught this doctrine over a period of years. It is worth noting that Brigham Young said, "How much unbelief exists in the minds of the Latter-day Saints in regard to one particular doctrine which I revealed to them, AND WHICH GOD REVEALED TO ME—namely that Adam is our Father and God." (Deseret News, June 18, 1873.) Clearly, this 'living prophet' is claiming that this doctrine came from God. Van Hale goes on to explain that perhaps Brigham Young meant this as Moses was called a 'god' to Pharaoh, etc. Brigham Young nullified such an explanation by saying that Adam is the '. . . ONLY GOD WITH WHOM WE HAVE TO DO,' an unmistakeable reference to Adam as our Supreme Diety. This is something Moses would have never dared to do in representing God to those to whom he was sent. God would never have confused people by saying that Moses was God, and the only God with whom they had to do, nor would Moses have claimed this of himself. Brigham Young saw his Adam-God sermon in print. He knew the capital G was used for God, indicating the Diety of the one addressed, and he never warned against that usage or changed it. He undeniably meant that Adam was God. In Van Hale's tract he seeks to minimize the impact of Brigham Young's Adam-God doctrine. He says it was never in any official canon. (That would be true of many of the things Joseph Smith and other Mormon leaders taught that are believed by Mormons today.) Brigham Young only spoke on this doctrine a few times, he says. (Half a dozen time, with two sermons recorded, and 'hints' given elsewhere.) Question: How many times does a prophet have to give a revelation from God before it becomes authentic? In the Word of God . . . just once. Brigham Young said and wrote more on Adam-God, than the Bible does on the virgin birth.

Many Mormons disagreed with this doctrine at first, among them Orson Pratt. Many accepted the doctrine immediately, as we know from their diaries. (I recorded a few quotes in The Mormon Illusion, Bob Witte and the Tanners quote more from Mormon sources.) Others came to accept the doctrine later. Some had strong 'testimonies' as to the truth of the Adam-God doctrine, just as today some Mormons have strong 'testimony' that this doctrine is false. Some Mormons have a 'testimony' that Brigham Young never taught such a doctrine, all of which illustrates the fallacy of testimony to determine truth. It demonstrates the need to prayerfully depend on the Word of God, the Bible. Notice that *Spencer Kimball* called the Adam-God doctrine, *'false doctrine.'* When the 'living prophet' calls another 'Mormon prophet's doctrine,' 'false doctrine,' it proves one or both of them to be false prophets. Only a false church could be led for years by a false prophet as its leader. Deut. 18:20-22, gives the test for a prophet of God. No true prophet of God can give false prophecy. Enemies of God may claim that some of the prophecies of the Bible failed. None ever did. There were a few conditional statements that God said depended on man's response or actions or repentance. God is not the Author of confusion. The Holy Ghost does not contradict the Holy Ghost.

Remember that Brigham Young gave his first message on Adam-God in 1852. In 1854, he gave another powerful message shedding more light on the Adam-God doctrine, and making it clear that Adam fathered our spirits, and was the God and Father of Jesus Christ. It was in 1873, June 18, *21 years after his first message on the subject, and subsequent enlargements on the doctrine of Adam-God,* that Brigham Young *deplored* the *'unbelief'* of Latter-day Saints in this doctrine which . . . "I revealed to them, and God revealed to me." (While many Mormons accepted this doctrine, some were very uneasy about it, or did not understand how it could be so.) Without doubt, Brigham Young taught this doctrine as a 'living prophet' from God for Mormons to believe. After 21 years, he was very unhappy that some did not believe it!! It was not just a shallow, minor, doctrine of no consequence, as far as Brigham Young was concerned, or as far as many Mormons of his day were concerned.

Speaking of 'canon' or 'authority' or 'official' church doctrine, or a prophet 'speaking as a prophet' or 'scripture' or 'what a Mormon is obligated to believe to be in line for the celestial kingdom or godhood,' consider the following list.

Ira Ransom, in his Visualized Witnessing Notebook, asks, "Which is the correct view regarding continuous revelation?" (pg. 37). 1. Only the four standard works are revelation. 2. All that church authorities teach is revelation. 3. All that the church president teaches is revelation. 4. All that the church authorizes in conference is revelation. 5. All that the church president teaches in conference that is printed in a church publication is revelation. 6. There is no way to distinguish between what *is* and what *is not* revelation. Mormons run the gamut all the way up and down the above list as to what is and what is not revelation. Their 'living prophets' have only added to the confusion with contradictory statements concerning continuous revelation. To say then that Brigham Young's doctrine, sermons he himself declared were scripture, 'has never been a part of the Mormon canon of scripture,' as Van Hale does, bears little weight. What DOES bear weight and is far more in accord with Mormon doctrine and practice, is the following list given by the now President and 'living prophet' of the Mormon church, Ezra Taft Benson. 1. The prophet is the only man who speaks for the Lord in EVERYTHING. 2. The living prophet is more vital to us THAN STANDARD WORKS. 3. The living prophet is more important to us than a dead prophet. 4. The prophet will never lead the

Church astray. (!!!) 5. The prophet is not required to have any particular earthly training or credentials to speak on any subject or act on any matter at any time. 6. The Prophet does not have to say "Thus saith the Lord," to give us scripture. 7. The prophet tells us what we need to know, not always what we want to know. 8. The prophet is not limited by man's reasoning. 9. The prophet can receive revelation on any matter, temporal or spiritual. 10. The prophet may be involved in civic matters. 11. The two groups who have the greatest difficulty in following the prophet are the proud who are learned and the proud who are rich. 12. The prophet will not necessarily be popular with the world or the worldly. 13. The Prophet and his counselors make up the First Presidency—the highest quorum in the Church. 14. The Prophet and the presidency—the living prophet and the First Presidency—follow them and be blessed—reject them and suffer.

In speaking further of the 'living prophet and President,' Benson stated, "If we want to know how well we stand with the Lord then let us ask ourselves how well we stand with his mortal captain. . . ." Ignoring the obvious affront to hundreds of millions of Christians who are not Mormons, and have no 'standing' at all with the Mormon 'living prophet,' notice how this 'living prophet' reveals the supremacy of the prophet's teaching over standard works, the Bible, Mormon canon, or whatever. Therefore, in the light of this authoritative Mormon teaching from their own 'living prophet,' Brigham Young's teaching on Adam-God was absolutely binding on Mormons then, and should be now, unless he was a false prophet. Mormon records show that Orson Pratt fought the doctrine for years, but finally succumbed to Brigham and to the doctrine. Why? 'This dispute between the Mormon Prophet and his Apostle continued for several years. Because of his disbelief in the Adam-God teaching and in other doctrines of Young, Pratt was for years upon the point of being severed from the Church." (The "Journal of Pastoral Practice vol. 3, no. 2. 1979, pg. 101-104). The pressure was too much, and Orson Pratt finally gave in, although later still showed distrust in the Adam-God doctrine. According to a statement Van Hale reports by Apostle Amasa Lyman, not only was Pratt so threatened with excommunication, apparently at least one man was excommunicated because ". . . he would not believe that Adam was our Father and God." Lyman strongly disapproved of such action, but the fact that it occurred underscores that this was a doctrine taught by Brigham Young, and at least to some extent, enforced by the Church.

Apostle Wilford Woodruff, later the 'living Prophet' and President of the Mormon church, accepted whole-heartedly the Adam-God doctrine. This is revealed in his Wilford Woodruff Journal in a tense session with Orson Pratt, which took place on Jan. 27, 1860. Woodruff stood with Brigham Young in trying to convince Pratt of the truth of the Adam-God doctrine. In light of this, we are astonished that anyone could try to pass off the Adam-God doctrine as just Brigham Young's 'opinion.' Such Mormon organs as the 'Millennial Star' claimed, in Vol. 15, pg. 801, "The above sentiment appeared in the Star No. 48, a little to the surprise of some of its readers; and while the sentiment may have appeared blasphemous to the ignorant: it has no doubt given rise to some serious reflections with the more candid and comprehensive mind . . . ADAM IS REALLY GOD! AND WHY NOT?"

Note what "Women of Mormondom" records about this doctrine, on pg. 196 after referring to Adam as our Father and God, as Brigham Young proclaimed, "Both in mortal and celestial sense—he made the most important revelation ever oracled to the race since the days of Adam himself." Even more devastating is this admission from Minutes of the School of the Prophets, Provo, Utah, 1868-71, (pg. 38 of typed copy at the Utah State Historical Society). "The doctrine preached by Prest Young for a few years back wherein he says that Adam is our God—THE GOD WE WORSHIP—*that most of the people believe this* . . . (!!!!).

Do Mormons today believe in the Adam-God doctrine? By and large no, though some apparently still do. Then why bring it up? To irritate Mormons, to persecute them? As God is my witness, NO! THIS is why. Clearly, if Brigham Young was a true Prophet of God, Spencer Kimball is a *false* prophet. He declared the Adam-God doctrine to be false doctrine. Clearly, if Spencer Kimball was a *true* Prophet of God, Brigham Young was a *false* prophet. If either of them were false, the Mormon church has been shown to be a false church led by a false prophet.

According to Van Hale in his pamphlet, "What About The Adam-God Theory?" Prophets can differ in matters of faith and doctrine. (!!) In matters of opinion not specifically covered by God, this might well be true. In matters of doctrine or revelation given by God, this cannot be true. As a drastic example, imagine one prophet saying that God revealed to Him that Moses was God and Jesus a Satanic imposter, and the other prophet saying that God revealed to him that Jesus was God and Moses a mere man called as a prophet of God. God is not and cannot be the Author of such confusion in His prophets and in His Word. Van Hale cites the Interpreter's Bible, a study by 125 liberal scholars who believe the Bible only *'contains'* the Word of God. Van Hale apparently cannot distinguish between this view and the view of tens of millions of Christians and thousands of evangelical scholars who know that God and His Son Jesus Christ claimed absolute infallibility for the Word of God, as indeed His prophets did also. Imperfect knowledge of the Word of God, because prophecy was not yet fully completed, may have caused some of them to 'know only in part,' but it was their knowledge which was imperfect, never the Word of God. (I Corinthians 13:19; Psalm 19:7)

I do not wish to impugn Mr. Van Hale. I met him once and he seems to be a decent and intelligent and well-read man. However, his pamphlet reflects some of the later thinking about Adam-God and the Bible that seems to be coming more to the fore today among some Mormons. This view however, is not that held by many Mormons.

Chris Vlachos in his excellent booklet, "Adam is God???", records that Mormon Apostle Orson Hyde sided with Brigham Young in his dispute with Orson Pratt on the Adam-God doctrine. Hyde maintained that God's prophets cannot advance false doctrine, that if God's prophets could do this it would in reality undermine the entire truth and foundation of their religion. From this we can draw the conclusion that God's prophets cannot contradict one another. One of them would surely be giving false revelation, false doctrine, and would therefore be a false prophet, not a prophet of God.

Vlachos points out also that the Adam-God doctrine incontrovertibly establishes Brigham Young as a false prophet, and nullifies the claims to priesthood of all those who got their priesthood from him, as well as those to whom they in turn gave the priesthood. President Spencer Kimball was ordained an Apostle by Heber J. Grant, who was ordained by Cannon, who was ordained by Brigham Young. All twelve of the TWELVE APOSTLES of the Mormon Church received their ordination through Brigham

Young. This makes them false and causes them to lack the priesthood which Brigham supposedly had. This is why Mormons must face the Adam-God issue squarely and honestly. Mormons of integrity, and there are many such, can never rest with evasions and shallow explanations. Too much is at stake.

We believe the evidence is insurmountable. Brigham Young taught the Adam-God doctrine as a revelation from God to thousands of Mormons, in public speaking and writing, and expected them to accept it and believe it. He was grieved when they all did not.

However, even if this were not true, if Brigham Young merely taught this as an opinion, where does that leave us?

Can you imagine the Apostle Paul teaching and writing in the Scriptures as he was inspired of God, that Jesus was the Messiah, the Son of God, but privately expressing the 'opinion' that Peter was really the true Messiah, the 'only begotten Son of God?' What would that do to his official revelation from God given in Scripture, and to his own credibility? God would not call such a man to be His prophet, nor put up with such duplicity in His name in one recording His infallible Word. *Faults and failings in prophets have absolutely nothing to do with what I am talking about.* When a Prophet gave a revelation from God it had to be TRUE, or God's integrity would be compromised, His Word invalidated.

A man who gave inspired revelation from God as a Prophet of God, but did not believe the revelation he gave, and held a different opinion about who 'God' was would not even be a christian, a believer, much less a prophet of God.

Some modern Mormons such as Van Hale, make it clear that they do not believe the Mormon prophets to be infallible, *even in giving their revelations directly from God as they claimed. I imagine President Benson would be interested to know that.* Read those 14 points of Benson again!!!

Mr. Van Hale may also speak for some Mormons today who seem not to believe the 8th article of faith of Mormonism. "We believe the Bible to be the Word of God as far as it is translated correctly." At least, this is the deduction one would normally come to from his quotation *approvingly* of Rev. J.R. Dummelow ("One Volume Bible Commentary—?) pg. cxxxv. "We must not regard the Bible as an absolutely perfect book in which God is Himself the author using human hands and brains only as a man might use a typewriter. God used men, not machines—men with like weakness and prejudice and passion as ourselves . . . in the Bible we do not expect the actors to be real and natural. Because of our FALSE THEORY of VERBAL INSPIRATION we are puzzled when the divine is mingled with the human . . . it is a mine of precious ore where the gold is mingled with the rock and clay—the ore is richer in one part than another but all parts in some degree are glittering with gold." I mention this because other Mormons have written me similar quotes or sent me the Van Hale pamphlet.

God claimed "For the prophecy came not in old time by the will of man: but holy men of God spake as they were moved by the Holy Ghost." ((II Peter 1:21)

God claims the Bible came NOT BY THE WILL OF MAN, however 'fallible' they may have been, they were overshadowed by His infallibility. 2 Tim. 3:16 makes it clear, "ALL SCRIPTURE, (not just some, part divine and part human) is given by inspiration of GOD (not Man!) (literally GOD BREATHED!), and is profitable for doctrine, for reproof, for correction, for instruction in righteousness." This is why God could claim that not one jot or tittle of His word would fail, and why Paul could confidently confirm a doctrine on ONE LETTER of a word given thousands of years before in God's Word. I can dictate letters through a dozen different secretaries with different personalities and abilities, using each for that for which they are best fitted, using, not effacing, their various personalities, and SO CAN, AND SO DID, GOD!!

Van Hale's position seems to be that *even the original Scriptures as given from the Lord, possibly contained human error,* not to mention the thousands of years of transmissions and translations. It is too bad that those who read the "Interpreter's Bible" and the Higher Critics, which many evangelicals have read, by the way, do not at least achieve balance by reading the works of greater scholarship produced by some of the worlds foremost Bible Scholars. Gaussen's classic and irrefutable "Theopneustia" for example, or the works of Robert Dick Wilson, or even Josh McDowell's "Evidence That Demands A Verdict," and "More Evidence That Demands a Verdict." These evangelical Christian works ably meet and demolish the claims of the Higher Critics, the Interpreters Bible, etc. showing both their fallacy scholarship-wise, and their unbelief. It was Satan who first said, "Yea, hath God said . . . ?" and he is still at it, in whatever guise he can find.

In any event, Brigham Young taught that Adam was God. This is false doctrine, directly challenging "Thou shalt worship no other god: for the LORD, whose name is Jealous, is a jealous God (Ex. 34:14). It totally violates Deut. 13:1-5, and proves Brigham Young to be a false prophet. READ IT! It shatters John 17:3, "And this is life eternal, that they might know thee the only true God, and Jesus Christ, whom thou hast sent." (For a more thorough study of Adam-God, read Chris Vlachos, "Adam Is God???," Bob Witte's book, "Where Does It Say That?" Jerald and Sandra Tanner's, "Mormonism, Shadow or Reality," and Brigham Young's sermons on Adam-God in the Journal of Discourses.)

We recognize that Van Hale and his opinions on Adam-God, and on the inspiration of Mormon 'living prophets,' Mormon scriptures, and the Bible, do not officially represent the Mormon church. We freely recognize his right to hold those opinions. Because we have received several letters lately, holding the same position, and several of his pamphlets, we use him as a reference point. We do this not just to answer him, but to answer his general position, which less orthodox or liberal Mormons seem to reflect. On the surface, at least in the case of Adam-God, it seems to be just another futile attempt to distance themselves from the false and revealing Adam-God doctrine. First, many Mormons accepted the Adam-God doctrine. After Brigham Young's death, and benign neglect, the doctrine fell into disrepute, even though it was believed and held by at least one other 'living prophet' and President. Then for years, Mormons denied that Brigham Young ever taught such a doctrine, and the leadership, including Spencer Kimball, deliberately misrepresented the truth, even though they knew what they were saying was a lie. This says a great deal about Mormon leadership in general, as many other Mormon leaders joined them in this evasion and cover-up. When it became clear that this would no longer work, because of information given from Mormon historical sources, the Journal of Discourses, and by people like Jerald and Sandra Tanner, some Mormons began another defense. They admitted that Brigham Young had, after all, taught the Adam-God doctrine, but 1. It was a minor doctrine of little consequence. 2. It was just Brigham Young's opinion. 3. Prophets are not infallible, even when getting revelation from God, so something apparently got lost from God's giving the revelation to His 'living prophet' and Brigham Young's giving the Adam-God revelation to the LDS people! (This latter view is totally untenable, scripturally, logically I believe to most orthodox, faithful Mormons.)

We *do not* gloat over the Adam-God doctrine. It is heartbreaking to any who love the one true God. It is only one of many false doctrines once held by Mormons, but it is one that must be exposed. Neither sincere Mormons nor Christians can ignore its devastating implications or allow it to be swept under the Morman rug.

CHAPTER 6
God, Gold Plates, and Joseph Smith the Prophet

This Biblical Truth is that there is—one God, existing eternally as God the Father, God the Son, and God the Holy Spirit! Only thus can we possibly account for the many scriptures throughout the Bible declaring again and again that there is only ONE God, and simultaneously declaring that God the Father is God, God the Son is God, and God the Holy Spirit is God. We gladly and scripturally recognize that there are 3 persons in the Godhead, and that there is now and forever only ONE God! A deep and careful study of the Bible will confirm this. Two very helpful books on the subject are "The Trinity in the Universe," a classic by Nathan Wood, and "JESUS—a Biblical Defense of His Diety" . . . Josh McDowell and Bart Larson.

Just as space consists of height, length and breadth, three distinctions in ONE space, and just as EACH extended infinitely is ALL THERE IS OF SPACE, yet all three distinctions are absolutely necessary, (or one could not even build a house, for instance!), so it is with God the Father, God the Son, and God the Holy Spirit. ONE GOD, as space is One, with three distinct persons in the nature of the ONE TRUE GOD. This does not make three Gods any more than the three distinctions in space make 3 spaces . . . Space is

One, with 3 distinctions. Just as each distinction, whether one takes height, or length or breadth, when extended infinitely, is all there is of space, NOT one third of space, even so GOD the Father is not one-third of God, or God the Son, one-third of God, or God the Holy Spirit, one-third of God. Each is ALL THERE IS OF GOD! Yet they are three in ONE!

So too, it is with time—past, present, and future—three clear distinctions, yet time is absolutely ONE. God, being 3-in-1, and the Creator of this vast Universe, naturally affixed His signature, 3 in 1, to the basic elements! How marvelous!

So then, Jesus Christ is God, and always has been and always will be! He is one in essence with the Father. NOTICE: The Bible says that to know Jesus is to know God, to see Jesus is to see God, to believe in Jesus is to believe in God, to honor Jesus is to honor God, and to hate Jesus is to hate God. God is called the First and the Last. Christ is called the First and the Last. You simply CANNOT have two Firsts and Lasts in the ultimate sense this is used of God! Both are called THE Almighty God. Jesus forgave sin, and the Bible says only God can forgive sin. Consider that Jesus forgave sin as God, sins that were against God, and only God can forgive a sin against God!! Things that are said in the Old Testament about God the Father, are said in the New Testament about Jesus. The Father God is called our Saviour and Creator in the Old Testament. Jesus Christ is called our Saviour and the Creator in the New Testament. An elementary rule of logic is that things equal to the same thing are equal to each other. (If A equals B and B equals C, then A equals C). Jesus is thus, in this way as well as directly, declared to be God, as He claimed to be. No wonder Thomas called Jesus, "My Lord and my God!" John 20:28.

Another serious problem for Mormons is that Joseph Smith did not really use the Gold Plates which he declared God had preserved for him for centuries. There were the plates on which the Book of Mormon was supposedly written in 'Reformed Egyptian' an unheard of and unknown language then and now. As shown by Joseph Smith's Egyptian grammar, and by his 'translation' of the Book of Abraham from Egyptian, he could not translate any Egyptian, reformed or not. Every expert Egyptologist who has examined his translation from the now recovered Fascimile (re-discovered in 1967) material and writings Joseph Smith used in translation of the Book of Abraham, has declared his 'translation' to be totally fraudulent.

Entirely apart from that prophet-demolishing exposure, is the attested fact that Joseph Smith did not even USE the Gold Plates in translating the Book of Mormon! Emma Smith, Joseph's wife, and Oliver Cowdery, often acted as scribes to Joseph Smith as he translated. They, along with David Whitmer and Martin Harris, (Cowdery, Whitmer and Harris being the 'three witnesses' to the Book of Mormon) described *in detail* how Joseph Smith translated. He stuck his face in a hat with a stone in the hat and, ". . . something resembling parchment would appear." Hieroglyphics would appear on the parchment, with the exact, perfect, English interpretation underneath.

Joseph Smith would read the English interpretation, and Oliver Cowdery, or whoever was acting as scribe at that time, would write it. When correctly written, the heiroglyphics and its English interpretation would disappear. Then another portion of the 'manuscript' would appear in like manner. If not correctly written, THE WORDS OF THE PARCHMENT (MANUSCRIPT) WOULD REMAIN UNTIL EVERY LETTER, EVERY CHARACTER, EVERY

WORD, WAS PERFECT, EXACTLY AS GOD GAVE IT. (See David Whitmer, "An Address To All Believers in Christ." pg. 12.) Also corroborated by Emma Smith and the other 'witnesses' Cowdery and Harris. THE GOLD PLATES WERE NOT EVEN USED, AND WERE SELDOM, IF EVER PRESENT!! THEY WERE UTTERLY USELESS! Emma Smith, David Whitmer and Martin Harris declared that the plates were either covered up, or not present at all while Joseph Smith had his face buried in his hat peering at the seer stone as he translated. (Martin Harris interview in "Tiffany's Monthly," 1859.) Strangely enough, though the witnesses said at one time they saw and 'hefted' the plates, they weakened their testimony considerably in saying that an 'angel' showed them the plates, though supposedly in the custody of Joseph Smith. Harris and the others also said they saw the plates by the 'eye of faith' and Doctrine and Convenants' 17:5 says 'by faith.' Strange indeed. Stranger still, the gold plates, supposedly containing the 'Reformed Egyptian' account of the Book of Mormon, were not used in the translation of the Book of Mormon at all! We repeat, *the gold plates were useless!*

Even more damaging to the claims of Joseph Smith was the translation itself. Consider again the words of His scribes, who watched him in translation, were his main witnesses to the Book of Mormon, and wrote down the words for him as he gave them. If every word, every letter, every character, was given directly from God to Joseph Smith, as his scribes declared, and Joseph Smith certainly never said otherwise or corrected them, and if the parchment would not move on until every letter, every character, every word was copied perfectly, HOW COULD THERE BE ANY POSSIBILITY OF A MISTAKE? EVEN THE GRAMMAR AND PUNCTUATION WOULD HAVE HAD TO BE PERFECT, COM-

ING DIRECTLY FROM GOD!! (Unless one dares to lay this poor grammar and poor punctuation and spelling in the first editions of the Book of Mormon at the feet of God!!)

Early Mormons recognized this, and usually claimed *inerrancy* and *infallibility* for the *Book of Mormon*, as indeed, they would be forced to, considering the claims of Joseph Smith and his scribes and witnesses. Christians make that claim for the Bible, *because the Bible makes that claim for itself*, and outstanding scholars and the *precise fulfillment of its words in prophecy* have ably defended and illustrated the truth of that claim. History, geography and archeology have united to prove its incredible accuracy, even after thousands of years. The very opposite is true of the Book of Mormon. Joseph Smith claimed that the Book of Mormon was the 'most *correct* of any book on earth,' even more so than the Bible. He said that when he and the witnesses went out to pray concerning the Book of Mormon, they heard a voice coming from a bright light above them saying, 'These plates have been revealed by the power of God, and they have been translated by the Power of God. The translation of them which you have seen is correct, and I command you to bear record of what you now see and hear." (History of the Church, Vol. 1, pg. 54-55.) Over 4,000 changes have now been made in the Book of Mormon. How could this possibly be, considering all the facts listed above? Mormons point to the 'changes' made in the Bible, but these have to do with *translations from the original*, it was NOT given in *English*. The Book of Mormon has *no such reason*. It was given *Word, Letter and Character, Perfect, directly from God, If Joseph Smith and his scribes told the truth.* If they did not, then it is a fraud, and not worth considering. If they told the truth, then it is impossible to explain the changes, and the change in many modern Mormon's view of the Book of Mormon.

A Mormon friend from Longview, Washington wrote me recently, claiming that Mormons never claimed infallibility for the Book of Mormon!!! In the first place, God would never give something with flaws in it to reveal Himself, His Word, His Son, and the Way of Salvation for men. He overshadowed fallible men with His infallibility that His Word, the Bible, might be perfect, without error, and he said His Word was perfect, and that the scriptures could not be broken. Surely He would do as much for the Book of Mormon if it truly was the Word of God.

As a matter of fact, Mormon after Mormon, leaders among them, testified that the Book of Mormon was an infallible book, given directly from God. Given the claims of Joseph Smith and his scribes and witnesses, THEY HAVE NO OTHER CHOICE!!

Here is a statement by Joseph F. Smith, who became President and living prophet of the Mormon church, as recorded in the Journal of Oliver B. Huntington, pg. 168, typed copy at Utah State Historical Society: "Joseph did not render the writing on the Gold Plates into the English language in his own style or language as many people believe, but EVERY WORD AND EVERY LETTER was given to him by the gift and power of God. So it is *the work of God* and *not of Joseph Smith,* and it was done in this way. The Lord caused *each word spelled as it is in the book* to appear on the stones in short sentences or words, and when Joseph had uttered the sentence or word before him and the scribes had written it properly, that sentence would disappear and another appear. And if there was A WORD WRONGLY WRITTEN OR EVEN A LETTER INCORRECT the writing on the stones would remain there. . . . when corrected the sentence would disappear as usual." It is IMPOSSIBLE to be honest and get anything but *verbal inspiration from God* out of this. It is *impossible* to get anything but *inerrant infallible, letter, word,* and *punctuation, direct from-God, inspiration and revelation* from *Cowdery, Harris,* and the others, out of how they and Joseph Smith got the Book of Mormon!! Our friend in Longview accuses us of misrepresentation in saying that this is a clear claim to *the inerrancy and infallibility of the Book of Mormon!* You decide!!

Later Mormons saw the flagrant errors, obviously Smith's, not God's, in grammar, punctuation, etc. and as Mormon scholar B.H. Roberts admitted, "The old THEORY must be abandoned." First of all, it was not a *'theory'* but the *bedrock teaching of Joseph Smith and his scribes,* as to *how they got the Book of Mormon,* and as to its *verbal perfection direct from God.* If this was not true, then neither is the Book of Mormon.

The 8th Article of Faith of Mormonism declares, "We believe the Bible to be the Word of God as far as it is translated correctly; we also believe the BOOK OF MORMON TO BE THE WORD OF GOD." Notice that it does not say 'contains' the word of God, or give any warning whatsoever that it is not *wholly* the *word of God,* or that the human may be mixed with the divine so that the Book of Mormon contains human errors as well as the Word of God. This is dishonest misrepresentation if the Mormons now believe the Book of Mormon is not the inerrant, infallible Word of God, direct from God, then the Articles of Faith should *say* so! (Only 5% of rat poison is actually poison!) If Mormons no longer maintain that the Book of Mormon is the Word of God directly, as Joseph Smith and his scribes irrefutably claimed it to be, and most dedicated Mormons believed it to be for generations, they should say so up front in the Articles of Faith. Futhermore, in doing so, they should, to maintain their integrity, forsake Mormonism, because Mormonism stands or falls on the truthfulness of Joseph Smith about the revelation he supposedly got from God. If this is untrue, then Mormonism is untrue.

In Deut. 18:20-22, we find this simple and easily understood test for a Prophet. These people were not scholars, they were ordinary folks like you and I. They needed an infallible test they could apply to determine God's prophets from false prophets. This is exactly what God gave them. "But the prophet which shall presume to speak a word in my name, which I have not commanded him to speak or that shall speak in the name of other gods, even that prophet shall die. And if thou say in thine heart, How shall we know the word which the LORD hath not spoken? When a prophet speaketh in the name of the LORD, if the thing follow not, nor come to pass, that is the thing which the LORD hath not spoken, but the prophet hath spoken it presumptuously: thou shalt not be afraid of him." Many of Joseph Smith's prophecies failed, something like 58 out of 64. Remember, it only takes *one* false prophecy to determine a false prophet, and Deut. 13:1-5 covers the eventuality of the occasional prediction by a false prophet which might come true. Joseph Smith failed that test also. He led away to other 'gods.' Let us now look at just a few of his many false prophecies.

Prophecy #1. Doctrine and Convenants 114:1, David Patten is told to settle up his business to "perform a mission unto me next Spring, in company with others, even twelve including himself, to testify of my name and bear glad tidings unto all the world." This prophecy was given April 17, 1838. On October 25, David Patten was shot and killed. The prophecy was false. He did NOT go on a mission "next Spring." My friend from Longview claims that this was not a prophecy, merely an instruction from the Lord.

It makes absolutely no difference in the final analysis. Would an all-knowing God, who declares He knows the future, the end from the beginning, call a man to go on a mission for Him, when He knew that man would be dead before the mission was even supposed to start? Would he so impugn His own character, and that of His prophet? Besides, his clear instruction was based upon the conclusion that David Patten would be alive next Spring, AND HE WAS NOT! It was obviously the prophet's mistake . . . not God's!

Prophecy #2. Concerning New Jerusalem and its TEMPLE being built in THIS (Joseph Smith's) generation. Mormons try to elude this in several ways, saying that Christ said the same thing about THIS generation concerning His coming etc. in Matt. 24. Turn to it and read the context. He spoke of the budding of the fig tree, after having given many signs which would occur, and said, "When ye see ALL these things, know that it is near, even at the doors." THEN he said, in v. 34, "THIS generation", obviously the generation which saw ALL the signs given, the budding fig-tree generation, would see the fulfillment of His promise. Also, according to Bible scholar C.I. Schofield, the Greek word used here for "generation" may be used in the sense of "race", or "family", meaning that the nation or family of Israel, the Jews, will be preserved, 'til all these things be fulfilled,' and that promise has been wonderfully fulfilled to this day.

Remember, the promise Joseph Smith supposedly got was in ENGLISH, and should be abundantly clear, without any of the problems of translation. When Joseph Smith said 'this generation' he meant what the English words meant . . . THIS GENERATION! The generation of which he was a part! NOW turn to D&C 84, and read the prophecy of Joseph Smith IN ITS CONTEXT. It is clear exactly what

Joseph Smith said and meant. The prophecy was clearly understood by his apostles and leaders, and the people who heard him and those who read his prophecy.

We know for a fact that Joseph meant the generation that was then alive when he spoke. Many of the faithful ARE ON RECORD declaring that very fact. Joseph Smith NEVER corrected them. Why not, if they were wrong? It would be unconscionable NOT to correct them! Apostle after Mormon Apostle, some of whom heard the message, and read the reports of the 'revelation,' declared that Joseph Smith meant exactly what he said; the current generation of Mormons alive when Joseph Smith gave the prophecy would not die before the fulfillment of the prophecy. See Journal of Discourses, Vol. 9, pg. 71, Vol. 10, pg. 344, Vol. 13, pg. 362. Joseph Smith's Prophecy in the History of the Church, Vol. 1, pg. 315-316. Apostle Orson Pratt spoke for many Mormons when he stated conclusively, "The Latter-day Saints just as much expect to receive a fulfillment of that promise, DURING THE GENERATION THAT WAS IN EXISTENCE IN 1832 as they expect that the sun will rise and set tomorrow. Why? Because God cannot lie. He will fulfill all His promises." Pratt was speaking at the time of the New Jerusalem, Temple prophecy. (Journal of Discourses, Vol. 9, pg. 71.) The city was NOT built, the Temple was NOT built in "THIS GENERATION." The prophecy was obviously false. How is it that NOW, after the prophecy has failed, those of today who were not in close contact with Joseph Smith, and did not hear him, claim to know what he meant better than those who knew him, heard him and were in close contact with him? Face it, Mormon friends, the prophecy failed. Joseph Smith is a false prophet.

Prophecy #3. Joseph Smith prophesied that the brethren should go to Toronto, Canada, and told them that they would sell the copyright of the Book of Mormon. They went, but could not sell the book, and called Joseph Smith to account. Do you know what Joseph Smith said: "Some revelations are of God, some are of men, and some are of the devil." Apparently Joseph Smith could not tell the difference! (An Address to All Believers in Christ," David Whitmer.)

Unfortunately for our Mormon friends, Mormon 'living prophets' and Apostles have the same problem. Apostle Parley Pratt prophesied that in 50 years there would not be an unbelieving Gentile upon this continent. Heber C. Kimball prophesied that Brigham Young would become President of the United States. Oliver B. Huntington, (from whose Journal we get the Moon revelation of 6 ft. tall men dressed like Quakers, living to be about a thousand years old, from Joseph Smith,) was told in this Patriarchal blessing, given by the father of Joseph the Prophet, that he would preach the gospel to the inhabitants of the MOON! Where do you suppose Joseph Smith's dad got THAT idea, certainly not from God?! Why didn't his son correct him? (Diary of Oliver B. Huntington, Utah State Historical Society) Also "Mormon's Young Women's Journal," Vol. 3. No. 6 of 1892.) Joseph Smith's prophecies, as well as those of other Mormon 'prophets' are indubitably false. Even if we accept the plea we have gotten from many Mormons, that not all the prophecies were meant as prophecies per se, and perhaps some were not, and that some were conditional, and no doubt some few were, it is an entirely hopeless case. Some 58 out of 64 failed, and even if we discount 30% of those, just ONE false prophecy forever brands a man as a false prophet. Joseph Smith, irrefutably, was a false prophet.

CHAPTER 7
Facing Further Facts and Fruits of Mormonism

There are many, many other serious problems behind the image of Mormonism, and I will mention just a few of them. The Book of Mormon and the Pearl of Great Price, and the Bible, on the one hand, and Doctrines and Covenants on the other hand, place Adam and Eve and the Garden of Eden on opposite sides of the earth at the same time. God, who is NOT the Author of Confusion, would never inspire such contradiction. Surely GOD knows where the Garden of Eden was! Genesis 2:14, B.M. 1 Nephi 5:11, PGP Moses 3:8-15 with D&C 116, 117:8. See also *Mormon Doctrine*, by Bruce McConkie, pg. 19-20, 303.

Incidentally, the Book of Mormon has *no* historical, or archeological proof, no authentic maps, no certain geographical locations in the new world. Not one of its massive 38 American cities have *ever* been found: 25,000 archeological sites verify and corroborate the Bible's cities, kings, nations, etc. *Bible 25,000* - Book of Mormon - 0."

Mormons continually violate God's express command forbidding Geneologies. 1 Tim. 1:4. "Neither give heed to fables and endless geneologies." Titus 3:9, "AVOID foolish questions and GENEOLOGIES." Mormons do not realize that geneologies have fulfilled their purpose and are now FORBIDDEN!

Mormons have raised up a dead Priesthood, which was NEVER given to or practiced by the New Testament Church in this age of grace, after it was formed at Pentecost, in Acts ch. 2. There is NO official Priesthood and NO TEMPLE in the New Testament church. The temple was for the Jews, for blood sacrifices, etc. 1. Priests had one MAJOR purpose: to offer blood sacrifices UNTIL the Lamb of God, Jesus, came to shed His blood, ONCE FOR ALL! 2. There is no official Priesthood or order of Priests in the New Testament church. This was DONE AWAY WITH after Calvary, when Christ shed His blood on the cross, and rose again. He now is our ONE AND ONLY HIGH PRIEST. No other Priest is ever even so much as mentioned, in connection with the New Testament church, in decades of writing by the New Testament writers, as they wrote on the church. Not once is any priest whatsoever mentioned in the numerous times offices and officers of the church are mentioned. Priests are GONE! All such priests today are false priests, however nice and kind and sincere they may be! Their 'Authority' is imagined, conferred on them by descent from a false prophet. There are no priests since Pentecost in the true New Testament church, except that now all Christians are declared to be priests. 3. All Christians are now declared to be priests. (1 Peter 2:9, Rev. 1:4-6, and Heb. 7:21) Christ is our one and only HIGH PRIEST FOREVER! Whatever do we need with official priests now, since He came and shed His blood for us!

God has forbidden a Church leader, Bishop, Elder, Deacon, to be the husband of more than one wife, in this age of grace in His New Testament Church. (1 Tim. 1:1-12.) Joseph Smith, Brigham Young and other Mormon leaders had more than one wife. This nullifies ALL THEIR CLAIMS of AUTHORITY for themselves and their successors!

Joseph Smith is on record as calling his three main witnesses to the Book of Mormon, "Thieves and Liars!!" He also said, David Whitmer, Oliver Cowdery, and Martin Harris, are "too mean to mention, and we would like to have forgotten them." (Times and Seasons," Vol. 1, pg. 81, Elders Journal, pg. 59, Senate Document, 139, pg. 6, 9. Also History of the Church, Vol. 3, pg. 232.) Joseph Smith brands these three men, his main three witnesses to the Book of Mormon, "Thieves and Liars," and then asks us to believe their "Testimony," about the Book of Mormon! Some Mormon friend may object, "Yes, but Abraham lied about his wife, calling her his sister." He did, indeed, but it was at least a half-truth, as she was his half-sister, and Abraham did this to spare his life, or so he thought . . . though that in no way excuses it. Abraham was called to account for his half-lie. He did not live a life characterized by lying. It was in no way the bent of his life. Indeed, it *cannot* be for a child of God, because God changes his heart, and he abhors lying, even if in a moment of weakness, temptation or fear, once, or a few times in his life, he lies. No one would dare call Abraham a liar, certainly God would not, nor would any other prophet of God. Liars, God says, cannot inherit the kingdom of God, and Abraham, God tells us, is in Heaven. Thieves and liars are not in heaven, and this is what Joseph Smith called his three witnesses. He also called them *'mean'* and said he wished he could forget them! Think long, prayerfully, and carefully about that, Mormon friends. These are the men whom you are to trust with your eternal destiny.

Brigham Young said, "I have many a time, in this stand, dared the world to produce as mean devils as we can; we can beat them at anything. We have the greatest and smoothest liars in the world, the cunningest and most adroit thieves, and any other shade of character that you can mention. We can pick Elders in Israel right here who beat the world at gambling, who can handle the cards, cut and shuffle them with the smartest rogue on the face of God's footstool . . . . We can beat them, because we have men here that live in the light of the Lord, that have the Holy Priesthood, (!!!) and hold the keys of the kingdom of God. . . . We can do that. We can pray the best, preach the best, and sing the best. We are the best looking and finest set of people on the face of the earth, . . ." (Brigham Young, Journal of Discourses, Vol. 4, pg. 77, 1856.)

The Bible says we can know false Prophets by their fruits, in the context, primarily by their doctrine, their teaching. We have tested the Mormon prophets and found them wanting. But some think of fruits also as being the behavior, the kind of people produced. Let us consider the fruits of Mormonism in its heartland, Utah. At the very outset, let me say, and truthfully, that I believe the great majority of Mormon folks to be fine, decent people, although, in God's sight, before we come to Jesus Christ, we are all sinners needing a Saviour. This is no more and no less true of Mormons than it is of any of the rest of us. I have read that the murder rate is lower in Utah. If this is so, it is highly commendable. I personally believe that the alcoholism rate is lower. That too, especially in this age, is commendable. However, there are other, less favorable statistics. Utah is 70-72% Mormon, and once was almost entirely Mormon. Yet, the divorce rate in Utah has topped the U.S. average for all but about 3 years since 1900: Deseret News, Wed., Feb. 11, '76, reporting on one year, says "Utah Divorces Top U.S. Average." This seems to me to be difficult to fit into the 'happiness is the family home evenings' image Mormons seek to create. "Utah teen suicides lead U.S. average," . . . "Rate among Utah teenagers has consistently led the National Average." (Deseret News, Sept. 3, '79.) The Deseret News also reported on Friday, Sept. 21, '79, that the rate of suicide for Utah women nearly doubled from 1960 to 1970. "Seven out of every ten children born to teenagers in Utah are conceived out of wedlock." (Ogden Standard-Examiner, Sat. Eve. Dec. 15, '79.) Also, child abuse is epidemic with 5 times as many murdered children in Utah as the national average! (Salt Lake Tribune, June 26, and August 13, '82.) In addition, Dee Goar of the Women's Crisis Center, of the Ogden YMCA, stated that a woman living in Utah had a higher chance of being battered by her husband than anywhere else in the Nation. She gave statistics to back up that claim, stating that figures showed one-third of the homes in Utah experience violence in their homes, the highest rate of spouse abuse in the Nation.

In regard to teen-age pregnancies in Utah, some Mormons have suggested that Utah girls, especially Mormon girls, do not PLAN to have illicit sex, and also, do not get abortions in nearly the proportion girls in other states may, and this may account for the deplorable 7 out of 10 statistics. I grant that, and it certainly is to their credit if they do not get abortions, yet this is still an incredible moral lapse hard to explain if Mormonism truly changes lives. Mormonism concentrates on children, teenagers and youth.

Some Mormons claim that Mormons married in the temple have only one-fifth the divorce rate of the national average. Good for them. However only a minority of Mormons are married in the Temple and that the most dedicated Mormons. Billy Graham recently said on National T.V. that only one out of 300 truly dedicated, born again Christian marriages ends up in divorce. Write him, ask him!

Others argue that the Utah divorce rate, while higher than the national average, is the lowest in the mountain west states, where divorce is traditionally high. But if Mormonism is the One True Church, and Utah has been its heartland and showpiece in the Nation for generations, and if the life-changing power and teaching of God is there, shouldn't it be *not just a little better than the worse*, but the best in the nation?

Another tragic fruit of Mormonism, are the estimated 30,000 polygamist, now forbidden and outcast by the same church that taught them to be polygamist, living in Utah, Arizona, etc. This is a direct result of Joseph Smith and Brigham Young's teaching on the practice of polygamy. This too, is part of the fruits of Mormonism.

I might add here, that while I believe Mormon people are a sincere and decent folk, by and large, no different from the rest of us in their need of the Lord Jesus Christ, no better and no worse, *I cannot say the same for many of their leaders*. Years of research has convinced me of the duplicity of Joseph Smith, Brigham Young, and many other of the top leaders, although possibly not all of them. Many of these leaders have known the truth about Joseph Smith, Adam-God, the Mountain Meadows massacre, revealing documents, etc. and they have covered up the truth, altered documents, and misled the Mormon people. (Please read *"Mormonism, Shadow or Reality"* by Jerald and Sandra Tanner, for thorough documentation from Mormon sources.)

To some extent, we have dealt with the Mormon claim that the Gospel and true Christianity disappeared from off the earth about the first century, until it was 'restored' by Prophet Smith in 1830. 1 Tim. 4:1 tells us that ". . . in the

LATTER times SOME shall depart from the faith, giving heed to seducing spirits and doctrines of devils." The very existence of Mormonism and other groups totally different from Biblical Christianity certainly prove this to be true. Unwittingly, the Mormons have called themselves the LATTER day Saints, identifying themselves with those who in the LATTER times would depart from the faith! However, there is nowhere in the Bible, history, or human experience a time of TOTAL APOSTASY, only SOME departed. Jesus plainly said the "gates of Hell would not prevail against His church," and He does not lie!! He also said He would be with His church continuously, always, which would have been impossible and futile if His church had disappeared as Joseph Smith and Mormon doctrine claim.

In addition to this attack on all Christian churches by Joseph Smith, he and other Mormons teach that all other churches are false, that they are ". . . all wrong . . . all their creeds were an abomination in His sight: that those professors were corrupt . . ." PGP, Joseph Smith 2:18, 19. Naturally, Joseph Smith claimed that God said this . . . in no other way could he have established credibility for his "restored gospel." Joseph Smith and Mormon doctrine go on to teach that the Mormon church is the One and Only True Church on earth, and men can only reach the highest 'heaven,' degree of glory, exaltation, and/or become Gods, through the Mormon church. Ora Pate Stewart cried, "All will be damned who are not Latter-day Saints." Apostle Orson Pratt in the Mormon organ, the Seer, pg. 255, asserted, "Both Catholics and Protestants are nothing less than the 'Whore of Babylon,' whom the Lord denounces by the mouth of John the Revelator as having corrupted all the earth by their fornications and wickedness. Any person who shall be so wicked as to receive a holy ordinance of the gospel from the ministers of any of these apostate churches will be sent down to hell with them, unless they repent of the unholy and impious act." Lately, Mormons have been much more careful with their rhetoric, but the *underlying doctrine* has not changed one iota.

Remember, Jesus was so very kind and tender toward any repentant sinner, no matter how vile his sin. He was extremely stern and condemning to those who were self-righteous in their religion and scorned all others as being less righteous than they were. The Pharisees, and religious Jews who depended on their own goodness, plus their zeal for God, were out and out condemned. Mt. 23:15 "Woe unto you, scribes and Pharisees, hypocrites! For ye compass sea and land to make one proselyte, and when he is made, ye make him twofold more the child of Hell than yourselves." v. 27, "Woe unto you, scribes and Pharisees, for ye are like unto whited sepulchres which appear beautiful outward but are within full of dead men's bones, and of all uncleanness." v. 33, Jesus says, "ye serpents, ye generation of vipers, how can ye escape the damnation of Hell?" Jesus *loved* these men enough to *tell them the truth*. He later died in brutal, bloody agony for them, as well as for all men, and some of them finally realized they were religious, but lost, and turned to Him alone for salvation. This included such men as Joseph of Arimathaea, and Nicodemus.

For the very same reason, I tell Mormons the truth, that they may cease to depend in any part on their own righteousness, or the Mormon church, but may turn to the Biblical Jesus alone, and be saved. The Mormon problem is virtually identical to the Jews problem, as explained in Rom. 10:2,3: ". . . They have a zeal for God, but not according to knowledge." "For they being ignorant of God's righteousness and going about to establish their own righteousness, have not submitted themselves unto the righteousness of God. v. 4. . . ." "For Christ is the END OF THE LAW FOR RIGHTEOUSNESS to every one that believeth."

Mormon friends, here I would like to ask a simple question. This is by no means meant as ridicule. (For instance, I have not even used the 'Salamander' letter material, or Hofmann's deceiving church leaders with fraudulent documents. Much could be said about church leaders supposedly led by divine revelation, spending church money to buy fraudulent documents. Much could be said about Joseph Smith's occult connections. I have not used this material which is potentially extremely embarrassing to Mormons.) The question I do want to ask, however, is because I do not grasp the logic of an event in the Book of Mormon. It is quite possible I may have missed something, but frankly, it looks like a mistake to me. The Book of Mormon people, the Jaredites, crossed the ocean to America in barges, with "a hole in the top, and also in the bottom." (Book of Mormon, Ether 2:20.) They were directed to make a hole in the top and bottom of these airtight barges so they could breathe, by the Lord Himself, according to Joseph Smith. Then, if the water flooded in, they were to stop up their breathing holes! I am sorry, but as an ex-sailor, it seems to me that the only successful trip these barges could make would be to the bottom of the ocean! I would like some Mormon's explanation of this . . . but please, don't bother trying to justify this story by pointing out the supposed deficiencies in the Ark. Scholars like Henry Morris, in "The Genesis Flood," ably and completely answers those usually baseless objections, and shows the dimensions of the Ark as Biblically given, to be roughly the equivalent of some of our best and most seaworthy ocean-liners, such as the Queen Mary.

Now let us get to the heart of the matter. Every miracle Jesus Christ performed was instantaneous, and this is true whether in the healing of the body or of the soul. Lazarus did not have to come alive gradually by a process, or do any good works, but simply responded to the call of Jesus instantly, and instantly passed from death to life. So it is with the sinner when he passes from death to life. Eph. 2:1, "And you hath He quickened. (MADE ALIVE), who were DEAD in your trespasses and sins." The New Birth, Salvation, is Instant, the results last forever! Literally millions of Christians can tell you how God saved them instantly, changed their lives, made them sure of heaven, filled them with love, delivered them from alcohol, drugs, illicit sex, child abuse, depression, fear, and from Hell!

One of the things which grieves me most about my Mormon friends, is that their view of Heaven resembles the biblical Hell, and that is heart-breaking. The highest exaltation, heaven or degree of glory for a Mormon, is to become a god on a planet with his wife or wives, populating that planet by sexual union with them. (It sometimes seems that Mormon women's highest exaltation boils down to being virtually eternally pregnant, or at best sharing her beloved husband with another or many others. Anything less than this 'Highest Exaltation' on the other hand, leaves the Mormon women pretty much as a relatively insignificant servant to those more 'worthy.')

Mormons believe there are millions of planets to be inhabited by Mormons who become gods, each Mormon god having his own individual planet. These planets may be millions of light years apart. Since Mormons believe both God and Jesus to be limited in time and space to one place by a physical body, they do not believe that God is omnipresent, as the Bible teaches. He can only be in one place at a time. With millions of Mormon 'gods' on planets scattered throughout the universe, an exalted Mormon may not see Jesus or be with God for millions of years at a time! The Bible indicates that to be separated from God is Hell; to the Mormons, it is Heaven!

The Mormon Heaven is in truth the biblical Hell, minus only the flames. The Christian longs to be with Jesus. The Mormon longs to be a god on a planet, for all practical purposes, separated from Jesus forever! Jesus told all true Christians that He would come again, ". . . and receive you unto Myself; that where I am, there ye may be also." John 14:1-3. 1 Thess. 4:17 adds that when Jesus comes for the Christians, ". . . so shall we EVER be WITH THE LORD."

This is the true heaven, and highest exaltation for a child of God, to be with Jesus and all the true saints of God in glory forever!!!

Beloved Mormon friends, Jesus Christ can save you and make you perfect forever in a moment of time! Heb. 10:10, ". . . WE ARE sanctified through the OFFERING OF THE BODY OF JESUS CHRIST, ONCE FOR ALL." (God is obviously speaking here of Christians. Sinners, until they are saved, are not sanctified by the blood of Christ from His broken body on the cross.) Also, sanctification is used in two ways in Scripture. One is instant, when we are saved, set apart for God. The other use is dealing with our growth in Christ after salvation, sometimes called progressive sanctification. This use here unmistakeably refers to instant sanctification. Now note . . . and rejoice!!! Heb. 10:14, "For by one offering He hath PERFECTED FOREVER

THEM THAT ARE SANCTIFIED."!!! When Jesus saves us, in God's sight we are perfected forever!

Your position in Christ will be perfect, the moment you are truly saved, your practice will be guided by the indwelling Christ to conform more and more to that position He has FREELY given you by His offering on the cross for you!! Never again will you enjoy wallowing in sin, when Jesus comes to save you, sanctify you, make you a child of God, and dwell within you. He makes you a new person . . . He said so, 2 Cor. 5:17. If and when you sin, after salvation, it will be your greatest burden until it is confessed and forsaken. The indwelling Christ, and your new nature activated by the Holy Spirit and His Word, will see to that.

Now, Mormon friends, we come to the real reason why this book, (and the 3 books in 1 book) was written. Rom. 10:1, "Brethren, my heart's desire and prayer to God for Israel is, THAT THEY MIGHT BE SAVED."

All of these books have been written to help Mormons see their urgent need of the Lord Jesus Christ. I would gladly dispense with all else except the chapter, THIS IS THE WAY, if I believed Mormons would read it with understanding as to the biblical Jesus and their need of Him alone for salvation. The material in this chapter, THIS IS THE WAY, has already turned many from darkness to light. Please turn back and read it, or re-read it, and let God speak to your heart. Truly, as God is my witness, THIS IS THE WAY!

CHRISTIAN OUTREACH
P.O. BOX 750
SALT LAKE CITY, UT. 84101